TRESPASSERS

by the same author

TRESPASSERS

A Memoir

Julia O'Faolain

faber and faber

First published in 2013
by Faber and Faber Ltd
Bloomsbury House
74–77 Great Russell Street
London WC1B 3DA

Typeset by Palindrome
Printed in England by CPI Group (UK) Ltd, Croydon, CR0 4YY

A CIP record for this book
is available from the British Library

ISBN 978–0–571–29492–3

2 4 6 8 10 9 7 5 3 1

CONTENTS

PROLOGUE: LOOKING BACK

'Why do you never tell us about yourself?' asks my husband when shown a draft of this prologue. 'Who are you? Do you even know? If you do, why not tell us? Is the answer so awful?'

It isn't, of course. I have had quite a good life. Maybe that's the trouble. To write a lively story you need some darkness, even fear. Anger is good, too. It stirs things up. So when I write fiction, I put in energising elements. But this time I am meant to be telling the truth, which is – as my mother told me when I was four – that I belonged to a southern Irish generation which could expect to be unprecedentedly comfortable and safe. Or, as she put it on other occasions, I had missed the excitement, which so often comes at a cost. Since then I have seen signs of this on recognisably Irish faces glimpsed in places as disparate as Los Angeles and London, where confrontations with angry taxi drivers and the like can reveal dangerously wounded personalities. 'Watch it,' I am sometimes tempted to tell bystanders who might not guess at the harrowing home or school lives with which my compatriots often had to deal and which can lead to hair-trigger reactions. Some wounds can go on hurting.

'Then tell about them,' my husband encourages. 'Indulge in a bit of narcissism.'

'I suspect it only works with the help of a dash of religion,' I argue. 'You need that to help manage your rage.'

'What rage?'

'The rage of people who suffer from bruising recollections.'

'Do we know anyone like that?'

I name two ex-Catholics and an ex-communist. We notice this

at the same moment and laugh. Excessive hopefulness, we tell each other, can be hard to handle.

One memory-bruised Irishman we knew was now a well-heeled Los Angeleno in his forties who probably rarely thought of his childhood. However, something on the day we met must have revived old angers, for he was soon stamping up and down the pleasantly spacious flat where he was entertaining us while cursing the sadistic monks who had run his Irish boarding school more than twenty years before and made his teen years a hell. Alarmingly, a resentful, possibly half unhinged, delinquent seemed to have replaced the suave man whom we had met earlier at a lunch, when our common Irishness had seemed to be a good reason for spending the next few hours together.

My young brother had gone to that same monks' school which, though reputed to be the best in Ireland, had turned out to condone such practises as letting boys drag one of their number into the woods to be flogged. What Stevie had done to provoke such treatment we never knew, though he did have a knack for annoying people. My mother blamed my father for failing to teach him caution before sending him to school, and he blamed her for regarding the need to do so as a male concern. Then, without more ado, they took Stevie away from the monks. Maybe, she suggested on our drive home, the monks had heard that our father was an anti-clerical journalist and had made Stevie suffer for this.

All this was some time back and, since then, schools have had to change their ways. Home life, though, has, if anything, grown worse, at least in England, where social workers seem to be in constant trouble for failing to save infants from their mothers' murderous boyfriends. About what happens in Ireland these days I am not up to date, and in California, when we lived there, the maltreatment of children kept going in and out of fashion. I remember an evangelical bookshop in the Westwood part of Los Angeles, when we moved there in the late Sixties, whose front window was filled with copies of a book entitled *Do You Dare to Spank?* An American psychologist to whom we let our London house went to the opposite extreme when we complained about his sons having sprayed our stairwell with buckshot. 'English people,' he snapped defensively, 'hate children.'

Coming back to the query about who 'I' am, I am a writer who has lived in London, Dublin, Rome, Florence, Paris, Los Angeles, Portland (Oregon), and, more briefly, in New York and Venice. Of these, it was the Italian cities that most influenced me. France – thanks to French having been my first foreign language – was my first love. But I was older and more capable of judging the world for myself when I lived in Florence with Lauro. Besides that, political debate when we lived there in the Sixties was a lot livelier and more heated in Italian newspapers than in French or English ones. And copies of *l'Unità* and *Rinascita* were regularly pasted on to walls all over Florence, so that members of the working class could keep abreast of current events. Eurocommunism, a phenomenon of the Seventies and Eighties, thrilled us by its openness to change and its promise to democratise the party. This horrified stodgy elements in the French Communist Party, and must have set Stalin spinning in his grave. It didn't please the hard left either. They still aimed to overturn capitalism by revolutionary means.

But the discomforting variant in the new situation made it clear that some meant what they said and others didn't. The question was: did we? Were we parlour pinks? I thought about this question more seriously than I had felt the need to do before, and decided that, though ready to be a 'Eurocommunist', this wasn't my fight in the way the Irish Civil War had been my parents' fight.

What upset me and my friends, first in LA then later on when we were back in London, were the neo-colonial wars which people like Tony Blair promoted by their shameless mendacity. Naively believing that mass protest marches might make them think twice, we walked in them all, and were utterly disillusioned by the cynicism of the Blairite 'Labour' Party, with its criminal collaboration – by 'rendition' and so forth – in the dirty war that was being waged in places like Guantanamo and Abu Graib.

Justice and truth are what an electorate should be able to aim for, if only by voting for a small, honest party which has some hope of playing an effective role. However, Italian corruption (*Tangentopoli*) followed by the advent of the appalling Berlusconi, put an end to any such hopes, which was heartbreaking when one remembered the brilliant journalism which had supposedly taught a generation of Italians how to think politically. Meanwhile, Ireland, too, turned out to be in corrupt hands both political and ecclesiastical.

But who, Lauro nags, years later, as I struggle with this prologue, do I feel the inner Julia turned out to be?

Well, I have given no thought to the inner Julia and am more interested in observing other people's behaviour than my own. Unlike him, who likes to quote Plato about how the unexamined life is not the life of a man, what I want to know is what other people get up to, what they do as much as what they think. That's my examining.

Having published seven novels and four collections of stories, I look into them to sort out the themes which interested me. Politics is one of these and fairness another; bullying, too. So is Church tyranny and those who opposed it, for in any community, there is likely to be, with luck, someone who stands up to bullies, as my father used to do in the years when a repressive RC Church lorded it in Ireland.

WE GO TRESPASSING

In 1933, when my parents came home to Ireland after seven years abroad, the economy was a shambles. Jobs were scarce so, rather than waste time and spirit seeking one, the survival mode commended to my father, whose first book had appeared the year before, was to write another, eke out the advance, and find a place where he and my mother could live cheaply and make their own entertainment.

Chat was a staple source for this and, by luck or design, not far from the house they found in rural County Wicklow lived other refugees from the jobless job market. A short walk off, the landscape painter Paul Henry was turning out his trademark blue mountains; in the house next to ours Michael Farrell, whose doorstopper of a novel, *Thy Tears Might Cease*, would appear thirty years later, was writing and rewriting it; while his wife, Francy, wove the tweeds which she would sell under the name *The Crock of Gold*. Michael O'Donovan, an old Cork friend best known later by his pen name 'Frank O'Connor', was working as a librarian in Wicklow Town. He spent frequent weekends with us, when he and Seán took walks, sang duets in eccentric Italian or recited old Gaelic poems and compared their translations. Each was said to have 'a lovely *blas*', which is Gaelic for a good Gaelic accent.

At this time my parents were revelling in an Irishness which, when they had been living in Boston and London, must have seemed precarious. They could so easily have stayed on in either place and had, they told me later, even thought of going to China. But the pull of home proved strong. My father's name, Seán Ó Faoláin, was a manifesto, for like many of his Republican comrades

I

he had started life with an anglicised version – John Whelan in his case – which he shed in his teens when romantic nationalism led him to join the Irish Volunteers, later renamed the IRA. My mother Eileen's name, too, had been Gaelicised from Ellen, and it had been she who first introduced him to the West Cork hills, where they learned Gaelic from native speakers. Next came the Anglo-Irish War, in which weapons were so few that young men like Seán had to be content with unglamorous back-up work. After that followed a truce, talks with the English, a treaty, its repudiation by de Valera, civil war (in which Seán at last got a gun), defeat, disillusion and then, in 1926, a fellowship to Harvard University. Now, home again and hopeful, they were seeing things through the bifocal lens of nostalgia and anticipation.

Meanwhile I, who had been born in London, allegedly spoke my first words with English intonations and had a supercilious – i.e. English? – expression while in my pram. Perhaps they misinterpreted a look of shock. They had engaged a French au pair to look after me, so not only had the sounds around me changed twice – more often, if you count Gaelic – but also I could hardly have failed to find Seán and Eileen unnervingly fanciful. They loved folk tales which scared me rigid. Consider 'changelings': bogus children, whom the fairies substitute for real ones. The mother who suspects such a switch must place the interloper on a red-hot shovel over a fire, whereupon, if it is a changeling, it will fly up the chimney. A woman, said my mother, had actually done that not long ago and been had up in court. Eileen was stirred by the persistence of folk culture. However, when I began having nightmares, she denied having said such a thing. Nonsense! I distrusted her but, hooked on terror, begged for more tales. When my father forbade them, they took on the allure of the illicit, and I scrounged for them behind his back.

'If I tell you stories, you'll get nightmares,' Eileen would worry. 'And your father will blame me.'

'I won't. I won't. I promise I won't.'

But, of course, I did and I woke the house with my shrieks. Again and again Seán had to reassure me by looking under the bed, where I was convinced a family of witches hid, waiting for him to go away before attacking me. Witches, fairies, ghosts and goblins did not, he patiently repeated, exist. 'They're all *pretend*,' he assured me. He lowered his candle to show me empty space. As soon as I was alone in the dark, though, I remembered that the pretend could outmanoeuvre the real. I had learned this from our maid, Kitty, who dealt with facts like a sharper with cards. Telling secrets was her passion.

'Now, don't tell yer Mammy I told ye. She'd crease me.'

'*Would* she?'

'Have me guts for garters. She would. Annyway, it's all cod. I was only coddin'. Aren't you the silly to believe me!'

Goaded, I would cheek her. 'You're a cod yourself! Cod! Cod!'

'Temper! Language!' Kitty would be all ladylike decorum. 'I'll tell yer Mammy!'

I took to waiting by the front gate for my parents to come home, so as to face them with a quick confession: 'I called Kitty a cod. I spilled my milk.' Getting my account in first took the wind from Kitty's sails.

The narrator, I was learning, takes control.

Even our cat had Irish credentials. He was called Pangur Bán (meaning White Pangur) after the cat in a poem doodled by an eighth- or ninth-century monk down the margin of his manuscript. It must be the Gaelic poem most often rendered in English. Here are scraps of Robin Flower's version:

> I and Pangur Bán my cat,
> 'Tis a like task we are at:

Hunting mice is his delight
Hunting words I sit all night.

Oftentimes a mouse will stray
In the hero Pangur's way;
Often-times my keen thought set
Takes a meaning in its net.
'Gainst the wall he sets his eye
Full and fierce and sharp and sly;
'Gainst the wall of knowledge I
All my little wisdom try.

So in peace our task we ply,
Pangur Bán my cat and I

On wet days when Frank O'Connor was visiting, jets of verse like this were apt to volley through the house with as much vim as when, on dry ones, his and Seán's squash ball bounced off backyard walls. Meanwhile, with catlike diligence, Eileen would be washing small slugs off vegetables while planning to trick me into eating food which, I now think, must have been at least as bad as I thought it at the time. Maybe it was worse? The home-grown greens would have been cooked with soda, as was the habit then, making them as bright as a St Patrick's Day rosette, bitter and usually overdone.

But this was true, too, in all the houses we visited and, when we went on holidays, it was true of the hotels. In Ireland back then only breakfast and afternoon tea could be relied on to be good.

Why else, in the Forties, when I spent a first summer with a carefully chosen Catholic family in war-harrowed France, would I be so astounded by their tasty salads and potato soup? How, I would marvel, had they, who had meat only once a week, turned simple, non-rationed raw materials into delicious gratin Savoyard, matefaim, crêpes and compotes of various fruits? Mirabelles, griottes, myrtilles . . .

Did the sun bring out those flavours? If it did, no wonder people had once worshipped it. I felt like doing that myself when I brought basil seeds back from France and raised the seedlings on a cold Irish window sill, only to find, when the leaves finally appeared, that they had no taste at all. In those days my mother and her friends, back from their own post-war forays abroad, were exchanging tips about buying such things as olive oil which no one at home had tasted for years. This being so, how could we trust ourselves to distinguish between rancid oil and good? We belonged to an emerging class whose emergence had been set back by the Troubles of the Twenties, the hungry Thirties and the war. During their 'austerity' years, the English, too, lost culinary skills, but their austerity could not be compared with ours. Theirs was a belt-tightening measure. But the true name for ours was 'penury', and it went back a long way. (Think of Swift's *Modest Proposal*. And Arthur Young's claim to have seen worse penury in eighteenth-century Ireland than in the Balkans.) In the light of such memories, de Valera's personal austerity, when in office, compelled respect and would be sadly recalled when his successors' greedy corruption became impossible to hide. That, though, was still far in the future.

In wartime summers, I got glimpses of that old penury when we went on holiday to Lake Gougane Barra in West Cork – by then almost a family shrine – where Seán and Eileen had done their courting while attending a Gaelic summer school, and where later he had gone on the run during the Irish Civil War of 1922–3. In an ecstasy of patriotism, they had learned the language fast, unlike myself who, though I did well in Latin and French, earned mediocre marks in Gaelic. It's fair to say in my defence that the nuns in my Dublin schools weren't keen on it either. In fact in my senior school a lay teacher had to be brought in to teach it, a rare event which lowered the subject's standing.

Fearful of cutting a poor figure in Gougane, I reminded myself annually how to say in Gaelic 'I don't understand Gaelic' along with other practical phrases not supplied in our school readers. These concentrated instead on proverbs, prayers and poems about visionary maidens described in terms unlikely to be of use if I met and recognised a Gaelic speaker. Language recognition in West Cork could be tricky in those years, due to a widespread lack of teeth and a habit of gargling vowels in the throat. 'You', an old man whom I had annoyed by saying I didn't understand Gaelic mocked me, 'have neither Oirish nor English?' Having decoded his spittly sounds as English, I worried that he might be right and I be turning into that despised hybrid, a West Briton.

Forgivingly, he shared a meal with me. Lunch? Dinner? For all I knew, it could have been his only meal of the day. It consisted of boiled potatoes unloaded in a ring onto a scrubbed table. No plate. No cutlery. Just a splash of buttermilk. Picky ten-year-old though I was, I knew enough about pride not to refuse. I had landed in his mountain cabin through some misunderstanding over catching up with a group from the local hotel who had gone snipe-shooting.

He and his potatoes were like pale, shrunken after-images of the Great Famine: ghostly escapees from someone's memory – though, on reflection, in the blight-ridden 1840s, his wholesome spuds might have constituted a small pocket of wealth. Amused by my encounter, my parents claimed it had served me right, as I had always been finicky about food and, when small, needed a mix of blandishment and threat to help me unclench my teeth, quell my nausea and swallow. This was why, back when I was still strapped into a high chair, Eileen used to sit with me at meal times and tell stories, some of which she would eventually publish. They were suspense-driven fairy tales with titles like *The Little Black Hen, Miss Pennyfeather and the Pooka* and *The Shadowy Man*, all aimed at my age group, which had grown almost old enough to have pocket money to spend by the time the books started to come out in England and the USA. At that time she must have been earning more than Seán, whose income had been hit by the war. Paper was scarce and English publishers were said to be unfriendly to writers who were not sharing the dangers of the blitz. Wartime readers, on the other hand, seemed eager for escapism, if only into the bedtime stories they could read to their children or hear Eileen read on Radio Éireann. She had woven in elements from Gaelic folk tales heard in Gougane, and may have called on knowledge of modern children's taste for fear and horror, too, gleaned while teaching in Boston and London.

Her first book used one of my favourite legends: the one about a fairy mansion which rises from the bog after dark, aglow with light and throbbing with music. Wise travellers avoid being lured inside or, if lured, refuse to eat anything they are offered. Those who do will never escape, but be carried off to *Tír na nÓg* when the mansion sinks back into the bog at dawn. The *pooka*, a fairy horse, which tries to get tired travellers to accept a ride on his back, and the empty coach, which pauses invitingly, play the same trick. Allegorical, or lending themselves to allegory, such tales draw force from their vagueness.

Once or twice Eileen took me with her into the Radio Éireann studio while she made a live broadcast. Perhaps this was a test – I had to stay utterly quiet – or, it strikes me now, her aim may have been to show me that women like herself were as capable as men. That was something she was keen for me to know.

She confided snippets of her personal history, too, some of which went back to the Troubles, which had petered out a year or so before first Seán, then she herself, left for Boston. One related an incident from her college days in University College Cork, UCC, when, at the time of the Anglo-Irish War, she and some friends hired a barge so as to have a picnic on the River Lee. Before setting off, men from their group went into a pub where Black and Tans in civvies overheard them make rash, incendiary remarks. That evening, when the barge returned from the picnic, the Tans were waiting and opened fire. Everyone on board dropped flat, but she, who craned her neck to look, got a bullet in it. She showed me the trace: a puckered hollow the size of a hazelnut which never disappeared. Later, during the Civil War, when Seán was Director of Publicity for the Irregulars and in hiding, she, who was his courier, was caught and jailed, and worse would have followed if an old UCC classmate on the winning side hadn't spotted her name on a list, crossed it off, and let her go. In those days, she said, fear kept you from sleeping, but also from getting fat or bored.

'You missed them!' she teased, while shoving a spoonful of lumpy porridge into my open mouth. 'All of them! The bad times and the good! And don't dare spit that out!'

Her moods had grown capricious, and Seán said that this was because her father had recently died. I was nearly five. I know because by my fifth birthday we had left Wicklow, but on that day we were still there. I can tell this by the shadows flinching and flickering in my mental motion picture of her, as she mentions Boston and an old fear lest Seán, whom she had gone there to marry, be having second thoughts: pre-nuptial doubts to which she would not again allude for fifty years. Maybe she had brought them up now as cover for a new fret. What kind of fret? All I knew was that it was as fitful as the draughts which whistled through that old house and on windy days could flatten candle flames and make an oil lamp smoke. Though the place was too remote for connection to electricity, we did have a wireless. It ran on batteries, and Eileen would sometimes sing along with the old songs that floated from it, then turn it off, with a brisk 'Ráiméis', which is Gaelic for 'rubbish'. When they first met, she and Seán had entwined their feelings for each other with those they cherished for the national cause. It was a heady bond. But bonds can chafe or fray, and back in 1922 theirs did both.

First the IRA split, and Seán, trusting de Valera's pledge to hold out for a thirty-two-county Republic, promptly joined his die-hard faction whose members fought, lost, retreated to the West Cork hills then, finding that they were now a burden to the people who fed and hid them, felt a shamed relief when the order came in April 1923 to dump arms. Seán himself has written about how by then he was demoralised, filthy, lice-infested and embittered by reports of summary executions and even torture being inflicted by one group of old comrades on the other. He turned for home. It was not the first time defeat left young men with a sour taste in their mouths, but the taste in his was as styptic as a sloe.

Even after the ceasefire a propaganda war limped on, and it was only in early 1924 that he, who had meanwhile been appointed Acting Director of Publicity for the whole imaginary Republic, received an order to give up even that. After the Civil War Seán went back to UCC, from which he had graduated three years before, worked for an MA, then got a job as a teacher in the small town of Ennis which – a shock – had neither a cinema, a library nor a bookshop. In the light of this, his elevation was dizzying when, on the strength of having published some short fiction in Irish and English, he was recommended for the Commonwealth fellowship which took him to Harvard.

He was happy there, as he would later be in London, where he taught at Horace Walpole's Strawberry Hill, then a teacher training college, whose fairy-tale architecture must have suited his and Eileen's mood as they began to pine for an Ireland which was never going to be the one they had imagined. Yet back they went in 1933.

Did they suppose that de Valera's ratting on his principles and taking the Oath of Allegiance to England's king, which he had sworn never to do, would be a sound basis for exercising the power he had finally won in 1932? Did Dev himself? Well, clearly – and correctly – he did. The choice was between doing that or skulking, for who knew how much longer, in the wilderness with neither salaries nor influence, as he and his followers had been doing until he ate his words, took the hated oath, led the followers into the Dáil and, once there, wrested power from his rivals.

Just as well, perhaps. Faced with a similar dilemma in 1924, Mussolini's opponents, whose leader had been murdered by Fascist thugs, chose the high-minded route, boycotted parliament – and ushered in twenty years of Fascism. Dev's choice was cannier.

The times, though, were censorious, as Seán found when his book of stories was banned in Ireland, and a group claiming to represent the Cork IRA, displeased by his having written it, summoned him to come and be court-martialled.

He ignored them, while possibly wondering why he had come back to his increasingly juvenile country. Hope was why. Hope and dream. In 1933 he published an adoring biography of Dev; then, six years later, a second one which took a revised view. The prologue to the first one opens like this:

Tall as a spear, commanding, enigmatic, his eyes so dark and deep that it is difficult to see their expression, his face deeply lined as with many cares, the face of a thoughtful man . . . this is the first impression one gets of Eamon de Valera . . .

Seán's magnificat may have embarrassed him even as he was writing it, for, two pages on, he cast a cooler eye, noting that Dev 'was the best loved and best hated man in Ireland'. Like many Irish republicans Seán, too, had reasons to love and hate the man whose courage in 1916 had dazzled his boyhood, but who, later, ruthlessly interned hard-liners for sticking to principles which had once been his. Dev's Oath of Allegiance had stuck in many craws, but what stuck most uncomfortably was his plea that an oath taken under duress was no oath at all. To cut the Gordian knot Dev needed to get into the Dáil, but, under the terms of the Anglo-Irish Treaty with Britain, couldn't get in until he *had* taken it – hence the casuistry about duress. Since he could have tried this shifty manoeuvre as early as 1922, and forestalled the Civil War, his delays were hard to forgive. But perhaps he learned cunning as he matured?

Another bone of contention was the power he gave to RC bishops whose arrogance, though he had defied them during the Civil War, he later condoned. Here is what Seán's second biography had to say about that:

Furthermore the Catholic Church, and the Church of Ireland, are both notoriously 'low church', puritanical and narrow-minded. To say this, naturally, will anger most Irish readers.

It is nonetheless a regrettable fact. Its effects may be seen daily in such things as the inhuman treatment of unmarried mothers, in the unimaginative control of juvenile houses of detention, in a stupid censorship . . . in the fanatical way in which such innocent amusements as dancing . . . are controlled . . . Etc.

These comments enraged Dev's followers who, on reading them, refused to have anything more to do with our family. As we were already on their opponents' black list, this meant, claimed Eileen, that we now had no friends at all.

The about-face had consequences even for me, whose godmother, Molly Fitz, had, in the early Twenties, become Seán's courier after Eileen's arrest. She too was caught, jailed, eventually released and subsequently married a man who was part of Dev's establishment, which was by then in office and presumably enjoying its fruits, since my most dazzling childhood memory is of a gift she gave me of two dolls, each – at a guess – fourteen inches tall. One was male, one female, so I called them 'the prince and princess', because they wore silky eighteenth-century costumes, and I say this not because I could have had such a thought then, but because even now I can picture the prince's taut stockings, smart breeches and waisted jacket.

Dressed as if for a white wedding, the sort Seán and Eileen didn't have when they married so quietly in Boston's Holy Cross Cathedral that they had to ask the sacristan and an assistant to be witnesses, the dolls made a perfect couple. Nobody I knew had a pair like that: a perfect image of married bliss. Molly had been a close friend, but, once Seán attacked de Valera, she had to break with us. 'Fraternising' with opponents was strictly forbidden after the Civil War.

'She was a generous godmother,' I remember Eileen sighing. 'She gave you lovely presents. You'd best look after them, for there won't be any more.'

And indeed I don't remember other presents, only the dolls, which someone said were French. In my memory they *look* French, like small aristos who could end up on the guillotine, a thought which may have been prompted by another memory. This is of my own hands twisting off one of their heads so as to get at its blue china eyes, then failing to fit these back behind their eye holes. They are attached to a wire which is hidden when they are in place. But I can't get it in. I hold on to the eyes. Whose are they? The prince's? I can't be sure. All I clearly recall is myself sitting on the ground outside our new Dublin house on a later birthday which, just as Eileen predicted, brought no gifts from Molly. Lying next to me in the long June grass are the mutilated dolls. I must hide them before anyone sees what I did for reasons I no longer understand. It's as if I had felt challenged to cock a snook at the godmother who has thrown me over and will not be back.

Why won't she? I am baffled. As I sit there fretting, it strikes me that lately there has been a lot of talk about something else I don't understand: treachery. Dev's, Seán's, Molly's and that of both sides in the Civil War. People keep using the word, which, as far as I can tell, has to do with people turning against their friends. So perhaps I too am treacherous, because the dolls now disappear. Perhaps they have been given to someone more deserving, like Kitty's nieces who have few toys and to whom Eileen has been threatening to give some of mine.

Has she done it? With the dolls? Better not ask. Perhaps they were so badly injured that she had to hide them from Seán.

I don't always grasp what is happening. Maybe I don't listen, or maybe my parents explain things confusingly. My mother's Aunt Kate certainly does. She has come to live with us but is unused to our ways. She used to live in Cork with Eileen's father, but, now that he has died, will live with us. Our first meeting starts out on the wrong foot.

Almost the first thing she does is scold me because I have gathered the hems of the new, short, poppy-red dress I am wearing, and raised them above my head. That way the dress works like a lantern, except that the light – it is a sunny day – pours in instead of out. As long as I hold up the dress, all I can see is redness, so I walk out our gate and along the road, feeling as if I were in the middle of a harmless but thrilling fire which has blotted out the world. I am too happy to give any thought to how I look.

Then I hear a scolding voice. 'Cover yourself,' snaps the aunt, and she says something about knickers. She is bossy but, Seán assures me later, has many weaknesses.

'Be kind to her,' he tells me. 'She's old and lonely. She needs you to like her.'

This flatters me.

Meanwhile, our time in Wicklow is almost over. We are shuttling between Killough and a house so new it is not yet finished. It is being built for us, just outside a village called Killiney, by an architect called John O'Gorman, and has been being planned for most of my lifetime – which is not, of course, very long, although it seems immensely so to me.

We have made countless trips in my parents' black Ford car to watch its progress, and its modern conveniences astound both Aunt Kate and myself, who have been looking forward in a delirium of joy to moving into it for good. None of the four of us has ever lived in a house so new that nobody lived there before us, a house painted white on the outside and primrose within. A house without ghosts.

Killiney, being in South County Dublin, is supplied with telephone lines, gas and electricity. This means that I shall no longer be left in the dark once my candle is blown out at night – an *enormous* relief which my parents pretend not to appreciate. They pretend not to because, while we're still in the old house, they are afraid to leave me a lit candle or matches or even an oil lamp lest I knock it over and burn the house down. I don't argue about this now. Why bother, since, once we finally move to the new house, there will be an electric switch in the wall next to my bed which, at the touch of a finger, will flood the room with light? The old, creaky, earwig-ridden room where I still sleep and where I cannot be quite sure that a family of witches doesn't live too will then be no more than a memory. Alleluia! Electricity is like having your own sun. I could worship it.

Kitty, who is not coming with us, is to take all the oil lamps when we leave, though not the candles. Eileen says we may need a store of those since sometimes electricity can break down. This shocks me. The sun doesn't break down. Why should electricity?

Until recently I was afraid to come out from under the bed-clothes after dark, and have been known to wet the bed rather than grope under it in search of a chamber pot. I manage to forget such lapses and, though ashamed, am addicted to the terror which provokes them.

Addicted! Eileen has told me this wonderful new word. Being addicted is like being under a spell so that bad things which happen aren't my fault. They are hers because she has made me too fond of the frightening tales she likes to tell before I go to sleep. That is because she is addicted too. Worse, when she and I go trespassing in the deserted estates which are now overgrown and have been taken over by owls, weasels, ravens and the like, we play a game which Seán has forbidden, but to which she and I are irresistibly drawn. This is how it works. First, Eileen hides in the bushes, leaving me to work up anxiety, then, having taken off her coat and pulled it over her head, she will suddenly appear in the middle of a yew or a laurel walk whose top branches have knit together so that, even at midday, it is as dark as a railway tunnel. Pretending not to be herself, she makes weird noises and mimes our joint idea of a witch. I run away. She chases me and sometimes I trip and fall. When this happens she, her face half hidden by the coat which she has turned into a hood, looms above me, still half playing at being a witch, and reduces me to thrilled, gibbering terror. The glass eyes of the fox fur which she normally wears around her neck now look down from the top of her head. Its teeth grin. When she pulls it forward, its jaws snap.

Don't I know it is she? Well, yes and no. After all, she may have a second, dangerous self which sometimes takes over. Maybe a demon has entered her? There are stories like this. She performs a sort of dance. Sliding out from under the coat, her pale fingers mimic tentacles and I both do and don't want to be more frightened still.

'Let's stop,' she says. 'You're getting too excited.'

'No, no, don't stop. Please, Mummy.' I am like a drunk worried about hangovers but unable to give up the booze. 'I promise not to have a nightmare.'

'You always promise.'

We are trespassing in an estate called Monks's whose owners have been absent for years. Perhaps they haven't the money to keep it up. We tell each other that they have forfeited their rights. Pinned crookedly to the jungly greenery are faded notices saying 'Trespassers will be prosecuted'. I mix up words. Execution? Persecution. With which are we being threatened? I think of the broken doll. Persecution is what the English did to Catholic priests at the time of Queen Elizabeth which, according to Aunt Kate, was worse than guillotining. Disembowelling. The rack. Being hanged, drawn and quartered. She has described these processes in detail and Eileen has told her to stop filling my head with such stories. But meanwhile she herself tells me about witches. That's different, she says, because witches don't exist. Don't they? I both do and don't want them to. What *is* prosecution? I don't know. And now, anyway, Eileen, tired of being a witch, is once again using her coat as a coat and, seated on a stone bench, is unwrapping a small snack.

As we eat it, she reminds me that we must say goodbye to our Wicklow neighbours before we leave for good: to the two Miss Griffiths, old ladies who sometimes invite us to their big, old house for afternoon tea with hot buttered potato cakes, and other treats; to the Dennehys who sell milk just a stone's throw from our house and sometimes give us a lift in their pony and trap; to Paul Henry and Michael Farrell and, most importantly, to Garret FitzGerald whose family – he has three older brothers – lives not far away.

Garret, with whom Eileen has persuaded me I am in love, is agile, curly-haired, six years my senior and disliked by Kitty. This is to be expected, since in almost all the houses we know, boys are to maids what dogs are to postmen: suspect, teasing, fond of pranks and hard to control. They track mud indoors on their shoes, untie the maids' aprons, tease them, and generally make trouble. I myself am full of admiration for Garret who is a champion tree-climber and may, I fear, visit us for the sole purpose of climbing our – but soon to be no longer our – vast old cedar. When he climbs high enough to be almost out of sight, he calls down tauntingly, 'It's nice up here.' I have never even touched the lowest branch. Desperate to do at least that, I run round and round the tree, calling up to him and feeling ridiculous. Eager as a puppy, I can't stop myself begging, 'Please, Garret. Come down. Give me a hand up. Please!' Around I go. I almost bark. I am tormented by the thought that once we leave Wicklow, I may never see him again.

Eileen, who will soon be preparing *The Little Black Hen* for publication, has put him into it. The story has the form of a folk tale, albeit one for primary-school readers. It is about an old woman's pet hen being captured by evil fairies and about the risky adventures on which two children embark to save it. Their names are Garret and Julie, and Eileen will manage to keep their story going through a number of later books. She has made us into a couple, handing me a fantasy Garret in lieu of the unattainable, real one.

Illustrations in the US edition of her book will show two barefoot children with brightly, not to say clownishly, patched clothes. This is not how Irish people, especially not those now running or hoping soon to run our young state, like to imagine themselves. Garret's parents are part of this group, the part opposed to de Valera, and Garret himself, when he sees the pictures, will – I hope jokingly – complain. Though he cannot guess that he will one day be Ireland's most distinguished Taoiseach, tree-climbing has given him a feeling for hierarchy. I, who am untroubled by patched skirts or trousers, am glad to see that, unlike the real Garret, the boy in the illustrations is the right height to be a friend of the pictured Julie.

Julie was my name at this time and would be until I was in my twenties when I would think it insufficiently dignified for my adult self and switch to Julia. On my birth certificate I am still Anna Julia to this day, but, for everyday purposes, my parents dropped the Anna when the aunt, after whom they had named me, went mad. Poor Aunt Anna! The rejection was a clear case of hitting someone when she was down, but, by the time I was told of it, I was Julie, and she was dead.

I had met her once. She called at our house in Killiney when my parents were out, and she and I went for a walk in the woods. She didn't strike me as being at all mad. If she asked my name, I must have said 'Julie' instead of Anna, so I suppose she guessed what had happened and felt hurt. I am sorry about that. Her name still has a bureaucratic grip on me, relentlessly surfacing on electoral rolls and wherever else birth certificates are consulted. 'Anna,' NHS employees sometimes call out when I sit in their waiting rooms, and often I don't realise that they mean me and fail to respond. Maybe they think my mind is slipping? Maybe Aunt Anna's offended ghost is amused.

My last memory of the Wicklow house is a sad one. It has to do with Pangur Bán, our partly white cat, who had led a decorous and, I hope, happy life with us, until one day a family of spoiled children who had three spoiled dogs dropped by. The dogs, which were not restrained in any way, chased poor Pangur around and through the house while I screamed at their owners in impotent fury, for I was fond of Pangur. Utterly rattled, he bolted up a chimney, didn't come down until long after the horrible visitors had left, and shortly afterwards disappeared for good.

Droppers-in would turn out to be even more of a nuisance in Killiney, where we were on a bus route and so, even during the war, when petrol disappeared, could be easily reached. People were still unused to phones and rarely alerted us. They just came. As Seán worked at home, this interfered with his writing, and on summer Sundays Eileen would feel obliged to produce afternoon tea and often supper. Habits were in transition between modernity and old, hospitable, rural ways and, as Killiney had a pleasant choice of sea views and places to walk, friends of friends whom Seán and she had made in Boston and London thought it a good place to visit. We grew to dread them and, once the shrubs which we would soon start to plant grew large enough to provide cover, would sometimes hide when the gate opened. That, though, would not be for some years.

For now it was still only 1937, and Eileen's mind was full of things like rugs, lined and interlined tweed curtains to keep out the cold, and the garden which she would soon start to create, with the help of a handyman, from the bare, tussocky, one-acre field in which the new house now stood.

'Your mother used to be fearless.'

My father stares in wonder at the medicines which she, hoping perhaps to cure any lingering puniness left by the Great Famine a century before, has marshalled by the door, so that I may fortify myself every morning before leaving for school.

Today he is seeing me off, and, with luck, will forget about the medicines. To distract him, I ask what changed her.

'Your birth! Remember?'

We laugh, because my birth was forgotten faster than most. It, or some side-effect, so nearly killed Eileen that no one took time to register it until the Somerset House record-book for its date was full and my entry had to be squeezed into a margin. This, plus the war, made it impossible to get a birth certificate in the Forties. So in 1942, when I was ten and due to be confirmed, our parish priest ruled that I couldn't be unless Seán made out an affidavit swearing that he was my father. Else people, the PP explained, might think he wasn't. Maybe, it struck us, he thought this himself.

Maybe I'm a love child, I told myself later, when the term cropped up in my reading and made my memories hum.

In the earliest of these, I am in our Wicklow garden, aged maybe three, staring in fascination at my cousin Denis, a towering five-year-old. Nothing happens. So why does the moment stay with me? Perhaps because I am amazed that there is such a thing as a cousin and that I have one. Not only does his presence enlarge our tiny family – *could* my Catholic parents, I will come to wonder, have used condoms? – but his visit feels like a convivial promise.

Sadly it came to nothing. Denis went home to England and stayed there until the war had come and gone and he had grown irredeemably English. Like his parents, he used the English form of our surname, Whelan, where we were Ó Faoláin. One good thing though: he and I were now of an age to flirt, and did.

Someone had taught me the phrase *cousinage, dangereux voisinage*. But I could see that he wasn't dangerous at all. On the contrary, he was a uniquely safe young male. Perhaps he had had the same thought about me.

'Cousin,' he kept saying, as though reminding himself of my harmlessness. 'Cousin!' He talked about the minutia of military service, told me how to get a really good shine on your boots, taught me to kiss, though I am not sure whether we actually 'French kissed' and whether, if so, the act was purely technical – like shining one's boots. The war had by then been over for three years.

We met again in the Seventies at his father's funeral – I shall come back to that. Then in 1991, when my own father died, Denis sent me a condolence letter, mentioning that he had changed his name to Michael. There was no return address, and I haven't heard from him since.

Denis, the name of the patron saint and first bishop of Paris, has Catholic connotations, which Michael doesn't. So Denis/Michael may have been cutting his roots. Why? I can only guess. He was a solicitor, and the Irish can't have been popular that year with the English legal professions, since three separate Irish groups, convicted of terrorism in the Seventies, had spent a decade and a half in jail, before their convictions were found to have been obtained by British policemen arresting them at random, beating false confessions out of them, manipulating interview records, and suppressing evidence. With honourable exceptions, members of the British legal professions lost face.

'Business as usual' was the verdict of most Irish citizens and a watchful foreign press.

But the Whelans were not Irish citizens.

Back in the early Twenties, when the Irish Free State was set up, Irish civil servants, including Denis's father, Augustine John, AJ, had a choice. They could go to England to work for the Crown or stay home and work for the new dispensation. The Whelans left. AJ became an English tax inspector and on his annual holiday, when he would come to spend some days with us, his handsome, bony, Jansenist face seemed to express awareness that what he saw before him were travellers on the road not taken. Was he thinking, we wondered, of Seán – his younger brother – as an anti-self whom he might resemble if he had stayed in Ireland? That seemed unlikely when one allowed for character. After all, when they both did live in Ireland, Seán had joined the IRA, and AJ the Civil Service. A tax inspector is presumably devoted to the status quo, whereas Seán, a writer and journalist, was for much of his life embroiled in polemics with the spiritual and temporal rulers of the new, young, divided country which he and his comrades had fought to establish.

So there was a definite flicker of mockery in AJ's smile.

But at whom was it directed? He might, after all, have been wondering whether to regret the thoroughness with which he and his family had shed their Irish Catholic identity. Denis, who had attended a minor English public school, seemed to accept its undemanding Protestantism, but, as far as I know, AJ himself displayed no interest in religion once he grew up. He had had a surfeit of it in his boyhood, when both he and Seán had it imposed on them by their pious mother and a zealous elder brother, who ended his days as a priest – indeed a monsignor – in New Zealand.

So when AJ, who was by then a widower, died, Denis was amazed to find that he had stipulated a Catholic funeral.

'We're counting on you', he told me when I arrived, 'to give the lead at the funeral Mass. Show the rest of us when to stand and sit and so forth.'

I, however, was unfamiliar with the rituals introduced in the aftermath of the Second Vatican Council, so our congregation's gestures bodied forth a dither of false consciousness. This, according to my mother, had always afflicted the Whelans as a penalty for aping the English. She, who could be a left-wing snob, alleged that they didn't even get this right. To her mind, they associated with the wrong sort of English anyway: soulless, golf-and-bridge-playing bank managers and their wives, some of whom she had met when she and Seán lived in London. She remembered them as conventional-looking women in twinsets who no doubt, in their innocence, mistook AJ for a wild Irishman!

As it turned out, her malice was only slightly off target.

The funeral was in a south-coast retirement town, possibly Hastings or Bexhill-on-Sea. The day was fine and, while the coffin was being lowered into the grave, something unexpected happened. One mourner, a woman who looked as though she might indeed play bridge and wear twinsets, began to rail against God. She addressed Him directly and angrily, raged at His cruelty in giving us the gifts of life and love only to then take them away, and, like Laertes grieving for Ophelia, looked ready to leap after the coffin into AJ's grave. Her speech was so articulate and persuasive that, if I had been God or His priest, I would have felt deeply uncomfortable.

I can't remember whether Denis and I mentioned this episode over lunch in a local hotel, but we did marvel at what might have provoked it: his father's surprise return to the bosom of Mother Church, a move by then less common than it had once been among renegade Catholics. Surely, though, AJ's reasons could not have been theirs? Wasn't it likelier that he had admired that Church's talent for putting on a good show in the same spirit as he had admired the British Empire? Distancing himself from the reckless tolerance of the Church of England was consistent with his earlier backing away from the splits and cock-ups endemic to new states. One does not *join* what might become a sinking ship.

Afterwards, reflecting on AJ's reticence about all this and on his woman friend's distress at losing him, I came to see that he must have harboured contradictions which none of us had imagined. Though clearly not 'wild Irish', he had known how to respond to the wild Englishwoman whose passion spoke in his favour. My father too was a passionate but reticent man, and it strikes me now that Denis may have been one too. He may have disappeared so as to pursue passions about which it is no business of mine to speculate.

Or he may – I had better face up to this – have simply found me unlikeably lacking in *pietas*. Family feeling. Solidarity with kin. People who have been raised without those can develop a craving.

Just now, looking through some old letters, I found one of his. It reports that he has been to Ireland in search of distant relations – Whelan roots – and met our very ancient, common great-grandmother with whom his letter urges me to get in touch. When it reached me I was living in California and must have written back explaining this. Secretly, I was probably relieved not to have to meet a relative with whom my parents had long lost touch and about whom I knew little. Perhaps he sensed this and disapproved. He could not have guessed at the hard truth concealed under my mother's jokey hyperbole when she said, as she sometimes did, that Seán's polemics with some of the men who ran the Irish church and state had turned us into pariahs.

Members of a diaspora as varied and populous as ours – there are far more of us outside the Republic than in it – risk disappointing each other's expectations.

As long as we lived in the wilds of Wicklow without a telephone, visits could be a surprise. The pleasantest of these, from my point of view, was that of Pamela Travers, the author of *Mary Poppins*.

'Tell her it's your favourite book,' my mother whispered excitedly. I guessed that it was hers, for she had read it to me twice.

Miss Travers's face is masked in my memory by one of those mist blobs which disguise witnesses in police documentaries, but her visit proved influential, for when the war came and cash in our house grew increasingly scanty, Eileen, as I mentioned earlier, took a leaf from Miss Travers's book and began writing childrens' stories herself.

By then we had moved to County Dublin, where a more troubling encounter was triggered when I heard someone talking about how Seán in his youth had made bombs. Bombs? Daddy? Amazed, I consulted my mother, who said, coldly, 'Ask him.'

She and he were not getting on just then, but I would not learn why until their tiff had been patched up and could be disguised as political sparring over de Valera's decision to intern a number of his own hard-line followers, including some of our family friends. Yes, Seán told me, he had made bombs for the IRA. 'More than twenty years ago. Someone had to. We were fighting a war.'

In this memory I am about ten, and the new war known to

us as the Emergency is in full spate. We, however, are neutral – most of us anyway. From what you hear, some people aren't. Some people are spies.

'Your mother', Seán tells me, 'needs her mind taken off things. You should try to cheer her up.' And skipping into his study, he closes the door.

So she and I go trespassing, as we used to do in Wicklow, where in the hungry Thirties there were a number of Anglo-Irish estates whose owners, unable to keep them up, had locked the gates and left for London. A year or so after they did this, neglected greenery would explode, wildlife go on the rampage, and my mother and I climb in past signs telling us not to, so as to enjoy the anarchic spectacle of tilting gazebos, overgrown yew walks and untramelled flowers. As half the pleasure to be had from these incursions lay in testing our nerve, we murmured tales to each other about man-traps which could break a poacher's leg – or our own! In the old days, Eileen warned, gamekeepers used to hide these in undergrowth where, for all we knew, one might still lie. There was nothing like this where we now lived in orderly South County Dublin.

What there was, though, was a boarded-up, Disneyesque, turreted Victorian Gothic castle into which we had not ventured until now, because a caretaker was known to live in its gate lodge. Thick trees hid it and abutted on woods belonging to a section of what might or might not be Killiney Park. Boundaries were becoming increasingly unclear and perimeter walls were crumbling. So we climbed one, then dropped into an orchard where leaf mould muffled sound and cidery fruit rotted pungently. Eileen was starting on a fresh tale of brutal, old-time gamekeepers, when, seeing a movement among the apple trees, I grabbed her elbow.

'Mummy, a gamekeeper!'

She was looking in the wrong direction. 'In those days,' she mused, 'they . . .'

'No! Now! Here. There's one. Look.'

Sure enough, a man emerging from the trees had hailed us. He had a gun. Not a gangster's gun but the sort my father used for shooting rabbits. He wasn't pointing it, but he was definitely advancing towards us. He wore a tweed coat so prickly it brought to mind the withered nettles goose girls spun and wove in some of Eileen's stories. His eyebrows were a yellow stubble and his face was lumpy, as though it had indeed been stung by nettles.

'Hullo there!' By now he was close, and Eileen must have seen him. So why didn't she move?

'Let's run!' I urged her, then bolted in panic and neither paused nor turned until I reached the damaged wall where we had come in. Still no Eileen. Where *was* she? Cautiously, I retraced my steps, then hid behind a clump of bushes to see what was happening.

He had a hand on her arm. Could he be taking her into custody? That was a word I knew from the wireless. No. He was handing her a notebook, then screwing the top back on a fountain pen. Moving from tree to tree, I edged close enough to hear my father's name and that of a magazine he had recently started up.

They were *chatting*! Could they be? They *were*! Catching sight of me, they laughed, then, as though pitying me, shook their heads. Nervously, turning away, I noticed that I had got a run in my black school stocking. A long worm of pale flesh showed through. Sheepishly, I sidled forward to hear the man say that he was one of those whom Dev had led and then let down. 'He's a splitter,' he told Eileen. 'He split the movement.' Next he told us that he had read Seán's recent attack on Dev for doing this and wanted Eileen to take him a message of support. As for our trespassing, well, no harm done if this was the end of it.

'The old people used to say,' he quoted, ' "Every dog is allowed one bite".'

Perhaps to apologise for the comparison, he presented her

with a bag of apples which he must have filled earlier, for it had been lying on a bench. Next, looking her in the eye, he warned gravely that we should not come back, then, leading us through a shrubbery and down an avenue to the gate lodge, opened a gate and let us out on the road.

On our way home my mother was unusually quiet. When I asked if the man was a gamekeeper, she said no, a caretaker, and that we mustn't breathe a word about what had happened. 'I'll tell your father,' she said, 'later.'

'Did the caretaker give you a message for him?'

'He did.'

'Which side is he on? The caretaker? Daddy's or Dev's?'

'No side,' my mother told me. 'He has no side. Now remember you're not to tell a soul. Have I your promise?'

'Yes.'

I was confused though. She had handled the caretaker with impressive coolness, so why didn't she want anyone to know? How indeed had she known that he would be friendly if she introduced herself to him? Had he known who she was already? Maybe they had seen each other in the pub or the village shop? Maybe they had talked?

I didn't want to think so.

Then rumours started. The milkman, it seemed, had told the Gardaí that something queer was going on in the castle. The caretaker, a lone man living in the gate lodge, was taking too much milk. A crate? Two? I forget. But the place was raided and – shades of my father's bomb-making days! – it came out that bombs were being fabricated there by members of a rump IRA which was in opposition to the government.

'Fifteen men they found!' Great-aunt Kate, who had been talking to Bridie the maid, revelled in shock. Bridie was on a network. She talked to other maids, some of whom had come from the same orphanage as herself.

'I heard six.' My mother, drawing on my father's experience in *their* war, thought six quite enough for a bomb factory. But nobody knew for sure. It was a great time for hugger-mugger.

Great-aunt Kate, who was now ninety, said bomb-making must have got a sight more complex since my Daddy's day, and seemed pleased rather than frightened by this. Perhaps she thought of bombs as lightning-conductors for the random evil that threatened us all, but especially people her age. Some of that had now been averted or at least stalled.

'A whole crate of milk!' She began to count on her fingers. 'They'd only use it in their tea or porridge. A whole crate! Sure that would be enough for thirty men! Half could have got away.'

'Maybe one had an ulcer? Ulcer victims are great milk-drinkers.'

Did the bomb-makers belong to the pro-German or the Communist wing of the outlawed movement? Perhaps the wings combined? Nobody knew, but passengers on our bus liked to speculate. It wasn't true that they cut my mother dead. Gossips were too keen to probe to do that. As for the war itself, the 'Emergency' whose name somehow denied what it signalled, reality and illusion had begun to blend.

I began to wonder if they had ever been separate.

SEAN READS *THE LAST SEPTEMBER*

Here is a quote from one of de Valera's more remarkable radio broadcasts delivered in 1933:

The Irish genius has always stressed spiritual values . . . That is the characteristic that fits the Irish people in a special manner for the task of helping to save western civilization.

Being a year old when that claim was made, I knew nothing of the risk that saving the West might become part of a Fascist agenda – as it might have that same year, when Irish citizens, enticed by the Blueshirt movement, were flirting with Fascist plans. Luckily, these foundered when General O'Duffy, the potential Führer, lost his nerve.

A more tenacious spectre, however, was haunting our young Free State. When hopes of achieving a pious, all-Ireland Republic also foundered, hypocrisy – 'the tribute vice pays to virtue' – grew exponentially. Coercion ensured that our population would at least seem to be amassing enough prayer-power to help save the West – and that my age group would grow up in an age of pretence.

So how trust anyone's memories?

I have been rereading Seán's defiantly named memoir, *Vive Moi*, which he rewrote towards the end of his life. To spare my mother's feelings, an edition published in the Sixties had made no mention of his love affairs.

Later, though, when he sensed love and identity slip away, he wrote an expanded version for publication after his death. This one too, though, missed completeness, not just through the paradox of that planned, posthumous gasconade, but also because, while wistfully reliving old loves, it failed to consider how they had affected my mother, or how best he and she might, in the time left to them, manage their mutual unhappiness. Instead, as his narrative advanced, her image receded – rather like those of the old comrades who vanished from group portraits in Stalin's Russia. She was stoical, as women of her generation often had to be. Her health, perhaps because of this, broke down, and Seán, who, it now turned out, both needed and was exasperated by her, lived with her until 1988, when she died. Then *he* fell apart, got dementia, lusted impotently after a youngish woman who encouraged him so rashly that he lost his bearings, fought with his housekeeper, ran into the street inadequately clad – some said not clad at all – to rage like Lear at the human condition and shock the neighbours who wrote to tell me this.

When I flew back from California where I had been living, they invited me to tea so that I might be warned against the dangerous woman and hear how effectively they had concealed Seán's sad antics from the editor of a national newspaper who lived in the same street. They were proud of having preserved decorum by keeping the incident out of the press. Virtue's tribute had yet again been paid, and I, for once, was glad of this because, although Seán had fought hard against the wretched Censorship of Publications Act and other petty curbs, he also, when in his right mind, cared as much as anyone about privacy.

Which is why, when I was growing up, I knew none of his secrets. These emerged piecemeal, sometimes indecorously and, as often as not, confusingly, as secrets tend to do.

Confusing moments, as it happens, can be the ones which stay with you.

The rue Montpensier in Paris runs along the side of the Palais Royal garden, a place pulsing with memories of intriguing ghosts. It belonged to Philippe Égalité, the revolutionary duke who was guillotined by fellow revolutionaries in 1793, and whose illegitimate daughter, Pamela, married Lord Edward Fitzgerald, a blue-blooded Irish rebel whose story has striking echoes of her father's. Lord Edward too plotted against his own class, and was then betrayed and apprehended with such violence that he died of his wounds in a Dublin jail. Just as compelling is the memory of Desmoulins, the firebrand whose speech delivered from a café table top outside the same Palais Royal sparked off the French Revolution. And so is that of the looting and arson which later revolutions unleashed there in 1848 and 1871. The memory which comes to me, however, when I find myself in the rue Montpensier, focuses on Seán. It is of a baffled moment when he and I came out of one of its restaurants, and having lunched too well and probably drunk a little too much, and being dazzled by sudden sunlight, I took a while to notice that he was weeping. This must have been in the autumn of 1953, so Seán, who shared the century's age, was also fifty-three. He was embarrassed and apologetic, so I refrained from asking what was wrong.

I was shaken, though, for, being socially backward like most of my compatriots, I had always relied on him to be worldly and in control. He had been my mentor when it came to affairs of the heart, and thinking back I see that I must have known more about his than I let myself know I knew, though I remember guessing that his tears had to do with a woman.

With hindsight, his marriage to my mother strikes me as providing a small but telling illustration of how people in de Valera's Ireland felt obliged to live.

As was true of large parts of that society itself, disappointed idealism and a soured personal experience of its quarrelsome and rebelly past contributed to the glue which held them together. When Eileen died, it was seventy years since she and Seán had first met as eighteen-year-old enthusiasts in a Gaelic class in Cork City. Ironically, in those days, de Valera was soon to become one of their heroes.

Did Seán ever let himself see how badly and often he hurt her? I'm not sure. Did I? Of course I did, but when their estrangement was at its worst, I was living abroad and trying to stretch the postgraduate scholarships which were enabling me to spend as many years as I could at the universities of Rome and Paris. So I limited my trips home and, when I did make one, I felt unable to help, except once, about two years after the scene in the rue Montpensier. By then I was entangled in my first serious love affair, which Seán manoeuvred me into ending by claiming that Eileen had threatened to leave *him* unless he got me to leave my lover – a French, North African, Jewish, Communist activist, scandalously unsuitable in the eyes of the Ireland of the day.

'Your mother', said Seán grandly, 'is punching above her weight. She doesn't realise that she couldn't survive without me. And what's worse, having issued her threat, she'll be too proud to climb down. So it's up to you to get us out of this mess. You're the only one who can.'

This struck me as a mean passing of the buck.

'Why should I believe him?' I asked myself, and felt outrage both on her behalf and my own. But though his appeal might be a bluff, it seemed dangerous to call. Between us, I feared that he and I could indeed back Eileen into a corner and provoke her into some sort of craziness.

Could we though? Truly?

What made me think we could was a small secret of my own, a shy memory of how, when I was six, I had been in love with her. There is no other term for my feelings at the time. Shortly before my brother's birth, I became excessively attached to her, and something – I forget quite what – tipped this state of mind towards recklessness. Perhaps she had been talking too happily about the new baby she planned to bring home from the Hatch Street Nursing Home or had shown off her preparations with too much pride. There was, I remember, a softly draped and canopied cot in which I would have enjoyed sleeping myself, if it had been big enough, with next to it a Moses basket heaped with crocheted coatees, bonnets and tiny shoes. All new! The sight made me so jealous that I went straight into her garden, where I picked and ate a selection of brightly coloured berries which I had been warned were poisonous. 'Attention-seeking' I suppose this would now be called or, more charitably, a 'cry for help'. In the end it failed as both, when the berries turned out not to be poisonous after all. Nobody knew I'd eaten them, and I don't even remember being sick.

In 1955, though, what the embarrassing, old memory brought home to me was the danger of making people jealous.

At the same time, I began to wonder whether, despite what Seán thought, Eileen might do very well without him. Better perhaps. She could still go beagling in Wicklow with her friend Lily and to point-to-point races and country-house auctions. Couldn't she? For all I knew she might be happier? Maybe. But I couldn't risk being wrong, even though she was still an attractive woman who, I knew, had in their early years as a couple been its live wire.

But now he was a successful writer and public figure, while she was a middle-aged housewife, and I wasn't worldly enough to judge her chances of – well, what? – didn't people speak of 'Making a new life'? In Ireland, that didn't happen often. Not then. Not for women.

And Seán back then was still dangerously good-looking.

Someone might snap him up. They would certainly try. Quite recently I had noticed women brighten in his presence. He was burning with energy, long-legged and lean, with good cheekbones and an amused smile.

There are photographs to prove it.

For all I knew, however, he might have invented the story about her threatening to leave him. He was a fiction-writer, after all. Impish and a bit of a tease! When bored at a party, he was quite capable of opening a woman's handbag, if he found one left on a chair, and shamelessly examining the contents. I had seen him do this more than once. If caught rifling through it, he would laugh easily, claim that this was research, then chaff the bag's owner about secrets he would pretend to have found. Next, he might argue that writing and living needed to feed off each other. A good way to write a short story, he sometimes told young writers who came to tea, was to bring two narrative ideas together, make them interact and see what would happen. How could I be sure that he wasn't doing this very thing with Eileen's life and mine? 'Leave him, or she'll leave me,' was how he had started our conversation. 'I'm appealing to you for her sake.'

Was this true though? He could be manipulating me, just as Irish governments manipulated voters when they appealed to national pride, then forestalled further argument by banning abortion, divorce and contraceptives, and stepping up the censorship of films, newspapers and books.

All this to show that the Irish genius stressed spiritual values!

The notion that we were peculiarly virtuous was related to a view of history which held that not only the Reformation but also the Enlightenment had been disasters from which Catholic Ireland had been happily preserved. In return for this grace, we owed it to God, ourselves and the world to try to deserve it.

Citizens who failed to live up to the required image were rumoured to find ways of hiding their failures. And reportedly some of the ways found were so ruthless that when wind of them leaked out, the exposed cover-up risked generating a scandal greater than the one concealed.

For what if it came to be known – for example – that records had been tampered with to hide the fact that someone was a sibling's child by their joint father? Things like that did happen. In villages near ours, they were rumoured to happen often, and gossips claimed that it was common for official records to piously misrecord incestuous births by ascribing parentage to an unmarried mother's own mother or married sister. Today, Irish newspapers do report cases of incest, but back then the priority was to keep the Irish name untarnished. As a result, our only knowledge of that practice came from the Old Testament. But, as Catholics rarely read that, few learned of the misbehaviour of either God's chosen people or our own neighbours, and I only did so because I had Protestant friends.

So de Valera was able to go on hoping that our piety might yet re-Christianise Western civilisation, as Irish monks had done in the sixth century.

Did we swallow that? Not quite. Did we disbelieve it? Not quite either. One can live in a blur.

Yet Seán and a handful of friends tried, when they could, to draw attention to the undemocratic connivance of elected politicians who, even up to the late Fifties, took orders in secret from unelected bishops. They had no pipeline to this conspiracy. As investigative journalists must, they pieced together the few facts which were known and with the support of groups like the Irish Association of Civil Liberties – which Seán, Christo Gore-Grimes, and Owen Sheehy-Skeffington, among others, had founded in 1948 – managed to pierce some of the veils and scrims behind which laymen and clerics lurked, while running a country in which cant had become a necessary product, and humbug a civic duty.

To survive in such a place, and report unwelcome truths, you needed to develop guile. Seán did, and the one time he used it on me was when he persuaded me to test myself and my French lover by staying apart for a year to see if we would keep faith with each other.

We didn't, of course. Each of us blamed the other. And my parents' marriage staggered on for another three decades. Then they died within three years of each other.

So how – to come back to my question – when looking back on a delusive and deluded country, can I trust my own memory, or tell whether I saw anything clearly in the first place?

Wondering about this, I try to remember my young self.

'She's easily flustered and highly strung!'

That was what my mother warned my husband to expect when she met him first, which was two years after I and my Frenchman broke up, and four years after I began to doubt Seán's omniscience and savvy.

I had had doubts about these earlier, when he gave me a golden rule to help me decide whether or not to go to bed with a man. If I was to avoid self-dislike and moral squalor, I should, he advised, do so only when I was at least starting to fall in love. Properly, truly in love, he specified. This, in the Ireland of the day seemed benignly permissive, but it paralysed me. *Am* I in love, I would ask myself when the moment arose, then take my emotional temperature and freeze. Young men, taken aback by this, could be scathing. A handsome, charming but, to my mind, too matter-of-fact young Frenchman called Robert took me to dinner and then to the Bois de Boulogne, where he hired a boat and attempted to make love to me as we drifted into the dark. When given the frozen treatment, he said sourly, 'So, you're holding on to your little capital, is that it?'

He assumed I was a virgin, which by then I no longer was. The question bothering me was my emotional state, which depended on his and on the likelihood that feeling might play a role in this encounter – especially as I had just spent a year in Rome, where I had grown used to Italian readiness to indulge in patient, courteous, unconsummated foreplay, which allowed me and my male friends to warm ourselves in the glow of an old-fashioned *amitié amoureuse*.

The evening with Robert, an honest man and an adult, was a débâcle.

'She's the race-horse breed,' Eileen warned my husband, Lauro, when they first met. She had taught in Ballinasloe, whose schools closed down during the days when the International Horse Fair was on to let everyone get an eyeful of the world-famous horseflesh. I imagined tremulous muscles quivering in a paddock, and wondered if that was really how I struck people, old schoolmates for instance. I wondered about this again when, on one of my visits back from abroad, a group of them gave a dinner for me. Women only. This made sense, since, if our aim was to remember the past, why drag along husbands? Inviting old teachers might have been interesting, though. They were all nuns, so they and we had not been close. But now – it was the Sixties – convent rules had changed. So might we not get closer? No? Perhaps not. Yet some were clever women who, if born in more prosperous times, could have had enviable careers. Would they, I wondered, have liked to know that some of us thought so? Again, perhaps not. They might even have mistaken the praise for pity.

I didn't query either their zeal or their vocation – the divine call. But how can it be denied that the call was seldom heard once opportunities for women increased, even before the advent of the Celtic Tiger, as the Irish economy picked up?

The ones who benefited from generations of talented women being obliged to settle for teaching were, of course, their pupils. I know this because, in the Fifties, during the year I spent testing myself and my French lover, the Irish economy was at its nadir, so I went to London where I worked, among other jobs, as a supply teacher. This took me from a pretentious private outfit in St Albans to a rough one on the Mile End Road and in and out of many in between. Nowhere in this bird's-eye view did I find the attentive efficiency of the Sacred Heart nuns. I didn't see it later either, not in my son's English prep school, nor in Bryanston nor at the French Lycée, which he had attended earlier in Los Angeles. This is not a puff for the nuns: their schools are now either quite gone or staffed by lay teachers, and that change must have put paid to the attentiveness my generation enjoyed, since lay teachers have a home life, whereas our only rival for the nuns' attention was God.

Come to think of it, the Celtic Tiger's brief prance owed them something, too, since one reason why international corporations set up businesses in Ireland was our well-educated population.

It is fair to admit though that, at the second convent school I attended, while the humanities were splendidly taught, we learned no science at all. The school was new and had no lab, so, while waiting for one to be built, the Department of Education let us substitute Thomistic Logic for the science subject which should have figured in our curriculum. Even now, I sometimes wonder if this left my thinking a little quaint.

How would I know?

At my old schoolmates' dinner party, I marvelled as much at the intricately folded linen napkins as at the absent husbands who had presumably footed the bill for a display as immaculate as a feast-day altar. Perhaps I mouthed something about this, for a woman I didn't recognise asked if I remembered the time I had turned up for the Feast of the Immaculate Conception wearing the wrong uniform.

'You had on the grey everyday one instead of the white. You had to be hidden in the back. *And* you left your lily in the bus! Dropped it!'

'Oh God! Did I?'

'It wasn't for God,' she corrected. 'It was for Mary! *Mater admirabilis!* Tower of Ivory, Hope of sailors! She should have transformed herself into a clippie and patrolled the buses looking for your lost lily. If it had turned up, we'd have had a miracle to our name.'

Hooting with laughter, voices down the table from us chorused, 'Oh Mary, I give thee the lily of my heart. Be thou its guardian forever.' Former Sacred Heart girls, I remembered now, had a reputation for going to the bad in later life. As this notion seems to have stayed current longer among the English than it did with us, it may have titillated English boyfriends.

So, I understood, inviting nuns *would* have been a bad idea.

Every year on 8 December during our schooldays, we were each expected to bring a St Joseph's lily – one of those funnel-shaped ones a bit like a dentist's drinking cup – to offer to the Virgin. In practice we were supplying the nuns' flower arrangement, so it was no wonder that the loss of a lily under a bus seat was remembered. Ten shillings, I think it cost. Or five? Even that was a lot back then.

'You thought me odd?' I challenged my hostesses.

'Ah no,' they protested kindly. 'Just scatty.'

'Easily flustered?'

'No, no,' they soothed.

But clearly my mother had been right. Then I remembered that *they* had seemed odd to me. Several had chosen to go to Swiss finishing schools and none to college. Hence, perhaps, the origami-inspired napkins.

In our school timetable, Latin and cooking classes had invariably clashed, as though to emphasise that choosing between them marked a parting of the ways. 'Domestic Science' pupils seemed to cook what they liked, for I remember them as always making meringues. White as my lost lily, these would be laid out to tantalise our Latinist nostrils as we clumped hungrily past their kitchen. We were never offered any.

On a later return to Dublin, I was taken to another women-only party. This one was for Muslim girls who were there to learn English. I forget where they were from – Lebanon perhaps? – but I was impressed, both by their exquisite silks and by the flair of whoever had picked Dublin as a safe place for chaste young women. Earlier, Spanish girls had come for the same reason and, earlier still, while walking the Dublin streets, the poet Antonin Artaud had had a revelation to the effect that to cut out reproductive sex would, by abolishing humanity, save the world from sin.

That, an acquaintance told me, was a tenet of the ancient Bogomil heresy. Dubliners, then, knew things like that. Heresies, like science-fiction, offer an escapist view and also, judging by Artaud, the opposite.

It strikes me now that I may not have wanted our *mater admirabilis* to have the lily of my heart, so dropped it partly on purpose. Religion, in a country like ours, could become a trap. At the end of our final school year, nobody showed surprise when one or two quite worldly girls revealed plans to become nuns. I remember our hockey captain doing so, and that when someone said she had too much team spirit for her own good, nobody laughed. In the late Forties the farewell dance held to celebrate someone's entering a convent was sometimes still held.

So how easily flustered was I? Now that I am at an age when forgetfulness might signal the onset of dementia, I would be happy to know of other blunders made in my teens. Reports of old gaffes mean that I have got better, not worse. And what about

Eileen whom I abandoned to Seán's unreliable care? After I left, she focused her energies on choosing and elegantly translating tales from the Irish sagas and turning her garden into an asset which doubled the value of the house so that it soared during the Irish property boom. None of us benefited, though, since Knockaderry had been sold before this happened. That was my fault. She had offered to hold on to it if I would agree to come and live there after she and Seán died, and I refused. I hope she never learned what leprechaun's gold we might have had.

I console myself with the thought that for years she had enjoyed designing and working on the garden, which must have provided pleasure and therapy – not to mention pride. From 1937, when we moved in, she worked on it with the help of a succession of handymen and fed us as long as we stayed there on increasingly interesting vegetables, soft fruits and, eventually, apples and pears.

In 1937 Seán's mind, too, was on a house, but perversely it was less on ours than on the decline and fall of an Irish 'Big House' which the novelist Elizabeth Bowen had imagined from an insider's viewpoint in her novel *The Last September*, while he saw it from that of the rebels in his own story 'A Midsummer Night's Madness'. (Maria Edgeworth had, of course, got in long before either of them with *Castle Rackrent*.) Though Bowen's novel had appeared in 1929, it was only now, eight years later, that he came across it. That was the year when he and Eileen left the US for England, so he must have been too busy settling into his job at Strawberry Hill to keep up with new novels. Now, though, he did read it and was captivated. He thought of its author as 'an Irish Turgenev' – an immense compliment, coming from him: not only because Turgenev was his favourite writer but also, as he started to see that his own novels were less successful than his stories, he blamed this on the narrowness of social experience in the new Ireland where, as he would note in his memoirs, 'a great levelling had begun'. Comparing this new Ireland to Nathaniel Hawthorne's New England, his memoirs quote Henry James's reflections on the compassion one must feel 'for a romancer looking for subjects in such a field'. The quotation continues: 'It takes such an accumulation of history and custom, such a complexity of manners and types to form a fund of suggestion for a novelist.' This complexity, wrote James, was sadly lacking in Hawthorne's New England just as it was, Seán contended, in the new simpler Ireland.

As I type, my fingers slacken on the keys.

They itch to argue with him about the many powerful novels, even some of James's own, which owe their punch to the narrowness of choice open to their protagonists. What about *The Awkward Age* and *Washington Square*, not to speak of *The Golden Bowl*? Need simplifies, and, in those books it is need, rather than complexity of manners, which drives their characters' fate, as it does in *Vanity Fair*, *Madame Bovary*, *Ethan Frome* and great stretches of Dostoevsky's narratives.

Meanwhile, Seán began to think of Elizabeth Bowen herself as 'a dramatic character, strayed from perhaps *The Last September*, one of its young Irish girls become fifteen years or so older, married ... more aware ...'

The next – unacknowledged – step could have been to see himself also as a character, strayed perhaps from Stendhal's *Le Rouge et le noir*, which he adored, one of whose great scenes shows the educated peasant, Julien Sorel, forcing himself to take hold of his snooty employer's wife's hand and hold on to it long enough to test his nerve. Did Seán make the analogy? His memoirs don't say, but their musings about novel-writing conclude that 'the Czarist Novel' – remember he is thinking of Turgenev – 'was written by an élite, about an élite, for an élite' and finally admit that where this had been leading him was to stray, emotionally, albeit perhaps briefly, *into* a novel. Suffering from a nine-year itch (he had married my mother in 1928), he had developed a cerebral passion for his imagined 'Irish Turgenev'. They hadn't met, but to remedy this, an amused Derek Verschoyle, editor of *The Spectator* for which Seán sometimes reviewed, arranged a small luncheon party at his London club and, one may guess, prepared the ground by telling Elizabeth how keenly this ex-IRA man admired her. Seán was good-looking, and it seems that Bowen's marriage, though solid, was unconsummated. So he and she began an affair. 'Why', he later remembered wondering during that lunch, 'might I not learn as much from her about Woman as I had already learned from Turgenev about Writing?'

Interestingly, her next lover, the Canadian diplomat Charles Ritchie whom she would meet in 1941 and love for thirty years, considered her writing 'infinitely more exciting . . . and profound than E. herself'. Inspiring cerebral passions seems to have been her forte.

Seán describes a final visit to her in London on 31 August 1939, when, as they 'lay abed, passion sated', her husband rang to say that the fleet had been ordered to mobilise, 'Which means war.' It also meant the end of their affair, since neutral Ireland would now be isolated and Elizabeth, when she did come over, would be doing so – though Seán did not know this at first – partly at the behest of the British Ministry of Information, who were eager to have her report on how Irish people felt about the English threat to take back the Irish ports.

A letter from her to a former lover, Humphrey House, describes Seán without naming him and says, 'we are . . . very much in love. It doesn't feel like a love affair. It feels like a marriage . . . He is the best (I think without prejudice) of the younger Irish writers. I only read any book of his last summer . . .' She claims that she nearly wrote him a fan letter. Then that he wrote *her* a fan letter, so they met. This account of their manoeuvring is more hesitant and less Stendhalian than Seán's, but probably slightly arranged – as no doubt is his. After all, both were writers. She says nice things about Eileen, mentions her husband and my five-year-old self, and says that, as they would both hate to upset anyone, 'We are paying for our happiness by being very good. We are both, by nature, extremely secretive, which helps.'

The above information comes from their pens. All I knew at the time was that there was a bristle of tension in our house, that Eileen was restive and that Seán making trips not just to London but to Cork – and not to Cork City either, where his mother lived, but to Bowenscourt. Why, I heard Eileen ask, if he was going, as he claimed, to a house party, had *she* not been invited too? Airily implausible, he insisted that it was to be a professional gathering which only writers would attend. A likely story! And yet, given his view of Elizabeth as an Irish Turgenev, there was some truth to his claim. His interest was not only professional, but also a form of fieldwork.

Muted rows dragged on, and Eileen must at some point have met Elizabeth because, later, she disparagingly described her as wearing yards of fake pearls. No doubt they met at one of the dinners hosted by the Irish Academy of Letters, for Seán had meanwhile introduced Bowen to its founder, the aged Yeats, whom she apparently charmed.

Seán himself was mesmerised. He and Bowen had so much in common: County Cork, romanticism and its opposite, emotional doubleness, their restless age (when they met, both, like the century itself, were thirty-seven), short stories – they both wrote them, and she drew attention in her *Faber Book of Modern Stories*, which appeared that same year, to the fact that 'the younger Irish writers' had all carried arms. This remark fitted Seán's case almost too neatly as, having both made bombs and carried a gun, he had indeed 'carried arms', but, as far as I know, he himself never turned them on anyone. He was proud of his marksmanship, though, and shooting was for years to be one of his hobbies. The story of his which appears in Bowen's Faber anthology is *The Bombshop*.

It may have been their differences, though, which added spice. She belonged to the Protestant Ascendancy, but then so had Erskine Childers and *he* had run guns for the Volunteers, then become one of the hardest of hard-liners when the movement split. He was the man whom Seán replaced as 'Director of Publicity for the First Southern Division': an unwieldy mouthful in sore need of being compressed into a Soviet-style acronym. DIPFSOD perhaps? Such job descriptions were fated to grow glum towards the end of the struggle, when men began to be arrested so fast that more and more titles came to include the thespian word 'Acting'. Seán himself would, as mentioned above, end up as Acting Director of Publicity for the entire, visionary Republic in whose name he kept issuing hopeless appeals until he was released by its Acting President and could honourably give up. By then de Valera too was in jail, and Childers had been caught carrying a revolver and executed – partly, I heard it surmised long afterwards, because his dash and gallantry got up some noses. As romance peeled away, it became a nasty little war.

Did it interest Bowen? Her novels, Seán noted, regularly punish romance, and *The Death of the Heart* (1938) does so icily. Judging by her surprisingly overwrought letters to Ritchie, she deployed both halves of her divided self in fictional encounters between her naïve heroines and the cads who make them suffer. So treachery was another topic which she and Seán had in common. Though Ritchie was the model for the lover in *The Heat of the Day* (1949) who proves to be a Nazi spy, it is likely that the theme had already come up in the late Thirties with Seán. He, like many old comrades, was smarting both from the treacheries arising first from the Civil War itself and later from the spectacle of de Valera sidling into his opponents' Dáil.

De Valera lived and learned though, and Dev Mark 2 was no doubt a sharper statesman than the man whom Seán had once unreservedly admired.

We, meanwhile, had become pariahs – or so my mother said, meaning that we had lost friends. Soon, she warned, we might have none left at all, for not only would Dev's followers, who had been Seán's comrades during the Civil War, now join their old opponents in ostracising us, but Seán's articles in the papers were making new enemies. The reason why passengers on our bus looked away when we boarded it, she claimed, was because they were conformists and afraid to say boo to a goose, let alone to be seen consorting with relatives of someone who had written controversial pieces in the morning paper or blown the gaff on a clerical intrigue. 'Letting the country down' in public, I learned, was a mortal sin to the men and women on the Killiney omnibus, whose hackles rose when Seán criticised the government or wrote – though this must have been later, possibly even after the war – about the brutal beatings being administered to pupils of the Irish national schools. These state-funded schools were non-fee-paying, so the priests who ran them were unlikely to be disturbed by letters, such as the timid ones Seán got from parents torn between a lively fear of upsetting the all-powerful clergy and anger at the violent injuries school teachers routinely inflicted on children. Violence back then was taken to mean beatings only, and the word 'paedophilia' was not, as far as I know, pronounced. Later, though, I heard Seán's friend and solicitor, Christo, say that what went on behind closed doors would make a classical Greek tragedian blench, though no paper dared report it.

There was, however, no lack of handier targets, and heading the list was the Censorship Board, which would ban so many books over the years by distinguished foreign Catholic writers that it became a laughing stock. Seán attacked it relentlessly and, among his papers when he died, I found a letter from an Irish government minister, dated in the Thirties, granting him the right to import six copies of one of his own banned books for his own use. The letter by then was brittle with age and, judging by its prick-marks and puncturings, must at some time have been pinned up for use, perhaps, as a dart board to keep his *saeva indignatio* well honed.

He wasn't the only one lacerated by that. On the contrary, he had been unusually lucky, not only in getting away to Harvard, but earlier, too, during the fight, when thanks to his couriers' prudence he escaped being caught and interned as hundreds were. Emboldened, perhaps, both by this and by the contagion of US optimism, he had come home, borrowed money, chosen a congenial site and built a house. This was so odd a venture in those depressed years that people used to line up outside our gate to stare over it at what they called 'the queer new house'. Its queerness, even in retrospect, escapes me, though perhaps the asymmetry of the windows was unusual then, as were its open-plan interiors and uncovered joists, about which the gawkers must have been told, since they could not see them from where they stood. Maybe the builders had given them a tour?

'Djez see the inside?' I can imagine them marvelling. 'Ye'd swear it was only half finished, but the builders is after tellin' us that the owners is all set to move in.'

Curiously, the only really modern house in the neighbourhood belonged to another Corkonian, a retired music teacher called Breen. White, terraced, curvy and vaguely naval, its design made ours look positively dull. Perched on a ridge rising above and behind Captain Disney's ponderous, whelk-grey mansion, the Breens' house could, on bright days, look ready to levitate and take off into the clouds. Disney, from whom Seán had bought our acre of land, lived in what was said to be the dower house of 'the

Talbot Estate', a place whose seat had apparently disappeared.

There was nothing cloudy, though, about Breen's response, when asked for his opinion of my musical ear. He said I hadn't one, and that my dream of learning to play the violin should be discouraged. Indeed, there would be no point wasting money on trying to teach me any instrument more complex than a tin whistle.

Though disappointed, I continued calling on him and his wife, Daisy, when on my way to visit their neighbour, 'old Miss Smythe', a friendly spinster who, it strikes me now, must have been much younger than I realised. Women like her had been twice bereaved, once by the Great War and again by the drift to England of their kind. She owned a great number of cats and a garden where she grew interesting oddities, like yellow tomatoes and white raspberries: relics perhaps of a childhood spent somewhere equipped with gardeners and greenhouses. With hindsight, I can see that she was recognisably of Ascendancy stock.

During my first years in Killiney, I had nobody to play with while other children were in school, because Eileen, who wouldn't send me there until I was eight, was teaching me the three Rs herself. Having worked as a teacher in Boston, she used a phonetic method to teach reading, which seems to have gone in and out of fashion since her day. I can't imagine why. It worked wonderfully for me, who learned so fast that I had empty hours left to fill every afternoon, and whiled them away by dropping in on tolerant neighbours.

At first I mooched 'up the Gut', a lane where floors were earthen, TB was rampant and people were allegedly prone to gut each other on Fridays after closing time. When I caught lice there once too often and the Gut was banned, I began calling instead on a retirement home for old ladies run by a Mrs Gracie O'Reilly. Dotty inmates there were as lonely as myself, and maids told tales about them behind their backs. A Mrs Leahy was known to them as 'Leaky' because of her incontinence, and an old lady, nicknamed 'the Little Flower', was said to be a saint.

Sanctity was an obsession of the time. Father Traynor, a friend of Seán's who appears in several of his short stories, was known, seriously and gravely, in Gougane Barra as 'the Saint'. As I was not yet at school, he gave me my first Communion, and I wore a new, brown wool dress instead of the usual mini bridal costume. Curiously, I don't remember being disappointed about this, perhaps because Traynor was a lively and entertaining man whom Seán claimed to have frequently helped climb back over the seminary wall after dances in their Cork youth. Traynor was convinced, Eileen told us, that clerical marriage would soon be permitted and he planned to avail himself of the latitude.

'God help him,' she sighed and shook a wisely sceptical head.

To my secret satisfaction, her taunt about my having missed the excitements of war now looked like being disproved. A contingent of the Local Defence Force marched promisingly often past our gate. 'Left, left!' urchins jeered and, lifting small, plump knees, imitated the men as they stamped by: 'I had a good job and I left!' Petrol disappeared, and our car was put up on blocks. Fascinating black rubber gas masks with long snouts were supplied to us, then stored in the attic, never to be used, though blackout light bulbs were screwed in and blackout curtains hung lest German planes use our too brightly lit coastline to guide their bombing missions. A cupboard with a lock was filled with food, including tinned corned beef and Hershey chocolate bars, both of which we ungratefully despised, sent by friends in the US who feared we might be starving. Meanwhile, Eileen and a succession of handymen drew up a map of what now began to look like a garden, laid out paths, and strewed them with beach pebbles which we collected with a horse and cart in the small hours, lest it be illegal to take them. There was uncertainty about this. The handymen planted tough vegetables like kale, which I furtively fed by the armful to Captain Disney's half-dozen cows who, considering our field to be still theirs, regularly broke through our fence to get at more. I was blamed for this, and when we learned that we might be liable if a cow broke its leg, we reinforced the fence. Cleverly, the cows returned by night. Defensively, we wove thorny furze through our palings. No good. The cows were persistent and, when chased, panicked and charged across seed beds and cucumber frames. So we planted a hawthorn hedge and hammered pointed sticks into the ground to protect it.

Having grown friendly with the cows, I declared myself to be a vegetarian, but was thwarted in this.

Meanwhile, were we at war or were we not? Confused, I tuned in to adult anxieties. What was neutrality? Did I want us to be at war? I did! I did! I yearned for the excitement but concealed this, since adults, despite wistful memories of their own war, were clearly not keen on this one.

Jobs were still scarce, and a rump IRA had again split and was again plotting. It had by now been banned, unbanned, then rebanned, and one faction, no doubt feeling a need to give signs of life, declared its own war on Britain, then seized state-owned ammunition from a magazine in Phoenix Park. Mindful of English threats to take back the ports, de Valera's government promptly rushed through an Emergency Powers Act, bringing back internment which it had abolished seven years before.

Naturally, I didn't know any of this at the time, but gleaned wisps of fact and speculation from listening to adults' chat.

So for what did our 'Free' State now stand? Side-of-the-mouth comment raged as usual on the number 59 bus, whose schedule was now truncated, as was its route. Shortages became the great subject of chat, and fuel was especially scarce.

∽

What leavened our family's social life was that Killiney was a partly Protestant village and that, although Protestants had lost power, pull and, in some cases, property, few – apart from Erskine Childers' relatives – can have been lastingly affected by the sour, emotional fall-out from the Civil War. On the whole, any grudges they might bear for having been sidelined were concealed with such dignity that my mother was puzzled years later to hear two old Protestant friends of hers refer to 'them' and 'us'. Who, she was wondering, were the alien 'them', when it dawned on her that her friends meant people like herself. Local Protestants, unlike the ones in the North, were tolerant and liberal, but had doubts about our being so. They had a point. When it came to mixed marriages and the children thereof, the Irish RC Church was inflexible. The marriage had to be celebrated – though the word didn't really apply – at unconvivial hours in a hole-and-corner way, and all children born of it must, the Church insisted, be brought up as Catholics. When a Protestant parent refused to go along with this, there could be social repercussions, and once, notoriously, as late as 1957, in a place called Fethard-on-Sea, there would be a priest-led, full-scale boycott of Protestants and their businesses. So it seemed that the only tyranny in the country now was that of our own Church, which from 1940 on would be incarnate in our archbishop and primate, John Charles McQuaid, a man obsessed by petty concerns, who allegedly greeted the arrival of Tampax on the Irish market in 1944 by advising the Minister of Health against permitting it, lest it sexually arouse young girls. McQuaid was said to be so opposed to mixed marriages that he did not want Catholic and Protestant schools to play hockey with each other. Such encounters, he feared, could lead to Catholic girls meeting and possibly eventually marrying Protestant opponents' male relatives.

Were these fantasies his or ours? His lean fanatic's face and tight, drawstring mouth discouraged negotiation, and when my generation began to think of leaving school we learned that he had forbidden us to attend Trinity, the older and more aesthetically pleasing of our two universities, on pain of excommunication. 'A reserved sin!' Why? Because Trinity was Protestant and he didn't approve of Catholics fraternising with Protestants. By all reports, McQuaid was an odd fish.

In 1945 he bought a property at the foot of Killiney Hill, where he got an astronomer to rig up a telescope overlooking the beach. So, for all his inquisitorial ways, he had a soft spot for natural beauty. Human beauty? Perhaps. A biography by John Cooney, *John Charles McQuaid: Ruler of Catholic Ireland*, published first in Ireland, then in the US by Syracuse University Press, reports a rumour that he had been known to disguise himself and go cruising for boys. Another fantasy? Or another reserved sin? Gossip flourished. Nobody knew. The biography quotes Dubliners who, as boys, had been embarrassed by the prelate's notorious interest in explicitly discussing sex and masturbation so as to encourage them to avoid both. And it records one lurid episode with a small boy which Irish reviewers tend to dismiss on grounds that its source was an enemy of McQuaid's, and that there was no witness to it. But then attempted rape is rarely witnessed.

Interestingly, the outspoken biographer's Irish critics argue that his 'life' of McQuaid judges the 'Ruler of Catholic Ireland' – his subtitle – between 1940 and 1973 by today's standards. This, they imply, makes his assessments faulty and so does his ignorance of how Ireland was in those years. But, in the wake of the paedophile scandals now shaking the Irish Church, we must wonder whether these defenders themselves knew what, we now learn, was going on all over the country in those decades. If they did, they were guilty of connivance. If they did not, their criticisms are worthless. The Murphy report, whose findings are being discussed in the newspapers as I write, says that paedophilia was covered up for forty years in the Dublin diocese. In those years, covering up scandals would have been easy – especially in the light of another item which appeared in the press not so very long ago to the effect that Pius XII apparently made it a reserved sin – yet another one! – for anyone to accuse a priest of paedophilia. True or untrue? How to know after so much duplicity?

I lived in Killiney myself until the early Fifties and thereafter regularly visited my parents there until twenty years later, when they left it for the urban comforts of nearby Dún Laoghaire.

Partly perched on its hilltop, partly tumbling down it, the town seemed so sedate, sexless and sleepy that my great anxiety was, when the war ended, travel revived and foreign exchanges were arranged for me, that the Italian or French girl whose lively hospitality I had enjoyed in the Savoy mountains or the seaside resort of Forte dei Marmi would die of boredom in Killiney.

Yet it was a pretty place, just a brisk, fifteen-minute walk from hilltop to beach, lush, woodsy, part of the old Pale, close enough to Dublin for people to have gone there in the days before motorcars to build roomy houses amidst what by now were mature, semi-exotic gardens, redolent of empire and Mediterranean trips. Several had dreamy names like Capri, Khyber Pass and Sorrento, though native Irish owners tended to choose ones like Carraig Donn, Grianán, Cois Fairrge and, in our own case, the semi-Anglicised Knockaderry, which, in the original Gaelic meant 'the hill of the oakwood', in memory of an earlier house where Seán had holidayed as a boy. Our field for now had only very young trees, but across the road from it rose a wooded park, and downhill to the right, between the Vico Road and the sea, a eucalyptus wood anchored the soil above a near-vertical slope which descended to White Rock Beach, where the cliffs gleamed with mica, and the sand was finer than caster sugar. In Killiney Park, during the Thirties and Forties, children could be seen gathering sticks for firewood, then carrying them home in great bundles on their backs, which were often bent at right angles, like those of figures in a Bruegel painting. In winter, their fingers, like my own, were covered with chilblains. Fuel shortages were returning us to medieval conditions.

However, just under the crest of Killiney Hill Road was a row of workmen's cottages, one or two of which, thanks to the Mexican Gulf Stream, had palm trees in their small gardens. These, allegedly, had been built to house English servants brought over to work in the vanished great house belonging to 'the Talbot Estate'. What had happened to that house? And where had it been located? Nobody seemed to know, but the names of the families now living in the cottages were indeed English – Hall, Mason, Tyndal and the like – and the big house belonging to Captain Disney, who had sold us our field, was said to have been the dower-house of the same estate. Down the hill to the left, just off the road leading towards what Protestants still called Kingstown and we called Dún Laoghaire, there was a tall, see-through, lacy, stone remnant of a house said to have belonged to the Parnell family which later disappeared. Had it been burned in the Troubles, as happened to so many such houses in fact and perhaps more in fiction? Surely not, if its owners were in any way connected to the great Charles Stewart Parnell? But perhaps they had had the roof removed themselves so as to avoid having to pay rates? Information was sparse, in part because so many Killiney residents were retired and had spent their active lives somewhere else. Many of those living – or having recently lived – in the roomy villas either on the hill top or down by the sea also had English names: Judd, Johnson, Robinson, Murray, Waterhouse, Hone, Starky, Fagan, Williams, Nutall-Smith, Boardman, Gibbon and even an ancient Mrs Parnell, who was thought to be eccentric because she wore nineteenth-century outfits featuring hats, buttoned boots, long skirts and black lace such as I see girls selling and modelling nowadays in London's Camden Market. She was often in our number 59 bus queue, but no one had the nerve to ask her if she was connected to the ruined house. Perhaps we half thought of her as a ghost.

PROTESTANT KILLINEY

Killiney Protestants varied. Some had represented the British Empire in India or Africa. Others, having inherited houses too expensive to keep up, lived frugally, while still others were feudal in their ways, like Captain Disney, who invited neighbourhood children to skate and slide on his pond when it froze, organised a fête every summer in his fields, and was generous with callers at Hallowe'en. Some occasionally invited Seán and Eileen, along with other neighbours, to drink sherry on Sunday mornings after church, and some were what Eileen called bohemian, by which she meant that the wives wore slacks (which was then thought daring if you weren't actually riding an animal), drank openly in the local lounge bar (rather than discreetly in a cupboard-sized snug) and, once the war got going, were apt to get into conversation with the officers in civvies who came down from Northern Ireland to eat steak. According to Eileen, one of her friends, whom I shall call Lily, did more than talk. She picked men up and took them home. Eileen affected disapproval, but was soon wearing slacks herself – though never in town – and gave up letting herself be shut away in a snug. She and Lily befriended a German woman married to a Dutch journalist who lived in the village and felt isolated and lonely. After all, why not? We were neutral, weren't we? They were careful, however, about introducing her to either Captain Disney or Colonel Williams, who lived on either side of us, or to Gracie O'Reilly's son, Terry, who was in the RAF.

'She's not a great one for taking hints,' Lily told Eileen. 'So if we go into the pub with her, we'd better take her into the snug and keep her there. I'll say you're shy about drinking in public.

She'd never believe it of me, and if we tell her that the officer class would refuse to fraternise with her, she might blub. She's prone to that.'

Lily, having lived in Africa, sometimes made remarks which would now be considered racist and which, even in the Forties, could make people blush. A swarthy friend might, to her mind, 'have a touch of the tar brush' or have a baby to whom Lily would refer as 'her new coffee bean'.

I too had friends whom it seemed wise to keep apart. One was Lily's daughter, Jasmine (another alias), who had spent her childhood in Africa and was imaginative, independent, astonishingly beautiful, permanently angry, resented her mother (whom she called 'that sow'), adored her father (whom she felt that mother mistreated) and claimed to despise all humans and care only for animals. She had won prizes for painting lions and possessed a pony, a goat, two ducks and a dog, but seemed never to have any pocket money and apparently lived on boiled offal, which the butcher had probably been told was being bought for the dog. Like almost all local Protestants, except Miss Smythe, she and her parents lived in a high-ceilinged, formerly elegant, cold, unmodernised house equipped with a tennis court, vastly overgrown rhododendron bushes and a winding drive which established its claim to be a gentleman's residence. Cash, however, was short, as was the case with many Anglo-Irish families, and often when I dropped by Jasmine would have a large potful of lights on the stove which creaked and croaked like something in a horror film. It made ghostlike noises as it simmered and looked, as it rose and sank, rather like a folded grey mackintosh. At other times she would be cooking sheep's head, and would dare me to eat one of its eyes, mocking me when I refused the dare. Her *contemptus mundi*

was extreme. 'Look at those corpses,' she would say, surveying a beachful of pallid sunbathers in early June. 'Aren't they horrible?' She was frankly curious, though, about bodily functions and, as she was a year or so older than I, had no trouble persuading me to join in examining the parts of each other's bodies that we ourselves couldn't see. However, she refused to come trespassing with me, and so clearly disapproved of the practice that I felt that she and my new Catholic school friend, Marie, could not be introduced to each other unless I found some way of warning each in advance that flesh was sacred to one and property to the other. Marie, though less than totally averse to trespassing, would have greatly disapproved of being shown Jasmine's private parts. And I, now that I had finally started going to school to local Loretto nuns, was being cautious about Catholic rules which, it seemed to me, my parents had either got wrong or had forgotten. Catholics at the Loretto convent seemed both mildly hostile and timorous.

Yet it was with Marie, a quiet classmate of whom the nuns thought highly, that I managed to indulge the addiction to fear which I had contracted while trespassing with my mother. One day I persuaded her to try skipping school with me (this was called 'mitching'), but I forget how we spent the stolen time. Perhaps I took her to visit some of my old acquaintances, like Mrs O'Reilly, several of whose doddery charges, I now realised, were amiably off their heads. Or perhaps our truancy was on one of the days when we walked down the coast to a stretch of rusted railway tracks which had been abandoned when the cliffs along which they ran became eroded. There were places where access roads to the beach ran under, and at right angles to, the tracks. They must once have been supported by some sort of girder but were now as airborne as telephone cables. Stepping out along yards of slim, unpropped and possibly crumbling track was pleasurably frightening, especially when Marie, standing some way off on terra firma, kept calling to me to come back, be careful, watch out, and remember that the road below me was paved with stones.

'You'll be killed,' she moaned satisfyingly.

Eileen would have been no good as a companion here, where the risk was real, since she wouldn't have let me run it. Besides, she was always busy now with her fairy tales (which I had outgrown), her garden and my small, but demanding, brother. Amazingly though, Marie let me persuade her to come with me on a more dangerous venture. There was a large cave at one end of the White Rock beach, used as a lavatory by swimmers. Its smell protected it, since nobody, other than myself and the anxious Marie, was prepared to walk through to the back, where the smell stopped and a number of underground passages fanned out into the dark. At least one was so narrow that we had to crawl through it on hands and knees and to come out backwards, since we couldn't turn around. Another still narrower passage with a high roof led along a slippery clay shelf running halfway up an underground cliff, past the side of a possibly deep pool. The whole area was sculpted from compacted reddish mud, and we learned later that it had been a copper mine, though it had looked to us like blood on our first visits. Following the advice provided by adventure stories read in schoolgirl magazines, we brought along bicycle lamps, matches and candles, by which we would know, if they flickered out, that the air was no longer healthy. They never did, but the place was eerie, litter-free and, as far as we could tell, known to no one but us. Exploring it was an end in itself. We hadn't expected to find bones or treasure, and had no practical purpose except to test our nerve and defy the adult world's advice about being cautious and avoiding 'useless, commercial trash', which was how my parents described the school stories which, on the contrary and to our delight, had turned out to be so helpful. They didn't supervise my reading at all closely, so I had often been enthralled by books found on their shelves which were clearly too grown-up for me, since their more exotic meanings remained opaque. Among these were *The Seven Pillars of Wisdom*, *Mr Norris Changes Trains*, *No Orchids for Miss Blandish* and a novel by someone called Rayner Heppenstall, whom Seán must have known, for his novel was in galley sheets in our attic. Not quite understanding proved tantalising, and perplexity drew me on. It was a little like the excitement I felt when venturing into the copper mine, and reminded me too of the games I played with Jasmine. The books could have been written by near-aliens, or by the kindly, harmless, semi-human animals which she had invented for us to imitate so as to escape our banal selves. I don't know whether my parents would have minded the odd selection I had made among their books if they had noticed it. Probably not, since most of my favourites were perfectly orthodox – I revelled in the adventure stories of G. A Henty, Baroness Orczy, Dickens, Hugo and Dumas Père, as well as in the polite world of Jane Austen and the entertainingly ordinary one of Richmal Crompton. The failure to warn me against less suitable books may have hinged partly on Seán's dislike of the Censorship Board and partly on a Rousseauistic assumption that, just as falling into a fire was the best way of learning not to play with it, reading incomprehensible books would encourage better choices. At any rate, my parents' only prohibition targeted 'English trash', by which they meant a paper called *The Girls' Crystal*. They had not read it, but as it was for English children they suspected it of peddling alien values.

My third friend was Diana. A Protestant of a different sort from Jasmine, Diana was prim, slightly younger than myself, totally without a sense of humour and apt to deliver little speeches about manners, hygiene and the most appropriate way to blow one's nose. It amused me to tease her by pretending to be a wild creature who had never even seen a handkerchief, but her readiness to believe this spoilt my fun. Which of us, I had to pause and wonder, was mocking the other? Surely she couldn't be as prim as she seemed. Could she? She could. And yet it was she who got me into trouble with my school nuns. She lent me a book which was a source of unexpected scandal. The surprise was that this hadn't happened until now, since some of my parents' thinking would undoubtedly have upset the nuns. What I had not foreseen was that her book about someone called Darwin would do so even more. It was the first time I had come across his theory, so I elected to give my geography class the benefit of my discovery. The geography nun, who was older than the others, had decided, possibly with an eye to arranging short rests for herself, that in the course of the term, each girl in our class should prepare a brief talk on any topic she liked, so long as it had a connection with geography. I submitted the title 'The Galapagos Islands', which did not alert her to what was coming, so it was only after I had laboriously anatomised the unfamiliar heresy known as evolution that she began to worry. Perhaps she hadn't been listening at first, for she let me talk on for quite a while before asking if what I was telling the class was supposed to be fact or fiction. Perhaps she had just remembered that my mother wrote fairy tales.

'It's science, Mother.' You had to keep saying the word 'Mother' when you addressed a nun.

'What sort of science? Let me see that book. Where did you get it?'

'From a friend, Mother.'

'A friend? What school does she go to?'

'Glengara Park.'

'That's a Protestant school. Did you know that?'

'Yes, Mother, but her parents are friends of my parents.'

That gave the nun pause. 'Well,' she decided, 'I'll have to get advice about this. Let me keep it for a few days.'

It turned out that evolution was erroneous and forbidden, and that the chaplain wanted a word with me. This news, I suspected, would not please the nun, who disliked priests or government inspectors or indeed anyone looking over her shoulder. Intrusiveness, even by other nuns, upset her, but her resentment applied most specifically to men.

'Men,' I remembered her exclaiming on an earlier occasion, while drawing a large, free-hand map of Ireland on the blackboard, 'never give up a privilege. They hate letting women near the altar.' Her hand wobbled with feeling as she said this, and I noticed that her Ireland was looking more and more like a cross between our rather chubby chaplain and a teddy bear. I was puzzled at priests – who else could she mean? – wanting to keep her away from the altar. 'They don't think,' she warned, turning to address us, 'that *we* can think for ourselves.'

I understood this bit, for my mother too liked to think for herself and, if advised to do something one way, would often do it in another. Sending me to school three years late was an example of this, and so was her failure to kit me out in the right uniform. Sometimes I wished she would do things like other people.

'Who's the little girl wearing England's cruel red?' a nun named Mother Fidelia had called out at assembly on my first day, ensuring that every head turned to stare at my scarlet hair ribbon.

'You knew,' I reproached Eileen when I got home. 'You *must* have known it was the wrong colour.'

She was unabashed. 'Ask that nun,' she challenged, 'where was she when your mother was fighting for independence.'

She was torn, though, for, while there was romance in despising the new 'bourgeois' Ireland, she wanted me to do well in it, so was unsure whether to scorn or join the new order. Ambition, for me, won, though there would be U-turns, like the times when she sent me out on to the road to collect droppings for her rose-beds. Due to the petrol shortage, horses, carts and old, mildewed cabs had by then been brought out of retirement, so my bucket was soon heavy with steaming, yellow horse dung, some of it still sweetly grassy and fresh. When I told her how worried I had been, lest someone from school see me scraping it off the tarmac, her response was always, 'You should get rid of human respect.' To help me do this, she might then sing *The Red Flag*, which had been written, she reminded me, by a County Meath man. I wasn't sure whether she was indulging in self-parody, or if the parody was an excuse for savouring the corny but rousing words:

The people's flag is deepest red.

'Join in,' she sometimes invited, forgetting or choosing to forget that I had no ear.

It shrouded oft our martyred dead . . .

During the Civil War, she and fellow members of *Cumann na mBann* – the IRA women's auxiliary force – had sung that regularly while slow-stepping behind coffins at Republican funerals. Didn't that prove that the English had no monopoly of the colour? Nor of aggression. Nuns, after all, could be very aggressive. Perhaps this came from living in a pack. Like wolves?

'Be sure you tell me,' she advised out of the blue, 'if any of them give you trouble.'

'Any of whom?'

'Nuns.'

Confused and at cross-purposes, we stared at each other. In those days confusion was as common as mist.

Somewhat at random, I asked, 'What *is* a community?'

I had been hearing the word at school which was strictly divided between 'community rooms' – off-limits to pupils – where the nuns ate and slept, and those where we had lessons. Any girl, it was whispered, who ventured into the nuns' domain was violating the privacy of the brides of Christ and could be expelled. Perhaps even excommunicated? To see nuns in their underwear or with cropped heads uncovered would be a sacrilege.

Yet, it mightn't be. A girl called Ann in the class below mine lived in a house whose garden bordered the convent grounds. Sometimes, she confided, she hid in the bushes which formed a barrier between the two properties and watched nuns bathing in a sea-water pool. The high tide filled it, surging in over rocks.

'I saw Mother Fidelia,' Ann told us, 'wearing a long, thick nightdress and bobbing up and down in the water. That's all any of them do. Maybe they think sport is worldly.'

'Or maybe the nightdress is too tight?'

It wasn't tight, she told us. It floated to the surface when the nun bobbed down.

I saw her other listeners try, as I was doing myself, to visualise this. We couldn't help being fascinated. A taboo was being broken. And taboos in our twelve-year-old world – we must by now have been twelve – focused either on sex or, as in this case, on its rejection. That was what cropped heads and forbidden community rooms came down to. Sex was the satanic snake whose clammy neck the Blessed Virgin's triumphant foot crushed in paintings hanging in convents all over the city. It was at once absent and present. Just visible under the hem of her lapis-blue gown, its sly emergence seemed to be part of herself.

Finding this thought too furtive for words, we averted our eyes from each other, and fell silent.

Turning to the safe topic of sleeves, a girl called Stella insisted that these could be too tight to permit swimming. 'That,' she reminded us, 'was why women used to be allowed to serve under-arm at tennis. Their sleeves were too tight at the armpits for them to raise their arms. You see that in old photos.'

'How high did the nightdress float?' another girl wondered. 'Did it leave her legs bare?'

The imagined sight of Mother Fidelia's legs, fish-pale in murky sea water, was fascinating. The limbs, Ann claimed, had been tightly joined and as neat as a mermaid's tail. Mermaids must have died out like garments with tight armholes.

'Isn't that what your evolution heresy says happens?' Stella remembered. 'What, by the way, did the priest have to say about it when you saw him?'

'Not a lot,' I told her. 'He asked why I wanted to think my ancestors were monkeys, and when I told him that that wasn't what the book said happened, he didn't listen.'

A pious girl said, 'You're lucky he didn't burn it. Looking into things like that could be dangerous. So is spying on nuns.'

Ann, wanting the last word, said she had every right to sit in her parents' garden and look wherever she chose. This was true, so, though letting property rights trump religion made us uncomfortable, we didn't argue. She, who had actually glimpsed bare nunnish flesh, seemed less prurient than the rest of us, who had only imagined it – so how could we?

The religious order which owned our junior school wasn't the only one to have snapped up big houses which had been sold off when the Free State took over. Its grounds sloped down to the edge of the sea, and relics of old finery subsisted indoors, especially between the tall windows of what might once have been a ballroom. The chief relic, a mirror surrounded by gilded carving, stretched from the top of a marble console table to a lofty ceiling. It might once have been part of a larger display which had been removed by the nuns as being too worldly. The mirror itself could not be removed, and they were clearly glad of this for, when interviewing parents, they boasted happily about their school's charm. None of them, they were keen to point out, owned anything personally ('Not even our clothes,' they would say, and point to the ones they were wearing), for they had each taken a vow of poverty. That, though, did not prevent their rejoicing in the convent's good fortune in having attractive surroundings for pupils to enjoy.

Mother Fidelia, as head of the junior school, was particularly prone to rejoice. She was a pretty nun about whom I sometimes dreamed. Her flowing habit reminded me of Maid Marian's clothes in the film of Robin Hood, and, though sorry that the black habit was a touch funereal, I felt that this was compensated for by the strangeness – even mystery – of someone as pretty as she being a nun. So my feelings about her were mixed. Once or twice I began to develop a crush on her, only to remember and resent the ridicule to which she had exposed me on my first day in school. She hadn't done anything like this again, because Eileen had made it her business to let her know that she would not tolerate my being bullied. She had visited the school, talked pleasantly about her experience working as a teacher in Boston and London, and established herself as someone who might, if provoked, make trouble. At first I didn't understand that this was what she was doing even though, as she herself told me later, it was I who had signalled to her that this nun was dangerous. The incident with the red ribbon was only a small part of the picture which Eileen had been building up from my chatter. Having herself taught in a convent school in London, she was aware of the furtive and blatant improprieties that could go on in such places. In the English school, she told me years later, the head nun, a hard-nosed Kerry woman, had actually ordered one of the lay teachers to open the sealed envelopes containing state exam papers on the day of the maths exam, go through the questions with the girls and give them the answers. The teacher, being not only lay but also English and young, was so stunned by the experience that she did as she was told, then resigned from her job.

'There was a conflict of loyalties,' Eileen explained. 'You get that with nuns. In the mind of a woman like that, keeping English rules would always take second place. She'd see helping Catholic pupils to do better than those in secular schools as her first duty.'

'So she got away with cheating?'

'The lay teacher', Eileen guessed, 'may have despised her, then felt ashamed of this and so been too deferential. I, being Irish, could have stood up to the nun, but the English woman couldn't.'

'But you didn't denounce her either?'

No, Eileen admitted. She hadn't. She too had left soon after that to come back to Ireland.

I guessed that the old Irish hatred of traitors was the reason, but didn't ask. Instead I said, 'Well, there are no English people in our school.'

'Just as well.'

'Yes.'

Later, though, it struck me that there were one or two pupils from England who at the beginning of the war had been evacuated to the school and who, because their parents were far away, were vulnerable to bullying. One of the boarders had told me that Mother Fidelia patrolled the dormitories armed with a cane and sometimes savagely beat girls whom she caught talking after lights out – even more savagely if she caught them going into each others' beds.

Mother Fidelia? I was astounded.

'She's different with us,' said the boarder, 'from how she is with you. And she's especially hard on the girls from England.'

One night, hearing me talk in my sleep about cruelty and possibly worse, Eileen woke me up. I fell asleep again, however, almost as soon as she left the room, and plunged into a dream in which Maid Marian was beating me and turning into a nun. Confused by my own feelings, I began to feel guilty. Apparently I then went back to talking in my sleep, but when Eileen questioned me about my nightmare at breakfast, I said I had forgotten what it had been about.

I hadn't, though.

In school the day before, there had been whispers about some trouble that had broken out in the dormitories, about which the boarders didn't want to tell us. They were clearly shaken, and a girl whom I shall call Jill, one of the evacuees, was led into our classroom. We had been drawn up in a circle and she was now made to stand in the middle. She had pink weals on her legs, was wearing a dunce's cap, and her face was completely distorted and swollen. This terrified us. Such treatment had not been seen before. Not anyway by me, but not, I think, by any of the other day girls either.

'She's bad, a very bad girl,' said pretty Mother Fidelia gravely. 'I want each of you to say so in Gaelic.' Then she pointed to the member of our class who was to start doing this and did.

'*Is cailín dána í,*' the girl said sullenly. It was clear that she disliked doing so. 'She's a bad girl.' Our Gaelic wasn't up to dealing with situations of any complexity – and anyway we didn't know what this one was about.

'Louder,' commanded the ruthless Mother Fidelia. 'Say it again.'

The girl did, and so did the next and the next, until half the circle had agreed that Jill was bad and so, by implication, deserved what she had so clearly got. Then it was my turn. Impotence numbed and strangled me. I felt that I had somehow brought this on the victim by indulging fantasies about the horrible chameleon nun. She *was*, I now saw, a horrible woman, and the gleam of evil in her was what I had mistaken for charm. Whatever she was up to had nothing to do with keeping order, lessons, or the 'duty towards God', which I had heard her claim as her reason for punishing bad children for the good of their souls.

'*Say* it,' she ordered me impatiently when I hesitated, and gave me a look which at once reminded me of Eileen's warning about her being dangerous but also of the useful fact that I – was the nun forgetting this? – had back-up. '*Is cailín maith t,*' I said fast and loudly before I had time to change my mind. 'She's a good girl.' The pious bully, being as aware as I was that things could now turn nasty and even get into the press, spat out the word 'stupid' and moved quickly on to the next pupil. I knew I hadn't done much. My attempt at solidarity was not only inadequate, but might have hurt the victim by reminding her that other people had more support than she. This, of course, is speculation, and I never knew what she felt, as she neither blinked nor looked either at me or anyone else. She was totally expressionless, seemed inert and frozen and probably wasn't thinking of us at all. Why would she? We couldn't help her. Her parents were in England and must have been telling each other that that nice, friendly Mother Fidelia was looking out for their daughter who must surely be better off in neutral Eire than she would have been living with them under German bombs. By now, however, the war was coming to an end, and that stickler for etiquette, de Valera, had already astonished the world by paying a visit to the German minister, Dr Hempel, to condole with him on Hitler's death.

Meanwhile I left the school, though I forget quite how this came about. The incident with Jill must have taken place shortly before the start of the summer holidays – the nuns' sea-bathing indicates that. What must have happened was that Eileen's intuitions about Mother Fidelia, sharpened by whatever ravings of mine she heard when I was asleep, led her to remove me before the end of term. So I never heard how the trouble between nun and victim was resolved, because by the autumn I was attending a new school which had just opened in Monkstown, some miles north of my old one. It was run by Sacred Heart nuns and was calmly efficient, unlike the anarchic and intermittently brutal one I had left. It was also slightly out of line with the mainstream of Irish education. This pleased Eileen, even though the divergence was to the right rather than the left. Despite her devotion to *The*

Red Flag, she was relieved to find that my new teachers would be as different as possible from the erratic peasants in habit and wimple on whom she and I now turned our backs.

Memories of post-revolutionary France affected the Monkstown curriculum, which was short on Gaelic, strong on plainchant and required us to curtsy to the top nuns who, like my mother, adopted a high moral tone. Cramming they despised, for they aimed, they said, to *educate*, and exams were nothing to them if, despite getting us late, they could turn us into ladies and true Children of the Sacred Heart.

'You will all have to be unmade and remade,' said our Mistress of Studies as coolly as if we had been so many jumpers whose kinked wool she needed to unpick. It was clear that she knew she could do it, but also that she would have her work cut out. We would later discover that she had been chosen as a troubleshooter and brought from one of the order's houses in Scotland to set the new school on its feet and form us into a unit. She was a Latin teacher, too, and, as most of us had done no Latin at all, whereas my class should – if I remember aright – have been starting our third year of it, she had to start us off and speed us ahead to catch up. Which she did. She was good at her job and, now that Ireland has had two successful women presidents, it strikes me frequently that in the years when women like her had few opportunities to use their talents, there must have been many mute inglorious Mary Robinsons hidden away in convents. Our Mistress of Studies was one of them. Her name was Mother Hogan and she could have run the country.

She impressed my mother and, more surprisingly, Seán, who had till then taken no interest in my education. Now, however, he wrote Mother Hogan a letter saying, among other things, that he hoped the new school would have some lay teachers, since girls of my age might need access to women with some experience of the world to whom they could turn for advice.

Mother Hogan invited him to tea. I don't know what they said to each other, but the meeting seemed to have been a success. They must have amused and challenged each other, for I think there were subsequent teas. She wanted him to know that nuns were less unworldly than he thought, but may have been hampered in her argument by convent etiquette. If she stuck to the rules, she would not have had tea herself, but would have sat there watching him drink his. The tray, unless she countermanded the usual arrangement, would have arrived with a single cup and saucer, and departing from custom might have been tricky. I wonder if she did arrange for a second cup. I should have asked him.

Since he was in and out of trouble over libel, and had acquired a reputation as an anticlerical who didn't hesitate to assail the pillars of Church and State, it may seem odd that I was being taught by nuns at all, let alone by those belonging to an order which – as they would proudly inform us – had been founded to prepare the mothers of France to teach their sons to resist revolutionary thinking.

It was not odd, though, in the Forties.

I had to go to a convent because in those days schools in Ireland were denominational; almost none were mixed; and if you went to the wrong one, as my small brother did when a Protestant kindergarten opened across the road from our house, a priest appeared on the doorstep to protest. Religion was a tribal badge, and my parents wanted neither to leave the real Ireland, nor to relinquish their feeling for the ideal one whose image had animated the nationalist struggle.

Yet it is fair to say that Sacred Heart schools were less nationalistic than others. The order's Mother House was in Rome, and the curriculum approved there could probably not find much space for Gaelic. This context is unlikely to have been mentioned over the tea cup – or cups. But I could tell that the conversation had been enjoyable. I could tell it by Mother Hogan's brightening when she mentioned meeting Seán, and his doing the same when he mentioned her. He always liked clever women.

Patrick , you chatter too loud
And lift your crozier too high,
Your stick would be kindling soon
If my son Osgar were by.

If my son Osgar and God
Wrestled it out on the hill
And I saw Osgar go down
I would say your God fought well.

Frank O'Connor, *Three Old Brothers and Other Poems*, 1936.

Was St Patrick, Ireland's first bishop, arrogant, and did he, like many of his successors, lift his crozier too high? My guess is that, as he was more myth than man, nobody knows, especially as I recall my father's great friend, the Celtic scholar D. A. Binchy, telling us that colleagues of his had come to think that there could have been two or even three St Patricks. Of more immediate interest here is the likelihood that O'Connor's poem about the pagan Oisín (pronounced Usheen) defying the saint may have been fuelled by anger against recent Irish bishops.

Politically, their lordships were often autocratic. They had condemned the Fenians in the 1860s and during the Civil War ruled armed resistance to the new, legally elected government to be immoral, thus virtually excommunicating the whole Republican side. Some went further, including the bishop of Cork, who instructed his clergy to refuse Republicans the sacraments. This rankled bitterly with Seán's and Frank's comrades who, when defeated, on the run, and at risk of being shot out of hand if caught with guns, must frequently have felt in acute need of absolution lest, by dying in a state of mortal sin, they go to a worse hell than the one they were in, which was after all what the bishops had ordered their flock to believe. Knowing this, a number of Cork priests, some of whom may have had Republican sympathies, disobeyed their bishop whose ukase, as Seán later wrote, 'was considered by all Republicans an abuse of clerical power. It was never to be forgotten or forgiven.'

He himself did not forgive it, and when my brother and I were small, one of Seán's best-kept secrets was that, if he was a Catholic at all, he was no longer a full-time one. As there was nothing unusual about members of a household going to different churches, and there were three within walking distance of our house, it would be years before I guessed that on Sunday mornings he and Binchy were likely to be walking out Dún Laoghaire Pier when the rest of us supposed them to be at Mass: a shift designed to avoid giving scandal to Binchy's housekeeper, his and our neighbours and my brother and me. A similar ambivalence must have driven generations of Irishmen to take similar measures, some of whom believed in but no longer practised their religion, while others disbelieved but shrank from breaking with their community. Despite endless conversations on the topic, I don't know to this day to which category Seán belonged and I suspect that neither did he.

He was tough when it came to criticising the actual Church and State, but all toughness melted before the memory of his and Eileen's love affair with Gaelic culture and their first encounter with it by the shores of Lake Gougane Barra. So on wartime holidays we went back regularly to remember their youth, as old friends foregathered and danced and sang to old tunes, and Father Traynor, who planned his summer visits to coincide with theirs, said Mass in Gaelic in the small lake-island church which Seán attended, presumably more from friendship than fervour.

Years later I learned that anti-clericalism had been infinitely harsher elsewhere than it ever was in Ireland. The French Revolution, after all, had seen priests guillotined; Mexico, to this day, forbids any but Franciscans to wear clerical dress in public, and I met a man in Italy whose parents had given him the name Ateo, meaning 'Atheist'. An Irish equivalent – 'Atheist Murphy', say, or 'Atheist Ó Faoláin' – is imaginable only as a bar-room joke. This is partly because anti-clericals often remained friendly with ordinary priests who, in relaxed moments, were apt to confide that they suffered more from overbearing bishops than the laity ever did. And indeed it was when Seán went into print with jokes about how Bishop Browne of Galway bullied his clergy that Browne launched a libel action. Such was my mother's innocence and my own (I am going back now to when I was eight), that we were slow to see the danger of this, for I clearly remember us being cheerily hailed, when out walking, by young priests who asked us to relay their congratulations to Seán on his having stood up to the bully. We agreed light-heartedly. Soon, though, it grew clear that, given Browne's resources and the bias of English libel laws in favour of plaintiffs, Seán could not fight him in court. Neither did his publishers intend doing so. On the contrary, in a letter to *The Irish Press*, they disowned and apologised for his book. And I, as a child moved by impotent fury, became an anticlerical of the extreme sort which Italians call a *mangiaprete* or 'priest-eater'.

Seán had been rash – or else had been trailing his coat. 'Truly,' he had written of Galway, 'I never met such a place for scandalous gossip . . . I wonder, is it libellous to repeat the sad tale of the bishop and the curate, as I heard it in a Galway pub?'

One can only marvel at Seán's chutzpah. He proceeded to describe Browne as 'an arrogant-looking man, much in favour, I gather, with the de Valera government; not so much in favour with the clergy.' (Who, it is clear from what follows, were forbidden to go to the cinema.) 'At any rate,' Seán reported, 'one afternoon the blonde at the box-office heard a voice over the telephone asking if Father X was inside at the show. On asking whose the voice was and on hearing the thunder of "This is the bishop" the blonde said, "Yerrah g'wan out of that! Are you thrying to pull my leg?" Finally the bishop had to drive down himself, and the terrified blonde was sent in for Father X, who of course said to her, "Yerrah g'wan out of that! Are you thrying to pull my leg?" At last, so the story would have us believe, he was induced to come out, and the poor man found his bishop waiting in the foyer like a figure of the Wrath of God. One version of this awful parable for sinners is that the bishop whirled him off straightaway to his new parish at the back of God-speed . . . '

The above extract is from *An Irish Journey*, a travel book on which Seán and his old Wicklow neighbour, Paul Henry, collaborated and which Longman published in 1940, Paul supplying illustrations and Seán the text. The bit about the bishop echoes an oral tradition which contrasts with the high flown Yeatsian vision of Ireland. It strikes me, though, as I write this, that Yeats' s Crazy Jane poems echo the oral tradition too. He could be earthy when he chose – and give hell to bishops.

Here is Jane's view:

> The bishop has a skin, God knows.
> Wrinkled like the foot of a goose,
> *(All find safety in the tomb.)*
> Nor can he hide in holy black
> The heron's hunch upon his back,
> But a birch-tree stood my Jack:
> The solid man and the coxcomb.

But now Yeats had died, and the gentry who had presided over the Irish literary revival had passed the baton to native writers whose taste was for the specific, the realistic and the down-to-earth.

That same year, along with Peadar O'Donnell, one of Ireland's rare Marxist activists, Seán launched *The Bell*, a monthly magazine which promised that, with readers' help, it would focus on 'the realities of Irish life'. 'This is Your Magazine' was the title of Seán's first editorial, inviting contributions which might help it evolve. 'That', wrote Seán, 'was why we chose the name *The Bell*. Any other equally spare and hard and simple word would have done; any word with a minimum of associations . . . All our symbols have to be created afresh . . .' Meaning, I suppose, that they wanted no rags of old rhetoric, either Celtic or pious. Seán and Peadar were making a stand against the Age of Pretence. What *The Bell* needed, they told possible collaborators, were documentary articles about aspects of Irish life which the authors themselves knew at first-hand. Isolated by neutrality, Irish writers had both a need and an opportunity to renew themselves.

So, in among fiction and verse, the magazine published pieces which reported on, among other topics, the experience of living in an Irish slum, an orphanage and a prison, schoolteaching, migrant workers, a new hat factory set up in Galway by a Jewish refugee, the art of window-dressing, and three extracts from a forthcoming book recording the thoughts of the bilingual Tim Buckley, one of the last of the *Seanachaí* or story-tellers who lived close to Gougane Barra. Buckley, known as 'the tailor', though it had been some time since he had worked at the trade, was famous for his mental independence, which locals and visitors alike crowded into his small cabin to enjoy. However, when a writer called Eric Cross made a record of the tailor's musings and published them in English with an introduction by Frank O'Connor, the book was promptly banned as 'indecent and obscene'. Not only were the bewildered old tailor and his wife, Ansty, now boycotted by neighbours who grew ashamed of having enjoyed the old man's salty wit for years, but worse still 'three louts of priests', as O'Connor described them, came round and forced the old man to go down on his knees and burn his copy of the book in his own fireplace. Meanwhile the scandal sparked off a sanctimonious four-day debate in the Irish Senate, reading the official record of which was, wrote O'Connor, 'like a long, slow swim through a sewage bed'.

The senators' rancour was almost certainly due to pique at finding that traditional Gaelic-speakers, whom, as patriots, they affected to admire, were neither as pious nor as genteel as they had wanted to think. Indeed, when one speaker read out examples of what he considered to be the book's obscenities, another demanded that these be struck from the Senate records, lest members of the public start going through them in search of smut.

The year the tailor died, we took our usual holiday in Gougane, but, though we called to condole with Ansty (short for Anastasia) he had already been buried. Seán, however, wrote one of his best stories, *The Silence of the Valley*, about an imaginary visit to attend his wake.

Rereading extracts from *The Tailor and Ansty*, first published in *The Bell* in March 1941, I have just come on the tailor's thoughts about animals. 'There is a change somehow,' he tells Cross. 'The animals are getting more daring and more intelligent. They are thinking more and they are learning the way we think too. They are not stupid. It is we who are stupid to think they are . . .'

I was nine when I first read that. It impressed me then and still does, especially as more people seem to think like that now. Here in the West, anyway, animals have come up in the world.

Elsewhere in Cross's book the tailor observes that, though a number of people who dropped into his cabin had written books and taught in universities, 'the airiest, wittiest men that ever walked into me were the men who walked the roads', adding that 'if a man does not use his own eyes and ears and mouth and intelligence, he may as well be dead. There's no man living can't see a new wonder every day of his life, if he keeps his eyes open and wants to see.'

This implicit rebuke to bookishness reminds me of the prolific Maupassant's claim that he himself didn't need to read much because he found the raw material for his fiction by looking carefully at what was going on around him. He even trained both his mother and his valet to report to him on any drama they might come across which he could use in his stories. Perhaps the men who walked the roads performed the same service for the tailor?

Remembering this reminds me of my own mother's zestful talent for providing writer friends with copy. Eileen had a flair for spotting promising situations and working up what she heard, and I now keenly regret failing to write a tribute, while she was alive, to her bravura when playing this rarely acknowledged role which bridges the oral and literary traditions. Both O'Connor and Seán based short stories on her field reports and, at least once, years later, so would I. The piece I thought of writing about her was to have been called *The Straight Woman*, in memory of those music-hall actors, known as 'straight men', who fed comedians lines designed to help make rehearsed witticisms seem spontaneous. Oliver Gogarty, a Dublin wit and poet, actually got her to give him cues like this at one or more of Yeats's Irish Academy dinners. Perhaps all the old wits achieved their effects by such secret preparation? I remember reading that Mahaffy, who had been Oscar Wilde's tutor at Trinity College and was a friend of Gogarty's, had done something of the sort. So the tradition may always have been a collaborative one which the cult of an airy amateurism led artful wits to present as artless.

Gogarty was a surgeon as well as a poet, and one of Eileen's less cheerful memories was of his chatting away while taking out her tonsils without an anaesthetic. He showed them to her at once and was about to take them to the next room to show them to Seán, when she managed to rally and dissuade him, since Seán might have fainted. Doctors who examined her throat later told her that the poet had done a perfect job. And he charged her nothing.

As her stories were often about acquaintances, libel actions were a risk. Publishers, in the Thirties and Forties, were almost always English and so subject to the harsh English libel laws. Yet Dubliners continued to sue and to risk being sued, and it is hard not to think that this activity was providing them with some of the buzz and challenge that conspiracy had done for earlier generations. It was sometimes seen too as a handy source of cash. Yet not all libel victims could or did sue. Take the case of Gogarty himself, recognisably the original of Buck Mulligan in Joyce's *Ulysses*, but, although meanly lampooned by Joyce, who had sponged on him and then suggested the reverse in his novel, he did not sue. Perhaps, as *Ulysses* had been published in Paris, he couldn't. Instead, in 1937 he was himself sued by an uncle of Samuel Beckett's, who claimed that his grandfather had been described in Gogarty's semi-fictional memoir as a usurer and a man partial to little girls. Gogarty had to pay £900 plus costs, which doubled his loss. Passing on the pain, like a character in *La Ronde*, he then sued the penniless poet Patrick Kavanagh who, in describing a call he had paid on him, had written in *his* memoir, *The Green Fool*, 'I mistook Gogarty's . . . maid for his wife or his mistress.' Gogarty's objection to this seems to have been that the text brought the words 'wife' and 'mistress' indecently close. Since the unfortunate Kavanagh had only recently come from his stony, Monaghan farm, his innocence seems blatant, especially as not only Joyce but also Gogarty's own poems had portrayed Gogarty himself as a buck. One of those included in Yeats's *Oxford Book of Modern Verse* which had come out in 1936 goes as follows:

I will live in Ringsend
With a red-headed whore,
And the fan-light gone in
Where it lights the hall-door;
And listen each night
For her querulous shout.
As at last she streels in
And the pubs empty out.
To soothe that wild breast
With my old-fangled songs,

Till peace at last comes,
Shall be all I will do,
Where the little lamp blooms
Like a rose in the stew;
And up the back-garden
The sound comes to me
Of the lapsing, unsoilable,
Whispering sea.

Though the poem defamed its author's domestic arrangements more effectively than poor Kavanagh did, Gogarty got £100 in damages; the book was withdrawn, and Kavanagh, though he had been a frequent visitor to our house, must have decided that, as Dubliners were twisters, he would be one too and sue Seán for publishing a poem of his in *The Bell* without permission. Seán claimed that they had agreed viva voce that he could publish, but had no written proof. This must have led to speculation in the pubs, for, on running into Kavanagh in one of them, Michael Scott, the leading Irish architect of the day, asked him why he was being so litigious. The poet, in his splendidly gravelly and wistful voice, said, 'I might make a few pounds.' Scott immediately offered to supply these from his own pocket if Kavanagh dropped his action. Kavanagh took the money but went back on his word, so Scott said *he'd* sue *him* – and, as often happened in Dublin, the thing fizzled out. Libel threats, however, continued to amuse some and worry others, and I can still summon the perplexity I felt when, at breakfast one morning, Eileen laughed in relief on finding a sonnet in the *Irish Times* by a writer, called Arland Ussher, which called Seán a yahoo.

'Thank God!' she exclaimed. 'Now that Ussher's vented his rage he won't sue over the hatchet-job of a review Seán published of his book.'

Alerted to the volatility of Dublin's hungry jungle, Seán now arranged for the solicitor, Christopher Gore-Grimes, to vet for libel everything he was thinking of publishing. 'Christo', a yachtsman and a sportsman whose solicitors' firm was well established, may have enjoyed the risk of finding himself maligned – libelled even – by writers with whom this activity brought him into contact. Honor Tracy, who was to arrive in Dublin in 1946, wrote satirical novels, one of which described a character based on him as having 'bog water coming up through his Trinity accent'. Christo didn't mind. And Honor, a woman of nerve, went on to provoke a Kerry parish priest who promptly sued the *Sunday Times*, where she had reported on the extravagance of his living arrangements and the cost of his new bathroom. The paper apologised on her behalf, whereupon she sued its proprietor and became the only person I ever knew or heard of who simultaneously took on the Irish Church, the English libel laws and Kemsley newspapers and won. In those years of few jobs and less industry, libel actions were a lively form of gambling. My admiration for her was infinite. According to Google, she was awarded damages of £5,000. Think what that would have bought in 1954.

But before then a lot of Liffey water would flow under the bridges.

MY FIRST SUMMER IN FRANCE

Starting in 1940, *The Bell* was produced in what we called 'the hut', a small, pretty building at the end of our garden, covered by green shingles and containing a desk, books, a divan and a wide window. This looked out past several downward-sloping fields belonging to Captain Disney towards a pond where a solitary heron spent most of its time standing motionless on one leg. On the near side of the hut was a verandah, to which Eileen and I were sometimes allowed to bring a picnic. Usually, however, this territory was taboo, reserved for *The Bell*'s staff members, chief of whom was Harry Craig, who could put his hand to anything. He edited, subedited, wrote articles signed, according to need, with either his own name or a pseudonym, and queued for our bus tickets when we were taking a trip to Cork or, as we sometimes did, to Kilkenny. Over the years Harry helped Seán to make several garden features including a swing, a sandpit, a rose walk and a wooden seat the size of a cartwheel which encircled an old tree. He was also our star reader when we read each other poetry, as people in those years used to do. With a lilting Limerick accent and a penchant for love verse, he was a student at Trinity College, a parson's son, and a known heart-breaker, for news of whom female voices would beg with shy insistence on the phone. I think my mistrust of charm, which would be re-activated years later when I grew up and began spending time in Italy, must have first started when dealing with Harry's girls who breathed hot, furtive hope into my ear while pleading to have their calls switched to the hut.

This – Seán's memoirs remind me – had not, at first, been on the phone at all. He had thought of it as a writer's retreat, and, at the beginning, if someone rang who urgently needed to reach him, he had had to be summoned to the house by one of us walking out along Killiney Hill Road ringing a large cowbell which he had bought on a visit to Kentucky.

Soon, though, a phone extension was connecting hut and house, where Eileen and I briskly interviewed callers and weeded out time-wasters. Our life had grown busy and convivial, for we often had guests at lunch and tea, and regularly for open-house on Sunday nights. As a result, I became expert at making sandwiches and large salads of chopped beetroot mixed with US-donated corned beef which were our mainstay whenever we had to provide a meal in a hurry. Money was short, so, even on the Sunday evenings, no drink was offered until the end of the war, when Seán started keeping a barrel of Guinness in the back yard. Others, though, were hungrier than we, and men like Kavanagh were prepared to walk the ten miles from the city centre to Killiney just to drink tea and eat sandwiches, some of which they put in their pockets to sustain them on the walk back. Tea was scarce. The ration, half an ounce per person per week, was smaller than in England, but people who were hard up sold their coupons, so the rest managed. Unfair? Yes, it was. But large, needy families were probably better off than before, since now they had something to sell. Meanwhile fuel was next to non-existent, so we burned damp turf, whose smoke left a combustible deposit in the chimneys which sometimes caught fire and, in our case, left a crack in the living-room chimney breast which had to be covered by a decorative cloth.

In 1939 when I got my first bike, guests who arrived too early risked being asked to teach me to ride it. Harry Craig and a handsome Russian called Alexander Lieven were my favourite instructors, and the joy of their presence led me to drag out the learning process. Kavanagh didn't volunteer but wrote jingles in my poetry notebook instead. Other visitors whose comings and goings I can't date were Brian Inglis, Brendan Behan (definitely post-war), Valentine Iremonger, Conor Cruise O'Brien and his first wife, Christine, Norah McGuinness, Betty Rivers, David Marcus, Arthur Power and Geoffrey Taylor (formerly Phibbs) who took over as poetry editor of *The Bell* from Frank O'Connor, whose colleague he had been in Wicklow Library. Both used pseudonyms, Frank because when he was a librarian he didn't want anything lewd he might write – Irish authorities often found life lewd – being traced to him. Taylor meanwhile had already shed *his* name when he got caught up in a small but lively scandal. This had involved Robert Graves and Laura Riding and, though it ended with her jumping out of a fourth-floor window and breaking – or not breaking? – her back, had started in Wicklow when the painter, Norah McGuinness, who was then Mrs Phibbs, went off with David Garnett, and Geoffrey took up with the American poet, Laura Riding, who was at the time living with Graves. The two shared her, and the story has more versions than a folktale.

The next thing was that Frank ran off – these were the words always used of such events – with the wife of the actor, Robert Speight. One thinks of the rape of the Sabines, with Mrs Speight looking beautifully lewd as the unathletic Frank tries to hold her aloft.

But perhaps he borrowed a pony and trap? Cars were scarce. Indeed, I doubt if any of our Sunday guests had one, though John Betjeman, who was press attaché at the British Embassy and, unknown to us, also worked for the British Ministry of Information, may have done so, and so must Sir John Maffey, the British representative, who came at least once. Betjeman's letters, however, complain about having to take buses, so perhaps he didn't run a car for long. He used to send Seán letters signed in cod Irish as Seán Ó Betjemán and once invited our whole family to lunch at his country house. Or so I remember it. Only now, reading his daughter's edition of his letters, do I see what a drag this may have been.

'I have to see pro-Germans,' one letter complains to an English friend. 'Pro-Italians, pro-British and, most of all, anti-British people . . . I have to go about saying "Britain will win in the end" and I have to be charming to everyone and I am getting eaten up with hate of my fellow beings as a result. The strain is far greater than living in London under the blitz.'

Oh dear. He *was* charming and, when I met him again with Seán in the Seventies, he still was. I hope that on those later occasions he was under less strain.

It is clear from his published letters that Seán, Frank and Kavanagh were in the pro-British category and so in no need of conversion. Despite – or because of – that, he got them occasional jobs on the BBC, each of which involved a trip to London and a chance for a breather away from what Seán called 'the dull smother' of wartime Ireland. He seems also to have helped organise the 1942 Irish number of Cyril Connolly's *Horizon*, which published work by all three, most memorably Kavanagh's poem *The Great Hunger*, then promptly seized by the Irish police on the usual grounds of obscenity.

Inevitably, there was the odd row on our open-house Sunday evenings. After all, if you declare yours an open house, you can't then restrict your guest list to people who get along with each other. And in the Forties there were plenty of reasons for Dubliners not to do that, especially if one of them had reviewed – or failed to review – books by others, or was on the Left or the Right, or despised our neutrality or had killed someone's father in 1922 or 1923. But I, whose role was to hand around sandwiches and refill cups with tea, either never knew or have now forgotten why people got upset.

Once, though, our family got caught up in a row which I

remember with unpleasant clarity. This did not happen on home ground. We were playing away.

In 1946 Seán, Eileen, my brother Stevie and I paid our last summer visit to our elected Eden, Gougane Barra, which, on that occasion, turned out to be more like the biblical one than expected. It bristled with sanctimony and a hiss of suspicions which, like the snake, crushed in old paintings by the Virgin's foot, were of a frankly sexual nature. So there was a fall from grace ending with our being, if not quite cast out, pointedly ostracised. It happened as follows.

Seán had arranged to rent an old-style, though well-appointed, horse-drawn caravan in Cork City and drive it slowly west to Gougane, pausing en route to shop, cook, eat, sleep, drop into pubs and look up old friends. This was a romantic idea and also a source of cash, since he sold accounts of the journey to one of the Irish Sunday newspapers which serialised them as we proceeded west, allowing us to buy copies from rural newsagents along the way, read about our doings almost as soon as they happened and admire their snapshots of ourselves, the hired mare and the caravan. A useful side effect was that locals stopped taking us for authentic tinkers at whose marauding approach they had better rush out and gather up their hens.

'Are ye the Wards or the Redmonds?' village outposts had been challenging us before the press enlightened them.

Originally neither Stevie nor I was to have come on the caravan trip at all. Instead we were to have stayed as paying guests with the Butler family at their house, Maidenhall, in County Kilkenny.

Seán and Hubert Butler, who would be hailed with surprise as a brilliant and insightful essayist when his collected writings were published towards the end of his life, were allies. Indeed some of his early essays had appeared in the Forties in *The Bell*. And Conor Cruise O'Brien, who delivered the eulogy at Seán's funeral in 1991, would note that during the dark days of native Irish oppression, censorship and deference, three men had defended Liberalism. Of these, one was a Catholic, one a Protestant and the third, Owen Sheehy-Skeffington, an agnostic. The three – Seán, Butler and OSS – had supported each other in many skirmishes, and Stevie and I had been happily parked with the Butlers on earlier occasions. Indeed, a nightmare which I used to get must connect with one such visit. In it I am trying to straddle a runaway carthorse whose back is so wide that I come close to doing the splits as I cling to its mane while it gallops through a small Kilkenny town. The horse has neither reins nor saddle. A rope has been tied around its middle and a voice, which I think of as belonging to Hubert Butler, is noting – as it may well have done in reality – that I bounce when trotting 'like a pea on a plate'. I suspect this dream-memory was a conflation of two emotions: stress and indignation, arising from what happened when we left Maidenhall for Gougane.

The reason for leaving was that no sooner had we been dropped off with our hosts than Stevie fell ill with something troublesome, whereupon the Butlers got in touch with our parents asking them to come back and take us away. Which they did. But as Knockaderry had been let for two weeks, we couldn't go back there. So willy-nilly the caravan became a home from home for myself and Seán as we headed west, while Eileen and Stevie stayed in hotels and tried to keep pace with us by taking buses in the same direction. It was a rainy summer, so we were held up by floods and took refuge where we could, while doing our best to cope with rural setbacks, like the one when the mare got so bloated that she couldn't get between the shafts, and rustic wags – a Cork speciality – assured us that the way to deal with this was to stick the prongs of a pitchfork in her belly. I forget how we solved her predicament, but don't remember anyone doing that.

Then real trouble struck. On reaching Gougane we found that the recently arrived English writer, Honor Tracy, whom Seán had met through John Betjeman, was waiting at our hotel, which had no room to offer her. Small boys had already been sent in various directions to ask if any cabin had a spare room or bed. None did. It was the height of the tourist season; no booking had been made for her and she clearly had not been expected. Equally clearly, my mother was put out by her presence, and, judging by subsequent developments, some of the Dubliners staying in the hotel lost no time informing anyone who didn't know that Seán and Honor were thought to be what is now called an item. I, who was too priggish – and worried on Eileen's behalf – to admit to myself that I had guessed this, clung to the belief that their friendship was as innocent as the one he enjoyed with Mother Hogan. Honor was a touch too plump, and I thought of this as veiling her subtler attractions. At the same time I was drawn to her myself. She had a thrilling laugh and a directness which astounded me, since Irish women then were rarely straightforward about anything. Indeed, apart from Jasmine, she was the only person I knew who not only spoke her mind, but did so with wit and relish in a seductively musical voice.

Seán sometimes described her as looking like a Maillol sculpture and had once produced a photo of one to show what he meant. It reassured me. Men, I supposed then, wanted women to look like Greta Garbo, whereas Honor must have been one and a half times her size. Her hair was an agreeable carrot colour, and her amused smile had a perfection which, in those days of bad dentistry, you hardly ever saw. Earlier in Dublin, she had – I guessed even then – set out to charm me because she knew that Seán and I were close. Saying so makes her seem as calculating as an old-time villainess, like Madame de Merteuil in *Dangerous Liaisons* or Henry James's Madame Merle. Perhaps she really was like them and had to be, precisely because she didn't look like Greta Garbo. Or perhaps stating things candidly, as I am now trying to do, is always a form of betrayal. The vague, shifting view of her which I had held at the start was probably closer to the way things were. It is also more charitable. But then, as we were starting to learn, Honor did not aim to depend on anyone's charity. She would take what she wanted if she could.

When we had parked the caravan in the hotel yard, found someone to look after the mare, and were wondering what to do next, I could tell that my parents felt uncomfortable. Perhaps they were remembering that shortly before Honor first arrived from England, they had received a letter warning them that she was a dangerous woman who had bewitched the famous orientalist, Arthur Waley, under whom she had worked in the Ministry of Information. Perhaps the letter-writer had worked there, too, and been trained as an informer. The word seemed to carry no stigma in England. The Ministry sounds, doesn't it, like of something in a book by Orwell and almost too appropriate for such a letter? I forget the precise words this one used, and whether, indeed, it was anonymous, but remember clearly that they described Honor as having insinuated herself into Arthur Waley's life and ruthlessly taken it over. She was likely, said the letter-writer, to do this again with someone else, so the Irish, who were unaccustomed to snakes, had better look out because she was an accomplished one. I remembered Seán and Eileen laughing over the letter and wondering whether it had been sent as a joke or by someone whom she had displaced. Probably a woman. The thought made me wish I need never grow up.

Adults were hard-hearted, and when you dealt too closely with them, you discovered that you were too. I had recently noticed that Jasmine, who was now sixteen, was changing. She had grown friendly with a girl from the village called Marge, who spoke exclusively in slang. Excruciatingly repetitive, and, to me, largely unintelligible chit-chat made the two of them giggle uproariously, while the previously fastidious Jasmine seemed to have been replaced by a slut. Somehow I knew that most of their coded silliness had to do with sex.

Meanwhile, in the Gougane Hotel, someone voiced a suggestion which had been nibbling at all our minds. It was that Honor could sleep in the caravan while Eileen shared a room with Stevie who, though no longer as sick as he had been, might need to be near her. Seán would then have the other room which had been booked, and I could sleep on a settle in one of the cottages which turned out, after all, to be available.

Whether Seán slipped from his bed that night and into the caravan, I don't know, and perhaps neither did anyone else. But, true or not, word must have got around that he had, for over the next few days we were ostracised. Picnics and shooting expeditions were planned in our hearing. But, although the locals knew that Seán was handy with a gun, he was not asked to join them, and when a banquet was arranged to eat the game the shooting parties had bagged, we alone, of all the hotel's guests, were not invited to that either. Instead, we sat in another room with Honor and chose our dinner from the everyday menu. It was like *The Scarlet Letter*. A penitential occasion. Oddly, even my mother was excluded from the festivities – unless, from pride, she had voluntarily joined the ranks of the outcast. She might have done. I still don't know. But the thought strikes me that perhaps we *had* been invited to the dinner – after all, the hotel-owners were old friends – but that, somehow, it had been delicately conveyed that things would be easier if we came without Honor, and that we had refused this condition. The leader of the zealots, a now dead professor from University College Dublin (UCD) called McHugh, might have dragooned the shooting expeditions, but he would have had little or no clout when it came to interfering with hotel arrangements.

My main contribution to the state of play was an attempt the next day to stop Stevie accepting bottles of lemonade – 'minerals' – from the otherwise ill-disposed guests. I think of them now as the morals police who, either because they had had a change of heart and hoped to repair the breach with us, or because, on the contrary, they wished to deepen it, deliberately drew Stevie into their camp. He didn't understand what was going on, but being a pretty child with great, violet-blue eyes, long lashes and curly hair, was used to being petted by strangers and couldn't see why he shouldn't take what was on offer. Poor Stevie! My attempts to coerce his loyalty backfired, and he was soon dodging our party and cadging handouts from our opponents.

Meanwhile, it rained. Floods made the roads impassable; and until they cleared, there could be no question of our returning to Cork City. What I can't now remember is whether Father Traynor was part of the gang which sent us to Coventry. Was he even still alive? I know he died shortly after the tailor did, and that was in 1945, so it is more than likely that he wasn't.

Yet, among the images jostling in my memory of that visit, his wistful-but-friendly face is omnipresent. It brings to mind my parents' memories of their college days and of the dances to which he used to sneak from his seminary, relying on Seán's giving him a leg up later to help him climb back in. Surely he, who had liked having his cake and eating it too, would not have condemned Seán for wanting the same thing? Or would he? He might. After all, what he had always wanted was to be a married priest, but while Pius XII was pope and McQuaid was the Irish primate, it was clear that no such hybrids would be sanctioned. So Traynor could well have felt jealous of Seán's freedom, as well as indignant at his failure to cherish conjugal comforts for which he himself continued to hanker with decreasing hope.

His dilemma interested both Frank and Seán, each of whom wrote stories about it, as it would soon be safer to do when, with the arrival of television and easy foreign travel, Irish society gradually grew less introverted. Soon fiction would no longer be frowned on for using the word 'breast' instead of 'chest', and Christo Gore-Grimes, when assessing libel risks, would come to the conclusion that, as thinking evolved, the question writers should start asking themselves would no longer be 'could so-and-so sue' but '*would* he?'

Looking still further ahead: in the Sixties the Second Vatican Council would give serious attention to the needs of priests like Traynor, though in the end nothing would actually be done.

Oh dear! Or as Great-aunt Kate always said, 'Wirrasthrue', meaning 'Mary's pity', which I took to be a cry for help to the top female power who had, as always, a lot on her plate.

As we left Gougane I felt sorry for everyone except the morals police: for Eileen and Honor and Father Traynor – whether dead or alive – and Seán and even greedy little Stevie, who had drunk so many chemically coloured minerals that he got sick. Meanwhile I managed to deceive myself about what might or might not have gone on in the caravan and would – I would learn later – go on for some years in various venues in a world which was opening and expanding before us, now that it was 1946 and the Emergency over.

I don't know whether Seán or Eileen ever went back to Gougane, though his short story, *The Silence of the Valley*, creates a counter-reality in which Traynor and Honor are more vigorously and entertainingly themselves than anyone had been on that visit. Neither Seán nor Eileen nor I appear, but the story sketches Dinny Cronin, the hotel proprietor, with graphic precision. Stevie is there, too, excitedly watching Dinny fish for eels, as he had done in earlier summers, by throwing chickens' guts into the lake, then netting the black, phallic shapes which converge on them, and which the fictionally born-again Traynor seems to resurrect in the kitchen by throwing them on a pan so blazing hot that, though dead, they leap and ripple in the torment of a dance not unlike that of the damned in innumerable last judgements.

Officially Seán and Honor soon broke up, but the following summer both accepted publishers' contracts which led to their travelling on the Continent, and years later, when I was sitting with friends in a Dublin bar, the two came down the narrow stairs from a second-floor restaurant, and it was clear that they had been dining together. Discretion in Dublin was hard to achieve.

For a while Honor rented a small, stone Gothic Revival tower on the edge of Killiney village and lived there in ambush. She possibly aimed to stage a replay of what may or may not have happened in the caravan, but the village had Argus eyes and I can't believe Seán braved them often, if at all.

'What have you to lose?' I imagine her teasing him. 'Everyone thinks you're a sinner, so why not sin?'

People did think that, and when she wrote satirical pieces about Ireland for *The Observer* and the *Sunday Times*, they said, 'She could never have dug up so much dirt by herself. Seán must be helping her. He's letting down the country!'

Sometimes, when I boarded the 59 bus, she would be sitting in it, and I would have to decide fast whether more gossip would be generated if I did not join her than if I did. At first I usually did, but later, after she had been away for almost a year in Japan doing research for a book, it seemed easier not to, as conversations were tricky, and the simplest exchange could sound loaded, even 'How are your parents?', 'Fine thanks', 'Give them my regards.'

Contrasted with my frets, her poise was flawless. As we would see when she challenged and defeated Kemsley newspapers (this took four years), she was patient when she wanted something. And she wanted Seán. His identity, however, had been forged in his youth. It may not have been bliss to be alive and active in the Irish Civil War, but it had been unforgettable, and his relations with Eileen had been part of it, so he couldn't give her up. She was his witness and memory, or so I concluded. Moreover, being volatile, possibly to his regret, he seemed to feel a need to be pinned down. I don't know how he conveyed this, or why. Perhaps it was to reassure us both – or in the hope that I would reassure Eileen.

Yet, at the end of his life, he was again dreaming of Honor and telling me sadly, 'She was the best of the lot.' If asked, though, about Eileen, he would retort with aplomb, '*She* is in another category.' His tears in the rue Montpensier seven years after the Gougane visit must have had to do with his yearning to reconcile the irreconcilable. Like Laocoön and his sons struggling with Athena's serpents in the Vatican sculpture, Catholics of his generation had tied themselves in knots.

As for Gougane, I don't think my parents can have gone back there, since from 1946 on they took their holidays abroad. I, however, went back twice, first when Eileen died in 1988, and again three years later when Seán did, to scatter their ashes in the lake. Gougane is the source of the River Lee, so I liked to imagine the ashes being washed down to Cork City, past the site of the picnic where Eileen had been shot in the neck by a Black and Tan, then out into the Atlantic Ocean which she had crossed, possibly a touch tremulously, two years after Seán did, to keep their appointment to meet again and marry in Boston.

Meanwhile in 1947, when my school nuns arranged for me to spend my summers with a family living high in the Savoy mountains, I found what seemed for a while to be an Eden of my own.

At about the same time, our attention became riveted on some very Irish wrangles which began to target Hubert Butler, whose plight recalled that of Dreyfus in that, as a Protestant, he belonged to an unpopular minority. He was less vulnerable than the Frenchman, though, both because he wasn't in the army and the charge against him was not spying but what would now be called 'spreading disinformation', which, as a friend of mine would learn decades later, could land a man in jail.

Although Butler was an Anglo-Irish Protestant, and Seán a Catholic policeman's son, their careers had similarities. Both were born in 1900, opposed censorship and held beliefs which alienated their own communities.

Like Seán, Butler got a travelling scholarship after finishing his university studies, and, having earlier learned Russian, chose to spend the years 1934 to 1937 in Yugoslavia learning Serbo-Croat, while Seán spent *his* fellowship years at Harvard working on Celtic studies. Compared to Slavic languages, this choice sounds insular but, remembering how hope perished in the Civil War and that Seán had fought on the losing side to the bitter end, one sees that the dry tussle with Celtic philology may have offered needed respite. Happily, just as he began to see that his true vocation was to be fiction, sales of stories to *The Dial* and the *Hound and Horn* in 1927 and 1928 enlarged his world and led to fruitful friendships with both Richard Blackmur, the *Hound and Horn*'s editor, and Edward Garnett at Cape.

Butler's field of study had been chosen for calmer reasons – but the calm would not last. He himself noted that his sympathy for the Irish War of Independence was part of a wider interest in the break-up of empires which, in the wake of the Great War, spawned a dozen or so small nations whose hopes and outlook were similar. One of these was Croatia which got its independence at the same time as Ireland and was beset by similar clashes of culture and religion. So Butler knew about clashes.

He could not, however, have foreseen the rage that his discoveries would unleash in the Irish Catholic press when he went back to Croatia in 1946, read the wartime newspapers available in the municipal library of Zagreb, and learned that Archbishop Stepinac, whom the Catholic Church was presenting as a living martyr for the faith, had collaborated with war criminals during the years 1941 to 1945. Worse, Stepinac had been hand-in-glove with 'a Nazi-installed puppet regime which had waged a genocidal crusade against non-Catholics'. Butler did not report this at first. On the contrary, he gave a circumspect talk on Radio Éireann which drew criticism for what he had *not* said. He had not mentioned Catholic suffering at the hands of Tito's Communists. When reproached for this, he replied that one could hardly refer to the Communist persecution without mentioning 'the more terrible Catholic persecution which had preceded it'. This was a red rag to the bull-headed. *The Standard*, a vehemently Catholic Irish weekly paper, foamed at its many mouths, and its editor and foreign editor wrote diatribes against Butler and Radio Éireann. As neither editor knew any Serbo-Croat, they could only rely on theory: Catholics did not support forced conversions, so Stepinac could not have connived at those of two and a half million Serbian Orthodox. QED.

Butler then went back to Zagreb and found out more.

In 1952 he was invited by Owen Sheehy-Skeffington to attend a meeting at which the editor of *The Standard* was to give a talk on 'Yugoslavia – the Pattern of Persecution'. At the end of this, Butler rose to reply to the speaker, but the moment he mentioned the persecution of the Serbs, the nuncio, of whose presence he had been unaware, stalked 'magisterially' out and the meeting was closed. Butler's native County Kilkenny hastened to dissociate itself from his failure to grovel, as the Irish normally did, to the papal representative. 'All the local government bodies of the city and county', he reported, 'held special meetings to condemn "the Insult".'

Later clashes were more venomous, and later findings more damning. Members of the Croatian Catholic clergy turned out to have connived in genocide; then when the war ended, helped smuggle wanted war criminals out of Europe. One of these was

Artukovitch. A former Minister of the Interior in the 'viciously anti-Serb Orthodox Christian and anti-semitic Ustashe regime in Croatia', he had been the master mind behind the campaign in which 750,000 Orthodox and 30,000 Jews were massacred, and 240,000 Orthodox forcibly converted to Roman Catholicism. After the war, as Butler would later discover, Artukovitch had escaped to Austria and Switzerland and then, in 1947, to Ireland 'with the connivance of the Catholic Church and the Irish Government. A year later, armed with an Irish identity card, he left for the US.'

Responsibility had moved uncomfortably close.

The reaction in Kilkenny was to ostracise Butler's family, force him out of the local archaeological society which he had himself resurrected when it was moribund, and devise other malicious, gnat-sized assaults. The County Council expelled him from one of its subcommittees, and local businesses such as creameries refused to deal with him. There is a cartoonish pettiness to this boycott, but it cannot have been pleasant to have been on the receiving end of it. The American writer Paul Blanshard, a virulent anti-Catholic whose aim was to alert the US to the dangers of letting RCs take over, seized on the story and told it later in his book *The Irish and Catholic Power*. Was his book really 'virulent'? Malicious? I thought so then but was unlikely to be open-minded. I remember his visiting Knockaderry and that, from my shy station behind the tea trolley, I took against him.

In the Forties and Fifties, religion in Ireland was prone to generate malice. The faithful used to be warned by priests never to put foot in a Protestant church. If invited to a 'mixed' wedding or christening, you should wait outside. As rules are for breaking, Marie and I used sometimes to slip inside the Killiney Protestant church, a pretty building with a slim verdigris-covered spire, to breathe forbidden air. It did not take much more than that to make us feel we were turning into apostates. The church was just a stone's throw from our house, so on idle days we would sidle in and have a look at the austere, alien, but unexpectedly appealing, décor. It was not until I had been to France that I began to notice how weepy, bloody, triumphalist and florid our own churches' arrangements were. The lovely ruined ones, destroyed in half-forgotten wars, would almost certainly have been just as overstuffed with gimcrack gewgaws if they had survived, so we didn't regret their undoing. As it was, the sight of a wind-eroded, free-standing stone groin framing stretches of sky had a sorrowful appeal. The mix of fragility and tenacity was heart-breaking. Clonmacnoise especially – a roofless, sixth-century monastery in County Offaly – was surrounded by close-cropped grassland littered with white bones. Eileen and I drove there one winter's day, after dropping Seán in Cobh, where he would catch the liner for New York, then wandered for hours around the ruined buildings, without seeing another human being whom we could ask whether those bones were human. In my fading memory – this trip was a long time ago – there are skulls or half-skulls in the scatter and I remember thinking of the 'Alas, poor Yorick!' scene in Olivier's *Hamlet* before realising that the skulls must have belonged to goats.

Years later, when visiting Palmyra and Apameia, I felt some of the same excitement, although those much vaster sites were neither as empty, lonely or numinous. And no doubt neither, now, is Clonmacnoise.

A memory of an earlier visit to Maidenhall: I am walking to Sunday Mass with the Butlers' maids, one of whom is called Sally. She is teasing me, but not, I sense, in a friendly way. I am younger in this memory, but alert, as children can be in ways they do not try to freeze in words. My awareness flickers as Sally's mood shifts. Am I wondering, she asks, why I'm with the maids this morning and not with the Butlers? She launches this as though it were a trick question. Is it? I am used to maids doing this. There is provocation here. The maids are competitive. Some are quite young. Sally nags, asking where I think my hosts are.

Without thinking, I say, 'It's early. I suppose they'll go to a later Mass.'

She laughs with delight, and I guess that I have fallen into a trap. 'Mass!' she derides, '*Mass?* Dontcha even know they're Protestants?'

Clearly she hopes her information will deflate and shock me. I shrug. 'We know heaps of Protestants,' I tell her, 'in Dublin. Some come to Mass.' My claim, though mostly untrue, takes the wind out of her sails.

In this memory I am too young to know the words 'social class', but, contrary to a widely held belief, you can think without words, and I know what Sally is on about. If I have to go to Mass with the maids, that, she wants me to know, is because I am of the same stock as they, so I'd better not be stuck up. Like, she implies, should stick with like and not be too friendly with Prods. *The Standard* would no doubt agree with her. Not that I have ever laid eyes on it. Seán, who has had run-ins with Peadar Curry, its editor, doesn't subscribe nor, as far as I know, do the nuns. All they have in their parlour are stacks of a dry-looking magazine called *Studies*. It is run by Jesuits of whom they think highly.

The idea of Protestants going to Mass came to me from a poem of Betjeman's who, while slyly working in Ireland for the British Ministry of Information, had professed some – teasing or perhaps tactical? – interest in becoming a Catholic. When his wife actually became one, he was horrified and wrote a poem listing and lamenting the familiar, cosy, Protestant ways and habits she would now miss.

In early June 1947 Eileen and I haul a suitcase down from the attic and prepare for my trip to France. We are excited, though nervous about the family with whom I am to stay. They will surely, we tell each other, be kind. The Sacred Heart nuns, whose school the younger girls attend, have promised that they will. The family is large because Monsieur Morandy married twice, though both wives died. Between them they produced two boys and six girls. Guessing that the war must have left France in worse shape than the Emergency left us, Eileen and I agree that I must bring useful presents. After some thought, we opt for shoes and butter: two by-products of the cattle trade for which Ireland is noted. I can't carry six pairs, but reckon that if I bring two, there is a good chance of one or two of the girls finding their size. The butter is 'country butter' and available off the ration. Salty and orange-coloured, it is coarser than that sold by the creameries, and I am ashamed to be bringing such a primitive product all the way to Savoy. Eileen, however, claims she can't spare any of the ration and argues that, if the French won't eat what I bring, our own needs should come first. What I won't realise, until confronted by the Morandys' imperfectly concealed disdain, is that the shoes are worse than the butter. Wartime efforts to make Ireland self-sufficient have lowered standards so badly that we forget how clothes used to be. For years our school cardigans rubbed our necks raw, and the shoes I am to offer are as stiff as boards.

In school, when we complained, the nuns' advice was to offer up our discomfort to help the souls in purgatory to work off theirs. But that isn't the sort of recommendation you can write on a gift card.

Having packed my *Moran's French Grammar*, I consider buying a phrase book, but decide not to. Seán has one in Italian, and I can see that the phrases it features are unlikely to be of use to someone staying with a large family in the mountains. For instance, 'Waiter, two more Marsala milkshakes, please' could sound silly if what I need to deal with is a request to help dig, wash and peel enough potatoes for eight or, if I include Monsieur Morandy and myself, ten. I am hoping things won't be like that, but you never know. Reports have reached me of Irish au pairs being enslaved by ruthless foreigners. Technically, I am not in fact to be an au pair. The plan is that my visit is to be the first half of an exchange and that one of the Morandys will come to Dublin. This, however, won't happen and, although I will visit them four times, I don't think they pick up much English from me. Numbers are against them. I have to communicate. They don't.

So the ruthless foreigner will turn out to be myself.

Come to think of it, *why* won't one of them come? Don't they like me? Is it the cost of the journey or could they have been put off by the shoes? On each of my later visits, Seán will slip a modest amount of money into a letter to pay for my keep.

On this first occasion, he is to come with me as far as Chambéry railway station, hand me over to Monsieur Morandy then leave for Italy about which he has contracted to write a book. He suspects Graham Greene, his editor at Eyre & Spottiswood, of hoping for hilarious accounts of how an Irish Catholic copes with temptations devised by predatory Italian ones, meaning, I suppose, pimps. I must have learned that word from Honor Tracy, who used to shock us by translating enjoyable excerpts from Curzio Malaparte's lurid best-seller, *Kaputt*. Though maybe not? Due to Seán's efforts to forestall the censors, our house is full of banned books. Nobody minds my reading these. Even Eileen thinks I'd as well learn about the dangers lying outside the country. Pimps, she warns me, can be women. Beware of motherly ones who wear a prominently placed miraculous medal. She read that in some novel, and isn't above using literature the way she uses her *Home Doctor*.

Why not, I ask myself – especially when you hear how some writers use life.

When Seán called at Eyre & Spottiswood's London office, Greene, slipping out on some pretext, managed to leave him alone with a girl who, he said, would keep him company but who instead made a lively attempt to seduce him. Seán now thinks that the two had had a bet as to whether she would succeed and wonders if Greene does this with all his authors, or only with Catholic ones. It was he who first had the idea of Seán's going to Italy and writing about it. So, why the girl? Is GG a voyeur? And Seán a guinea pig?

Pondering these questions I guess that animosity between Irish and English Catholics might be to blame. *They* think of us as lowering their image. And *I* think of GG as using religion as copy. He does this brilliantly, which makes it more annoying.

Seán didn't tell me about the incident with the girl. I heard him talk about it to Dick Ellmann, the American writer and literary critic, who was often around in those years. Shortly after being demobbed from the US navy, he had arrived in Dublin and almost instantly became a family friend.

His impressive career as the biographer of Yeats, Joyce and Wilde was just taking off. But, not knowing at first with whom I was dealing – he had, I would discover, translated the poems of Henri Michaux – I agreed recklessly to write and exchange sonnets – happily soon lost. He had probably been asked to help with my homework so as to give Seán another half hour to finish an article. This, now that I no longer needed to be taught to ride a bike, was how I guest-sat people who arrived early – as many did, due to anxiety over a lack of buses. Sometimes I took energetic ones for a walk and swim, but don't remember Dick as one of those.

Two years later he and Mary were married. She had been teaching at Wellesley College, but gave this up to be with Dick in Ireland. Their three children were born in the early Fifties and at some stage they settled near enough to my parents to share a maid who, since telling tales is a maid's perk and privilege, told Eileen that Mary disliked Killiney and was homesick for Wellesley. Well, Killiney was a sleepy place.

In those years I was mostly away, so I missed getting to know Mary, which I regret. Her book, *Thinking About Women*, came out in 1968, has a cool wit and is, to my mind, the most elegant of the Second Wave feminist manifestoes. Sadly, an aneurysm of the brain prevented her writing another. She kept on bravely though, writing pieces for the *New Statesman*, and outlived Dick, who was struck down with motor neurone disease in 1987. This second blow was terrible luck, but at least he managed to finish his life of Oscar Wilde. I didn't see him once he fell ill, but before that Lauro and I spent a number of happy evenings with him whenever we coincided in Oxford, London or California. My last memory of Mary is at Dick's memorial service in New College, which she attended in a speedy wheelchair. Like characters in a Greek tragedy, they were both endowed with rare brilliance and stricken by rare adversity.

The Morandys lived up the mountains from the town of Chambéry in an airy, grey house called Le Sarvant, which in patois meant 'the genie'. It had a wide, curving stone stairway, a great, bright kitchen with a high ceiling, and several cellars where they stored wine casks and other equipment, including a contraption for shaking honey from its combs. They kept bees, grew vegetables and fruit, had vineyards, made their own white wine and were self-sufficient on a scale grander than de Valera's wartime campaign could ever have hoped to achieve. Only in one way were we in Ireland better off. We had meat almost every day, whereas they only had it once a week, and even then its origin was probably a black – or grey? – market. Monsieur Morandy made occasional forays further up the mountains to collect provisions from his 'butter man' – *mon bonhomme à beurre* – and similar providers. Back in Dublin, no such contacts were needed. Our shoe-leather might be tenth rate, and we might be short of fuel, paper, oranges, sugar and tea, but we did have meat. Which was to be expected. After all, the old Irish had always kept cattle, our great epic is about a battle over a bull and, during the Emergency, the availability of steak south of the border attracted visits from allied soldiers stationed up north. Back in the misty past, our lush grasslands must have made the breeding of cows and horses an inevitable trade. Later, the poor kept pigs and, until myxomatosis struck, rabbits. And in the Forties, when fishermen had no way of getting their lobsters to market, they sold them cheaply to whoever happened to be swimming off Killiney Beach. Watching the Morandy girls provide tasty meals without such raw materials, I wondered whether having such a plethora of them was why we had failed to elaborate an imaginative cuisine. All you needed to do with a steak, after all, was throw it on a hot pan, wait, then turn it. My parents wrote, gardened, read, took trips and entertained, but had no time for fancy cooking. Even unusual meat could puzzle us.

Once, during the Emergency, some benefactor sent us a freshly killed stag. Seán claimed it had arrived anonymously, a lordly gesture which makes me wonder if it came from Lord Moyne, a poet who had the wherewithal to donate such largesse. Other friendly lords – Wicklow, Longford, Dunsany – had either less reason to do so or fewer resources. Or the stag might have come from a charitable soul in some government department – forestry perhaps? – which had a right to cull deer. Meanwhile, how were we to dismember and cook it? Nobody knew.

In those days people ate game 'high', i.e. on the point of going off. This point, in the case of snipe and plover, was determined by hanging it by its beak and waiting until it fell. The stag, though, was too much for us. Captain Disney, when consulted, was equally at a loss.

'Hang it in the turf shed for a bit anyway,' he suggested, putting off the moment of truth.

So we did, and like the witch testing Hansel's finger to see if it and he were fat enough to eat, we poked and sniffed it regularly. Shamingly, we must have forgotten to do this at some point, for one day when we opened the turf-shed door, a maggotty glint told us all we needed to know. It had to be buried. We should, we now saw, have called a butcher the minute the gift arrived. We felt like the undeserving poor who are alleged to keep turf in their bathtubs.

Monsieur Morandy in the Forties looked like everyone's idea of a Frenchman. Lean and dark, with a trim moustache, he had served in the Chasseurs alpins and enjoyed reminiscing about meals he and his comrades had improvised under unpromising conditions. Even the least of them would surely have known how to butcher a stag.

'We used wine bottles to pound boiled potatoes into purée,' he told us. Recalling that cheerful male readiness to adopt impromptu shifts clearly made him wistful, but he liked domestic conviviality too.

During that first summer and later ones I would see him on innumerable, festive occasions – name days and birthdays – presiding genially at his dinner or luncheon table, filling glasses with his 'little' white wine and cracking jokes whose subversiveness expanded as the meal proceeded – subversive, that is, regarding politics and politicians. Never about morals. He needed those. After all, he had had to keep six daughters in order for years, which may have been why he tucked them away so far up the mountains, although his own work was in Chambéry. The eldest ones were now over twenty.

'Papa,' they warned me, 'is very strict. *Très, très sévère.*'

I guessed that this, if true, would not be in an Irish way, and saw I was right when he filled my glass with his 'little' white wine, then laughed uproariously when I said I had taken an oath not to drink until I was twenty-one. Why ever, he asked, had I? Everyone in the Dublin diocese, I told him, had to take it on their confirmation day. It was because we in Ireland drank too much.

'Pff!' he laughed with disapproval. *His* wine would do me no harm.

'Taste it. Good, isn't it? Have some more.'

But what, I worried, about the oath?

'Pff!'

Subversion delighted him. And by the end of that summer, he had so resolutely – and often slyly – topped up my glass, and introduced kirsch or cognac into my coffee cup, that I had become addicted to every sort of alcohol.

When I first met him, though, at Chambéry station, he seemed a little lost and glum, but neither of us knew how to ask if the other was all right, and Seán, who had a train to catch, had to rush off.

We, too, Monsieur Morandy managed to let me know, should

hurry. His car was outside. Over there. See? Better start out. People were waiting at home.

The drive into the mountains swerved sharply up winding roads, while spectacular views, some of them snow-capped, flashed abruptly in and out of sight. The car was *décapotable*. That was the first brand-new French word I learned that summer and, as if to celebrate it, the top was down. The sun's glare bounced off metal and mirrors, and it was a surprise, on reaching the great, thick-walled house, to find its interior as cool as a cellar. Shutters had been closed, and in the dimmed *salon* about thirty people turned to face me. Most were women. All wore black, and some wore ill-fitting clothes which made me think they might be nuns in mufti. An affable old lady who was one of the girls' aunts and spoke perfect English took charge of me. She introduced me to the others and, simultaneously, to the expeditious French mode of shaking hands with everyone within reach, working the throng like a politician. Already, on my way here, I had been astounded to see grown men kiss on railway platforms, and now wondered whether, since French manners were so showy, I should curtsy to the nunnish ladies. After all, in school we curtsied to the Reverend Mother, so I knew how to do it. Better not, though, since France was a republic.

The black-clad gathering was not in my honour. No. It was, the bilingual aunt told me, a funeral party which had earlier attended a Mass for the elder Morandy son, a keen mountain-climber who, years before, had fallen into a crevasse, and whose perfectly preserved body had now been uncovered thanks to a small avalanche. He had been reburied. There had been a lunch, and now people were starting to leave. She, though, would stay on for a day or so, to help me settle in.

'Then I'll go back', she gave me a plucky smile, 'to my retirement home for old ladies.'

Taking this for a joke, I laughed, saw that it wasn't one, and blushed. I had supposed her to be the family's mother-substitute, and was saddened to think of her being stuck instead in some grim institution probably run by nuns – handing them spare coupons to sell, washing her underwear in a portable basin, then bending, despite pains in her joints, to mop up spills. I knew about such places from Killiney village. Yet why could she not have stayed here, the way Aunt Kate had stayed with us?

By now, though, Aunt Kate, who had lived into her nineties, had been dead two years. And I rarely thought of her. Perhaps, by associating her with the Morandys' aunt, I was hoping to repay to the live woman the sympathy I owed the dead one.

Perhaps I would light a candle for her after Mass next Sunday?

Not knowing quite how things here worked made me uneasy.

I had guessed one thing right though. There *was* a mother-substitute. It was one of the girls themselves. Claude was neither the oldest nor cleverest. The two sisters who were had earned teaching diplomas and taught in schools further up the mountain. At this time of year they were home for the summer vacation, but in winter would be back above the snowline. Claude, meanwhile, stayed home and ran the house. She was quick, tender and funny, could slice a carrot as deftly with a knife as anyone can using today's electrical implements, and appeared to get all the satisfaction she needed from looking after her family. The others adored her, and I too would soon fall under her spell. Watching her cook was a delight.

However, life, as I now began perceiving it, was full of gaps. As I missed much of what was said, I thought of my view as being like the one people must get from inside those Moorish balconies whose carved screens conceal them from the street. The Morandys had cousins in Egypt who had sent photographs of these, and I guessed that, when sitting in them, their perceptions would be as porous and puzzling as mine became when the bilingual aunt went back to her convent, since the girls' attempts at English were as opaque as their French. Jacques, the surviving son, was keen on jazz which he pronounced 'jets'. Correcting him was tricky since he might have got his pronunciation from one of the clever elder sisters who, he now informed me, taught English. Did *they* say 'jets', I wondered but, fearing to embarrass them, didn't ask. I didn't correct them either when I heard one tell a younger sister that the English pronounced the word 'bouquet' as 'bucket'.

MADAME DE LA TOUR PIN
COMES TO TEA

One side-effect of my poor French was that at first I believed my hosts to be happy and that the place truly was an Eden. How could the thought not occur to me when I had seen, plucked and tasted my first peach and apricot on their terrace, not to speak of my first muscat grapes and mirabelle plums? In the evenings we sat outside enjoying the cool air and watching fireflies swoop. Sometimes a storm on distant mountains lit snowy peaks with pink and green lightning. Sometimes, earlier in the day, we bicycled down to Aix-les-Bains on the Lac du Bourget or up to high pasture lands, where the tinkling of cowbells was the only sound, or else equipped ourselves with baskets and dispersed into the woods to collect boletus mushrooms and wild strawberries. It was a paradise, I wrote in my letters home. All that first summer I held to this view. Quarrels were muted, and it was only in my second year that I began to tune into tensions reverberating just out of earshot. In my third one, a few things grew clear. Claude, the beloved 'little mother', had spent a month in Pau, on the other side of France, looking after an ailing aunt, and there had met a perfectly suitable man. They had promptly got married, and, after their honeymoon, she brought him to stay. They were still there when I arrived in June. But the atmosphere was stormy. She who, when I came first, had been the undisputed mistress of the house, had been elbowed aside. Resentments flared. By now my French was good enough to pick up snide remarks, but the reasons behind them were never spelled out. Was it envy? Anger with Claude for going away? Or possessiveness? Was money involved? Were the children of their father's two marriages at odds with each other –

over an inheritance perhaps? Or had she invited one of her sisters to stay with her in her new home so that she too might find a husband? If so, were the others jealous? And had the sister whom she had invited been forbidden to go?

Or did I, in my fifteen- and sixteen-year-old ignorance, get everything wrong?

Signs were hard to read. A hand of cards might suddenly be smashed down during a decorous game of bridge. Or someone might knock over her chair and run out to the terrace. Someone else might run after her. Sometimes there was sobbing. Then the game might take up again.

Surely Claude's attempt to reclaim her old position in the house could not have caused so much bad feeling? How could it have, if she and her husband were only here on a visit and would soon be gone?

I never discovered. But questions floated through my mind. Why, looking back on the many *fêtes* which the family had celebrated during my visits, could I never remember there having been a male guest – apart from Claude's husband? Not even the curé was invited, even though, judging by a glimpse I had caught through the open door of his house, he was painfully poor. He was by far the poorest priest I had ever seen, and could surely do with a free meal. Why did Monsieur Morandy invite no personal friends, only the aunts? Why, come to think of it, had they chosen to invite me who, being Irish, might be expected to have an undesirable accent? I wondered, indeed, if the bilingual aunt had been delegated to check on this. But what I began to think now was that, during the recent war, Monsieur Morandy might have made enemies. If he had and was still resented on some account, inviting someone from a neutral country would pose less problems than inviting one from England.

If I were writing fiction, this would be the point where my narrator would find something out. A sexual intrigue could come to light when Julie – I was still called Julie, especially in France – witnesses Claude's husband engaging in a tryst with one of the other sisters. Or voices, floating from an opened window, might name partisans who had hidden in this mountainous area. Had some family member denounced them – or become too friendly with them? Was the dead son's fate connected with some version of these events? Blackmail could have been threatened. The family's introversion could be due to their being ostracised. Dreams could interact, and a plot knit or unravel.

But I am not writing fiction.

More plausibly, Monsieur Morandy, having lost two wives and a son, might be more protective of his family than most fathers. It is fair to speculate that far. Especially as Jacques, who was eighteen in my first summer and longed to get away to Paris, talked more than once about how his father would do his damnedest to keep the girls from going there. 'He thinks it's a den of vice,' he once burst out bitterly. 'He thinks that any girl who goes to Paris is bound to end up as a lost soul!' He himself wasn't sure he could get away either. I don't know why. Perhaps he had repeatedly failed his exams? Something of the sort seemed likely, for I heard him weeping one evening in the room next to mine and being comforted by his father. Or else – this would have made things harder for him – he may have felt that he had to make up for his brother's death by staying home and taking his place? The father, who, the family agreed, had always been strict with them, was strangely tender in that overheard conversation. '*Mon petit Jacques*,' he kept murmuring, while I wondered if I should alert them to my presence by opening, then closing my bedroom door.

Was I becoming a snoop? Could trying to learn French turn me into one? Maybe imitating the way people talk – and so think – leads, willy-nilly, to abusing hospitality and burgling minds? Outsiders who try to become insiders *must* be a trifle suspect. The British Ministry of Information or some such entity had, I now remembered, invited people who had travelled on the Continent before the outbreak of the war to turn over their holiday snaps.

Spies?

⚭

An unexpected visit drove such scruples from my mind.

Madame de la Tour du Pin was a granddaughter of Arthur O'Connor, one of Napoleon's generals, and the mother of Patrice de la Tour du Pin, a major Catholic poet (1911–75) of whom even I had heard. The La Tour du Pin had had an earlier Irish connection, too, when a marquis of that name married one of the Dillons who had been part of an exodus known in Ireland as the Flight of the Wild Geese. These were Jacobite Irish officers who fought in the Williamite Wars, lost and left for France, where they founded the Irish Brigade which remained part of the French army until the revolution. Henriette-Lucy Dillon, Marquise de la Tour du Pin, wrote a lively memoir, describing her high times at the court of Marie Antoinette and her thin ones when she had to flee, for some years, to the US.

The lady who called on the Morandys and no doubt asked to see the little Irish girl may have heard of my existence from the nuns. We had tea. And to me who had read my way through the Dún Laoghaire Carnegie Library's stack of novels about the Irish Brigade, this was like meeting a descendant of the three musketeers. I imagine we talked English, and that I wasted another chance to show off my curtsy. Or I may have remembered how Frank O'Connor – always keen to cast down the mighty from their seat – used to say that the Wild Geese should not be mourned but blamed for running off and leaving their country leaderless. Eileen, on the other hand, enjoyed singing rollicking songs about them, but I, having no ear, could not produce one for

Madame de la Tour du Pin. Instead, I thanked her for her visit, and let her hear my best English, in case the Morandys asked her if I was teaching them to talk with a brogue.

They needn't have worried. At my junior school, an elocution teacher, called Miss Burke, on discovering that I was a mimic, had insisted on my taking her class.

'I must have that girl,' I heard her tell the nuns. 'I'll put her in for verse-speaking at the Feis Cheóil. She might win the medal.'

Might I?

Years of humiliation owing to my lack of a musical ear were instantly effaced. Miss Burke and I hadn't met before, because her class was in the afternoon and Eileen believed that afternoons should be spent in the fresh air. I had agreed to this, since most afternoon classes – singing, dance and playing an instrument – required an ear for music. But mimicry, it turned out, somewhat surprisingly, did not. So I joined the class, went in due course to the Feis Cheóil, where I parroted Miss Burke's posh accent for a poem by some Elizabethan poet and Seán's mimicry of Yeats for one of his and won two medals. Sealed by satisfaction, my accent changed forever, though the medals were soon lost.

Back in Ireland for the winter, even unprepossessing foreigners attracted me. For months a fat Belgian who wore a beret and sometimes took our bus confused me by the contradictory responses his accent touched off whenever I heard it. He sometimes made mistakes in English, and in my fantasy I intervened to explain that what he wanted was not a billet but a ticket. 'Do yez mean a billet-doux?' teased the fantasy bus conductor cheekily, and from there the imagined dialogue could go anywhere.

Then I met Stephane, a dark-eyed, lean, hollow-cheeked man who looked like the concentration-camp survivors who were being shown on the newsreels. And that, in a way, was what he was. He was four years older than I and, every Sunday, for what felt like a long time, while we walked on the beach or biked to Enniskerry or up the Dublin Mountains, he told me about the sufferings of the Jews, and how his parents had died in the camps, while he spent the war working on a French farm, and pretending to be a Catholic.

Raised, as I had been, to feel for suffering, both Christ's and that of the gallant Wild Geese, I was easily persuaded to extend compassion to Stephane's lost relatives. When this did not stop him obsessing over his pain, I understood that too. Victims harp on their woes. I knew this because I had learned off pages of Gaelic 'anger poems', as we all had. But I knew enough, too, not to compete in victimhood. Stephane's loss was too vast and fresh. Besides, Ireland had been neutral in the war, and I guessed that he must be holding back censure.

Ours was an odd friendship. We didn't flirt, and if we laughed, I don't remember it. He lent me books and took me to films about anti-Semitism. I felt accused. At the same time, I guessed that we were using each other, but couldn't quite see how. He, being older and clever, was teaching me new things, and, besides, I was practising my French. But what use to him was I? He was living with his Uncle Serge, whose wife had also died in the camps, having failed, like Stephane's parents, to get away to Ireland in time. Now, though, Serge and his daughter seemed well integrated in Dublin society. It occurred to me that, as their sorrow must have dulled or at least calmed over the years since their arrival, Stephane's fierce unhappiness might seem to them like a reproach. Perhaps he saw this and tried to hide it – but needed to express it, too, and did so with me?

His pretty cousin Rachel got married while he and I were seeing each other, and I attended the ceremony. The synagogue, into which, according to our Church's rule, I should not have put foot, struck me as rather grand, and so did the convivial congregation, none of whom I knew. This made me wonder whether, like Monsieur Swann, Stephane kept his friends from meeting each other. Why? Had I been right in thinking that he wanted to be melancholy with me and cheerful with his uncle and cousin? Eileen, who had written a piece on Serge's hat factory for one of the first issues of *The Bell*, had another theory.

'Remember', she warned me, 'that for both Fine Gael and Fianna Fáil' – the main Irish political parties – 'we *are* pariahs. When he got here first Serge would not have known that. Now that he does, he may prefer not to get too close.'

This, in the light of later events, was less paranoid than I thought. For some of the big beasts in Irish life, Seán was indeed a pariah. And the beasts rarely forgot a grudge.

Here is a slightly expanded account of a row mentioned earlier.

In 1948 de Valera's government lost an election to a coalition of other parties and in 1951 the new Minister for Health, Dr Noel Browne, tried to introduce a Mother and Child Scheme without a means test. To Irish doctors, this savoured of socialised medicine and, given the likely cost, was anathema to John A. Costello, the head of the coalition to which Browne's party belonged. Shrewdly, as Conor Cruise O'Brien would later note, Costello, 'to quash Browne's scheme, called in the help of the Catholic Church'. He did this by revealing that he had asked Archbishop McQuaid whether the proposed measure was 'morally sound' and, on being told that without a means test it was not, asked Browne to include one in his scheme. Browne refused. His party leader promptly demanded his resignation and soon afterwards the government fell. Browne then published the correspondence between himself, Costello and the Church, which threw light on the sort of stitch-up which was normally carried on in the shadows.

Controversy ensued, and Seán published an article entitled *The Dáil and the Bishops*, pointing out that, as was now clear for all to see, there was 'a parliament in Maynooth' – the country's chief seminary – 'and a parliament in Dublin . . . The Dáil had, when up against the Second Parliament, only one right of decision: the right to surrender.' As McQuaid's biographer, John Cooney, would observe later, 'Not for the first time the commentator who angered McQuaid most . . . was Seán Ó Faoláin.'

McQuaid bided his time. Then, eight years later (churchmen, as the old phrase puts it, 'eat their vengeance cold'), he tried to get the Taoiseach to withdraw an offer he had made to Seán – who had accepted it – to appoint him Director of the Arts Council. The Taoiseach, Costello, was only too ready to appease McQuaid. To make this easier to do, he asked Thomas Bodkin, a former director of the National Art Gallery, if he would take the post instead. Bodkin, who had witnessed Costello's offer to Seán the week before, refused. McQuaid, allegedly, spent an hour trying to twist Bodkin's arm, but failed. Since I never heard any of this at the time, Seán may not have either. At all events, he took the job, then in 1959 resigned from it when the Arts Council proved too underfunded to do the work for which it had been set up.

Irish struggles back then were apt to teeter into farce. A man with a nose for that was the sparky Flann O'Brien – alias Brian O'Nolan alias Myles na gCopaleen – who signed off a petition to the Council with the jeer, 'Arts Council my arts'. The petition was for a grant to take him to an island where he could write without fear of being distracted. It would, he promised, be an island without a pub. Seán wondered if Myles thought he had never heard of moonshine – in either sense of the term. My feeling, then as now, was that, no matter how little money there was (or how much poteen), Myles should have got the grant.

As well as three names, Myles allegedly used two hats. One was said to hang permanently outside his office so that his superiors, on seeing it, might suppose him to be at work inside, when he was in fact drinking in some pub. Men, in those days, did not go out hatless, and open-plan offices had, presumably, not yet been invented.

I was one of Myles's fans and regret never having met him.

I don't know why he never came to our open Sunday nights. It can't have been because he was obstreperous or a lush, for both Brendan Behan and Patrick Kavanagh, who could be both, were habitués of Knockaderry.

Like other passengers on our morning bus, I read his column in the *Irish Times* over the shoulders of anyone who would let me. It was entitled *An Cruiseen Lán* which is Gaelic for 'the full jug' and, though no doubt a metaphor, must also have referred to drink, since Myles was known to like his drop.

I, meanwhile, had grown impatient to leave school. Life there was so coherent that its oddities had hardly bothered most of us until now. But when we got to be sixteen and one of our friends was caught with a letter from a boy, and expelled with unpleasant pomp from the Congregation of the Children of Mary, the rest of us took against the nuns' rituals. The line in the letter thought to have given most offence was from a popular song: 'I'd like to get you on a slow boat to China.' Some of us wondered whether a more brutal quotation had touched off the furore. It was from a much older song which shows how backward we were. It ran:

> Here's to the girl who gets a kiss
> And goes to tell her mother.
> May she in a convent die (bis)
> And never get another.

We understood nuns being upset by that and a variant which ran:

> She should have her lips cut off . . .

I doubt if any of us knew enough anatomy to wonder 'which lips', but there was a sick chill to the words which made me lose interest in receiving the thick, silver child-of-Mary medal, which the nuns claimed would be a life-long passport to the society of former Sacred Heart girls. Wherever we went, they assured us, it would be a signal to people who shared our values and save us from taking up with the wrong sort.

'What sort, Mother?'

'Reds.'

Bad times, the nuns warned, were back.

This explained the great part played in our timetable by the invisible world. Not only was Religious Instruction the first lesson of the day, but polyglot pieties frittered away time needed, at least by me, to cram for outside exams. School was like an aquarium in which alien life was alarmingly close but, we hoped, safely glassed in. Was it though? Or were we at risk from a leakage of religious mania? An absurd notion, but one I must have entertained, for in my final year I told the new Mistress of Studies that I wanted no truck with ribbons or medals. 'Blue ribbons' were the insignia worn by girls who, in other schools would have been called prefects. I did not, I told her craftily, feel up to the responsibility. Chillily, she warned me against spiritual pride.

She had guessed that my energies were focused on winning a university scholarship, and that I didn't want to waste good cramming time on supervising junior netball or the like, as blue-ribbon wearers could be asked to do. Poor school spirit? Yes. And there was worse. Religiosity had begun to embarrass me. If someone made a showy sign of the cross when passing a church, I felt uncomfortable. The Morandys had never done this. I hadn't seen anyone do it in France, and suspected that we, in Ireland, had been landed with a 'mission-country' style of religion. Maybe Stephane gave me the idea? He, who had had to pretend to be a Catholic during the war, must have looked closely into our ways.

People who invoked God were more annoying still. 'God bless you,' they kept saying, as if they had pull with Him. Often they were old acquaintances of Seán's or Eileen's from Cork, a place whose yo-yoing accent was considered comical in Dublin. What if they did it when I was with Jasmine or Stephane? Or dredged up the old, prolix, greeting-dialogue: 'God be with you!' 'God and Mary be with you!' 'God and Mary and Patrick and Joseph and . . .' Who? They could string this out endlessly. How to stop them? Maybe I should pray against them? 'Dear God,' I might appeal, 'can't You, if You're there at all, stop them making a holy show of us?'

A convent education aimed to help us make our way first in this world, then in the next. In my case, the nuns told my mother, I needed another year in school. Bookish girls, they warned, could be backward in unforeseen ways.

Another *year*? Wearing lumpy, black shoes, lumpy lisle stockings and my hair in plaits! I couldn't bear the thought. After all I was *sixteen!*

In what I hoped would be my last term, we had a retreat during which there were no lessons. Instead we were each assigned a quiet space where we could spend the day trying to meditate. We could walk in the convent woods, if we preferred, and meditate there. Images showing the stations of the cross hung on the inside of the perimeter wall, and when D, one of the most frivolous of my friends, was spotted genuflecting to them, it was clear that something was up.

My mind kept jumping. I had told the nuns that I couldn't meditate and didn't want to be hypocritical by pretending – only to be accused again of spiritual pride. Annoyed, I set off for a walk in the woods. There was D, wearing her broad, blue petersham silk ribbon across her proudly tumescent chest and, just above her, seated on the top of the outer wall, half hidden by thickets of ivy and valerian, was the faun-like face of her current boyfriend, who was playing hooky from his own school and relishing a glimpse of a breast which she had half bared by undoing three shirt buttons and loosening the blue ribbon. I warned them that they were dangerously visible from third-floor school windows, then went back to my desk, took out my Horace and worked at it for the rest of the day. Hypocrisy, I saw, was exactly what was expected of us. Good! OK. Now I knew.

I got my come-uppance though.

Candidates for the scholarship exam were required to present their three best subjects, and mine were English, French and Latin. But I learned at the last minute that the Church Latin pronunciation taught in girls' schools was not accepted by the university or its oral exam. I was indignant, and wondered if the nuns had known this – and if not, why not. Perhaps God had answered my mocking prayer with some sly mockery of His own?

Meanwhile the state leaving-cert. exam was held in a nearby Dominican convent rather than in ours, where I was the only one sitting it. This exam, though of a lower standard than the university scholarship one, was nerve-racking for me because it included obligatory maths and Gaelic, at neither of which I was much good. Eileen, knowing how flustered I could get, now did something for which I would be grateful to her forever. If there had been a medal for heroic mothers, I would have nominated her. Knowing that I had acquired a taste for cognac while staying with the Morandys, and that Hennessy or Martell could settle my nerves, she called on her old trespassing skills, and arranged to meet me in the Dominican-convent shrubbery before each of the two dreaded exams to give me a few swigs from a pocket flask. This made me worry about the smell on my breath, displaced my anxiety and did the trick. I passed both exams.

I did less well in the one for the university scholarship, though; in fact, I failed to get it. A boy from a Benedictine school did. I thought of him as having snatched it from under my nose, because we had met as I came out of the oral and he was on his way in to display his superior pronunciation. As a consolation, I was given an 'exhibition' worth – I think – £25, while he got £125.

Abandoning the unequal rivalry with people like him, I left school, signed on at UCD, decided to drop Latin, took up Italian and won the £125 the following year. Not only that, I won summer scholarships to the University for Foreigners in Perugia for three years running. Walking down the Corso Vannucci during each of those summers with the local Perugian assigned to exchange Italian conversation with me for English, I was half tempted to start believing in God again, if only to thank Him for my lucky débâcle in the Latin oral.

Perugia is a hill town and charming, although living there all year round – I know from friends who did – would be deadly. But a summer visit, when the University for Foreigners is holding classes and arranging coach trips to look at art and architecture all over Umbria, provides a perfect way to get over those tongue-tied first weeks when one is trying to break through into a new language. As had happened with the Morandys, I only discovered the drawbacks on my second trip. Local young men, it turned out, were predatory. Local girls went home at 9 p.m. and stayed there for the rest of the evening. The freedom enjoyed by foreign ones to linger in cafés, dance on sun-warmed terraces or walk out along the shady streets convinced Perugians that the girls were shady themselves. Fair game. Tarts. This distinction, we foreigners soon learned, was not peculiar to Perugia. Young men in other Italian towns we visited made it too. But the sheer numbers arriving in Perugia every summer had got local men used to exploiting us to the hilt. I was there in an innocent time compared to what seems to have happened later, when terrorists used the university as cover and druggies made the place dangerous. In the early Fifties it was no worse than unpleasant. Guessing that not even foreign girls would want to lose their virginity, the men merely hoped to be masturbated. As this requirement was hard to explain to girls who knew little Italian, action had to take the place of words and could provoke rage, slaps and tears. The families from whom we rented rooms advised us to beware of local men, but did so indulgently, using tolerant metaphors, such as 'man is a hunter'. Clearly, we *straniere* told each other indignantly, the predators had been spoiled rotten by their own women.

We turned for company to foreign young men, but were still exposed to misunderstandings. A French Communist, called Jean, with whom I had chatted a few times over milkshakes or coffee, told me not to go to a drinks party planned by the English contingent which, he had heard, could turn into an orgy. I laughed and told him that drink was all Anglo-Saxons and indeed the Irish did. They didn't have orgies – well, the ones here weren't likely to. He wouldn't believe me and warned that if I went to the party, all was over between us. All what? No more milkshake-drinking? When I laughed at him, he left in a huff. So I went to the party, where, just as I had expected, people ate pasta, drank cheap wine and sang *Gaudeamus Igitur* and *The Foggy, Foggy Dew*. Jean must have had a spy among us, for the next day he approached me gravely, bowed and apologised for his suspicions. He was the first Communist I had met and reminded me disappointingly of the kind of Catholic who, in Ireland is, or was, called a Holy Joe. His spy must have left the party early, for Bill, an older man than the rest, had given me a lift home on his motorbike and made a pass when we got there. He was easily rebuffed. But Jean, if informed, might not have believed this.

∝

My friends in UCD were not Holy Joes, but, apart from the handsome eighteenth-century Newman House at 86 Stephen's Green, the place was drab. Notoriously, there would be no contraceptives available for years to come. Men and women were careful with each other, and the Fifties were impoverished years. Meanwhile, our summer jaunts abroad only served to show Modern Language students how much livelier things were in places other than Ireland, where a post-Famine fear of the woman who 'gets herself pregnant', so that the man is forced to marry her and divide the wretched bit of family land, survived subliminally into my time and made it a grim place for both sexes. Men drank.

Trained in this nursery, those of us who got abroad scrutinised foreign men for similar doubts regarding us, were circumspect in our dealings with them and, being recognised as wife-material – *des filles bien* or *ragazze per bene* – attracted quite a few offers of marriage. One or two girls I knew accepted, and I later wrote a novella, *Man in the Cellar*, about the imagined experience of marrying an Italian. Later still, an Irish woman who had fled from such a marriage told me I'd got it more or less right. I was pleased but deserved less credit than she thought, for in my winter in Rome I had had a *fidanzato* – a less serious connection than a fiancé – on whose more furtive doings I received reports from two Irishmen, whose solidarity with me trumped their male connivance.

My Roman year (1952–3) was funded by an Italian government scholarship and I spent it working for a two-year National University of Ireland travelling studentship which was due to come up the next year. Before leaving Dublin I introduced my friend, Grace, to Stephane, and not long after that heard that she had joined him in Paris and that they were in love. However, I then learned that when he told her he could only marry a Jewish girl, love had petered out. Years later, when married to someone else, she confided that, on her return from France, she had grown friendly with Stephane's uncle Serge, who told her something Stephane could not have wanted us to know. Although his father had indeed died in the camps, his mother had not. She was alive, remarried and had never been Jewish. 'Stephane couldn't forgive her,' Grace explained, 'for remarrying. He told Serge that that was why he could never trust or marry a Catholic.'

I was fascinated. So this was why he had chosen me as his confidante when I was fifteen. It had been because I was someone – perhaps the only one ? – to whom, after sustained brainwashing, he could talk freely and at length about a faithful – though imaginary – dead, Jewish mother. Anyone who knew his uncle's friends would have known this to be untrue. But with me he had been able to comfort himself with a consoling fantasy.

'Do you realise,' Grace was following her own train of thought, 'that this means Stephane himself isn't Jewish either? For Jews it's the mother who matters. The heredity comes through her.'

That made me think of my own mother. 'So,' I saw, 'it really was because we were pariahs! He *needed* a pariah! I bet Eileen had told him that that was what we were and so gave him the idea. I can just imagine her saying it! She could be quite obsessive about it.'

'Who are you talking about?'

'My family. It would take too long to explain. Tell me, though: did he make up for his mother's not being Jewish? Did he marry someone who was?'

Grace's laugh was sour. 'Can you believe that in the end he married a Catholic?'

When I knew it first, Rome's *centro storico* had traces of a rural languor which might almost have dated back to the era before 1870, when the pope was king. Vespas and Lambrettas buzzed about, but there was otherwise often so little traffic that, if I crossed the piazza di Spagna early in the day, Edward McGuire's archaic and shaky vintage car might be the only vehicle parked there. He and I had been introduced before we left Dublin and encouraged to meet in Rome, where we were both headed. Edward's father may have regretted filling his house with a seductive display of expensive French paintings when Edward announced that *he* meant to paint professionally rather than go into the family business. The father was said to be a talented amateur painter himself, but had devoted his life to making money. Edward despised him for this. 'He's a bloody businessman,' he sometimes murmured, 'so the least he can do is give me enough money to make me free to paint.' To buttress this decision, he dressed the part. The vintage car was a prop, and so were his unfashionable stove-pipe trousers cut from a tweed which matched his tawny curls. He had a life-size painting of a dead bird in his room, which reminded me of Patrick Swift's work, which in turn recalled that of Lucian Freud. In time Edward would paint some rather lovely paintings of owls and a number of portraits of poets, including one of Seamus Heaney, and a Stubbs-like one of Charlie Haughey on a horse with a gentrified house behind him. I'm not sure, though, whether he painted much while in Rome, apart from the dead bird. He claimed to want to paint me, but our sittings produced nothing. He kept his canvas turned away from me while he worked and, in the end, declared the portrait a failure. When asked if I could have a look anyway, he loaded his brush with green pigment and, quickly sloshing it on, turned whatever had been on the canvas into a cabbage. Like myself, he was an Irish – i.e. immature – twenty-year-old.

Why Edward wanted to paint me at all may have been because he had seen my portrait by Swift, whom he admired, in a one-man show which the Waddington Gallery put on just before Swift took off for Portugal with one of Dublin's more impressive beauties. Oonagh Ryan was one of several glamorous sisters, the best known of whom, Kathleen, had starred in John Ford's Oscar-winning film *The Informer* and Carl Reed's *Odd Man Out*.

Swift, who already knew the art worlds of London and Paris, was more alert than my UCD contemporaries and, in contrast with my parents' friends, was animated by a tigerish juvenescence. Sitting for him had been like watching a window swing open onto a previously unimaginable landscape. He talked while working about painters whose work he loved, launching their names with such verve that I remember them still. They were Francis Bacon, Johnny Minton, Alberto Giacometti, Frank Auerbach, Derek Hill and Lucian Freud, with whom Swift shared a studio on Freud's frequent trips to Dublin. He spoke with enthusiasm about Bacon, whom he portrayed as caring so little for success that he hid his best paintings from prospective buyers and destroyed quantities of his work. This may have been a legend or – more probably? – a validation of an attitude by which Swift himself would live more boldly than even Bacon did. It would be said later of Swift that he disliked the commercial side of his profession, and a close friend of his would claim to have found him too hiding paintings on a day when he was expecting a visit from a rich collector.

This backfired. Despite being praised in 1994 by Derek Hill as 'probably the most formidable Irish artist of this century', Swift, who had died eleven years before, is now often described as the most underrated Irish painter, even though that 1952 exhibition had been hailed as a triumph in an article in *Time Magazine*. 'Irish critics', wrote the *Time* reporter, 'got a look at the work of a tousled young man named Paddy Swift and tossed their caps in the air. Paddy's thirty canvases are as grey and gloomy as Dublin itself – harshly realistic paintings of dead birds and rabbits, frightened-looking girls and twisted . . . plants. Their fascination is in the merciless, sharply etched details, as oppressive and inquiring as a back-room third degree.' Remembering myself as one of those frightened-looking girls, I can report that the effect was carefully contrived. In Swift's portrait my flesh is indeed grey, and I appear to have nothing on, though I was in fact wearing a very proper jumper rolled down to create a décolletage calculated to cover both my embarrassment and breasts. If I look alarmed, it is either because of this or of his saying that before Cézanne felt able to paint an apple, he had to want to eat it – or words to that effect. Fascinated, I both did and didn't want to be eaten.

A large portrait of Swift's lover Claire painted the previous year and entitled *Girl with Thistles*, is also artfully designed. Claire, an American redhead who dazzled Dublin, is painted vividly, but in a way which belies her radiant self-assurance. She is slumped on a high stool, in a semi-foetal posture, while her hair and dress are reduced to Cinderella-like negligence. Pushed to the edge of the canvas, she is looking away from an opaque but luminous window, and her face, turned towards the viewer, seems ready to crumple into tears. Add some tall thistles and what you have is a memento mori.

The critic Tony Gray, quoted by *Time*, wrote that what Swift 'unearthed' from his subjects was neither 'a decorative pattern, nor even a mood, but some sort of tension which is a property of their existence'.

Not having the money to pay for it, I did not expect to keep my portrait, but at the private view an ex-RAF pilot, who was courting one or more of the Ryan sisters, bought her portrait and mine and, apparently on impulse, gave each of us her own. I am ashamed to admit that I have forgotten his name.

The tension detected by critics in Swift's portraits erupted that day and baffled those of us who didn't know what was going on. As I remember it, Paddy and Oonagh left the party that day suddenly and unexpectedly for Portugal, where they married, and it strikes me now that the ex-RAF pilot, who kept guying himself with jokes about shooting people down in flames, may have been courting Oonagh more intently and, in Swift's view, dangerously, than I guessed.

As I too left Ireland that autumn, and spent some years in Rome and Paris, I met neither him nor Swift nor any of the Ryans again. I did, though, run into Claire decades later at a party and learned that she was a poet. I had thought her so extraordinary that I was surprised to find her quite like the rest of us. Disturbing encounters can stay as fresh in memory's deep-freeze as that ice-pale window in *Girl with Thistles*.

Mine with her had been sufficiently upsetting for Swift to associate me later with fright. What happened was that at the end of a Dublin party I and a friend, whom I shall call John, were stranded without a lift, and Swift, whose studio was nearby, offered us shelter for the night.

What, John asked, about Claire, who had left the party early in the company of an older and irritatingly successful painter? If she came back, would she mind our intrusion? But Swift was so sure she wouldn't come that we accepted his offer. The walk to Killiney would have been about a dozen miles.

When John had constructed a barricade of pillows down one side of the one and only bed and motioned me into the furrow between it and the wall, we put out the light but couldn't sleep. I could feel him, who knew I had a yen for him, try to shrink as he moved as far as he could from any overtures I might make, while simultaneously trying to avoid making any to Swift who was on his other side. John claimed to be queer, but had been known to enjoy an occasional dalliance with a safely married woman.

While I was thinking about this, the light snapped on! John, saying he felt responsible for me, pulled the sheet over my head, and Claire's pleasantly mid-Atlantic voice produced a four-letter word. 'To think,' she followed it up, 'that I should come home to this! You have a virgin in my bed. A tight little virgin. And I could have had a passionate night with Louis! I left him to come home to you,' she castigated Paddy, while John's hand clamped my mouth. 'You clod! Get that virgin out of my bed. I won't have virgins in my bed!'

'Put a sock in it, Claire,' John growled. Paddy said nothing, and I, even if I hadn't been half smothered, was too paralysed with embarrassment to stir from under my sheet. Hearing Claire move around the room, I lay braced for a physical attack.

'I could have had a passionate night,' she kept repeating.

It struck me that she was having one now.

'Come and have one with me then,' Paddy coaxed. 'Come on, sweetie!'

'I don't want *you*!' Claire's accents grew increasingly cultured. 'I want John. I want to make love with John. His virgin won't mind, will she?'

'Shut up!' John was yelling. 'Can't you shut her up, Paddy?'

'Come on,' Paddy coaxed. 'I'll give it to you, sweetie. Let me give it to you.'

'I want John. You'll never get another chance, John!'

'Shut your mouth, Claire!' John was kneading my arm so fiercely that I would have bruises next day.

'Well, make love with your virgin, then,' Claire suggested. 'I won't have you lying there, masturbating unhealthily in my bed.'

John nearly throttled me, and Paddy must have got hold of Claire, because the light went out, and mattress-heavings took the place of talk. After a while those too stopped, and after another while John uncovered my head so that I could see the window, which had grown less opaque and had thistles in front of it, which were greyer and stiffer than in the painting. It must have been about four in the morning. Astonishingly, I fell asleep.

My last thought as I did was to wonder how many other Dublin Saturday party-goers had ended up in strange beds.

McGuire's work, though influenced by Swift's and Freud's, would be both more decorative and less tense. But to write this is to look years ahead. In 1952 I saw only the bird – and the cabbage.

He was clearly more attuned to commerce, which he affected to despise, than Swift, for I see from the Internet that he won a number of prizes.

His room in Rome was either in the via Margutta or the next-door via del Babuino, two bohemian streets celebrated in a song of the day in which a foreign girl remembers her Roman lover:

> Arrivederci, Roma!
> Goodbye – au revoir.
> Voglio ritornare alla via Margutta.
> Voglio rivedere la soffitta
> Dove m'hai tenuta stretta stretta accanto a te.

(I want to return to the via Margutta again. I want to see again the attic where he held me close.)

And so forth. It was a tribute to themselves paid by Roman men whose foreign girlfriends could never forget them. In up-market *trattorie*, the itinerant singers all sang it, especially towards summer's end, when young men brought their tourist conquests for a farewell dinner and, if singers failed to drop by, even waiters were prepared to burst into song.

Cheap eating places such as *tavole calde* and the philanthropic *mensa comunale* offered no such entertainment, but in them everyone talked to everyone else, and English- and French-speakers could make friends.

A series of what were called 'surprise parties' (pronounced

'soorpreezpartee') provided dressier occasions in private houses. I can't remember how I came to be on a guest list for these, though it may have been thanks to Edward, who was well supplied with introductions to what must have been a smart set, since the houses were comfortable, the Turkish ambassador's daughter was an habituée, and the rule that nice girls leave at nine was often ignored. Rome was more laid-back than Perugia – and the men behaved better.

Unfortunately someone – no doubt my father – had arranged for me to stay in a *pensione* run by nuns who *did* apply the 9 p.m. rule and threatened not to let latecomers in. For a while, I managed to sweet-talk my way around this, but in the end had to leave – regretfully, since the convent was in the city's heart and practically next to the Pantheon. It was conveniently close too to the fashionable Jesuit church, the Gesù, where at Sunday Mass a brutal but brilliant preacher regularly eviscerated the Italian Left to the glee of a well-dressed congregation which clapped like a theatre audience each time he scored a point. As long as I stayed in the convent, I attended these sermons assiduously, marvelled at their venom, was shocked by their worldliness, and wished I knew some Communists who could tell me how to rebut the Society of Jesus's arguments, if only inside my own head. People who roused such rage must, I felt sure, have something interesting to say. But I knew no Communists, and it was only when I moved to a room in the Prati, a district developed to house the city's expansion after it became Italy's capital, that I felt comfortable reading the left-wing press. I didn't want to hurt the nuns' feelings by leaving *l'Unità* or *Paese Sera* for them to find in my waste-paper basket.

ROME UNIVERSITY

I did, though, know one famous ex-Communist.

Ignazio Silone, a founder-member of the Partito Comunista Italiano (PCI), was married to my best friend's elder sister, Darina, who was acknowledged to be one of the most beautiful women in Italy and Ireland – she shuttled between them. Harry Craig, who was smitten, compared her to the legendary Queen Maeve, and years later, when I was scouting for Italian books for a US publisher, Italian editors grew misty-eyed when told I was Irish. Did I know la Signora Silone, Giorgio Bassani inquired wistfully. Was she as beautiful as ever? Of course she must be! *Senz'altro!*

As well as being beautiful, Darina was clever and unhappy. What man could resist the blend? She was generous, too. Not only did she take her sister, Eithne, and me to a Lancôme beautician, who taught us to make up our faces, she also arranged for Silone to invite me to dinner regularly during my Roman year.

The Lancôme session – of which he would have disapproved – must have been on one of my early Perugian trips, for in 1952 Darina herself was not around. Her marriage was clearly troubled, though she kept on faithfully translating Silone's novels, which by then were world famous. I had read and admired these as they came out, and was excited to be spending time with their author, even though the actual occasions were sombre. Eithne had warned me that he could be moody, so I wasn't surprised to read later that he suffered from depression. He even *looked* depressed, with five o'clock shadow, dark colouring and melancholy jowls. He warned me to be careful what I said in front of his and Darina's maid, who had been told that I was a relative because, being from the country, she would have been shocked to see him dine alone with a young woman who was not.

This didn't surprise me any more than his melancholy had. His novels were dark, and their characters tended to be victim figures: peasants who were at constant risk of being tricked, swindled and even killed by Fascist policemen – just as one of his own younger brothers had allegedly been killed while in jail.

Silone's contribution to *The God that Failed* had, to my mind, been one of the best in the book, which consists of accounts by six writers from different countries of their reasons for first embracing, then turning against, Communism. It had come out in 1949 and its recollections of Silone's native Abruzzi were sad, warm-hearted and angry. His mix of socialism and Christianity reconciled my own contradictions and, though that particular blend would not reach Ireland until liberation theology did, elements of it were already familiar from reports of French worker priests.

I have just reread his claim: 'Franciscanism and anarchy have always been the two most accessible forms of rebellion for lively spirits in our part of the world. The ashes of scepticism have never suffocated . . . the ancient hope of the Kingdom of God on earth, the old expectation of charity taking the place of law . . .'

I see no nostalgia here for the people's opium – especially as his next remarks, while acknowledging the difficulty of discerning 'the ways and means to a political revolution . . .', implicitly salute its necessity. The only choice open to people in the village where he grew up was, he insisted, either to rebel or connive with an exploitative and cruel system.

My guess that he would have taken a dim view of Darina's taking Eithne and me to have our faces done is based, more specifically, on his wondering, 'From what source do some people derive their spontaneous intolerance of injustice . . . And that sudden feeling of guilt at sitting down to a well-laden table, when others are having to go hungry?'

In the light of that, spending the price of two or more meals on a facial could hardly please him.

Yet he had married a woman whose looks and style excited his colleagues' envy. Worldly, then – or unworldly? He was, Darina told her friends, a complex and often inscrutable man.

This was truer than she could have known when she said it – and it would be years before the whole truth hit the headlines.

What I relished in his writing was the vivacity of the day-to-day experiences described. They belonged, as did the films being made at the time by de Sica, Rossellini, Visconti et al., to the great blossoming of Italian neorealism, but reminded me too of the local news which the Killiney postman, my mother's friends and our washerwoman would sometimes bring hotfoot from the village shop, and which my father would think of turning into a story.

Irish and Abruzzese history had a lot in common, although the wounds left by Italian wartime experience seemed uniquely raw.

'Everyone hates us,' a student I met in Perugia had lamented. 'We Italians let everyone down: most of all the Germans, who were our allies.'

That outspoken youth may have recovered faster than the one who would be the best man at Lauro's and my wedding in Florence in 1957. Roberto's father had been a Fascist and died at the front, and he himself became a vociferous, guitar-strumming Red after being beaten up by Left-wingers who may have been trying to purge shames of their own. More than fifty years later, Lauro ran into him on a stopover in Florence. They had a drink together and Roberto, now a leading historian of Fascism, sent us a memoir he had recently published about his still unassuaged distress over the father, who, as his memoir pointed out, had

had perfectly honourable reasons for fighting and dying for his country, even when its leader was Mussolini.

'Several old friends', Roberto told Lauro, 'cut me dead in the street when I published that.'

Silone's trouble with disappointing creeds did not only apply to Communism. By 1961 he would be describing himself to an interviewer as 'a Christian without a church and a Socialist without a party'.

I can't remember whether I nerved myself to ask him about his ideas during those shy dinners at his house in the via di Villa Ricotti, but I remember admiring him in spite of Eithne's reservations. Indeed, it was because of him that I got into conversation with some unshaven and shabbily dressed Abruzzesi students at a restaurant in the university campus and found that the end of Fascism had not done them much good. They were so poor, they told me, that they only came to Rome to do their exams, then left. They couldn't afford to stay and attend lectures. Instead they bought roneoed copies of these to study at home.

Absenteeism was not confined to students. A number of fashionable professors, while drawing salaries for teaching in Rome, were working and drawing larger ones in the United States.

Mario Praz, for instance, whose lectures I had hoped to attend, though officially listed as teaching in Rome that year, was actually, I learned from the janitors, in the US. These *bidelli* seemed to be the only people who knew – or were prepared to admit – what was going on.

'That', a student told me, 'is because it's bad luck to mention that gentleman's name. He has the evil eye, so you, who just named him, had better *fare le corna.*' Illustratively, he folded his two middle fingers, leaving the index and little one sticking out like horns. 'It wards off evil.' I wondered whether he believed this. Half believed, I guessed. I was used to half belief.

Unlike French ones, Italian university students addressed each other with the *tu* or familiar form and called each other *collega*. This seemed promisingly emancipated, but when the Abruzzesi tried to flirt, I found myself in an uncomfortable position. They were like escapees from Silone's novels: poor, possibly hungry, despised and able to afford only the cheapest university meals. How could I snub them? On the other hand, wouldn't it be unwise and indeed unkind to encourage them?

I told a persistent one that I had to get back to the convent, where I still was at the time, and when he, unaware perhaps of the 9 p.m. rule, started waiting all night outside its front door, I speeded up my move to the Prati.

Meanwhile, who should turn up but Harry Craig, who was in Rome to ghost-write the memoirs of a veteran of the Spanish Civil War, called – I think – Donald Armstrong. Harry had always been a Man of the Left, though always at a remove. So being a ghost-writer for a veteran of a lost war was completely in character.

He took me a few times to our embassy – or rather ministry. In those years, Ireland had to count its pennies, so we had few full ambassadors. In Rome, however, we almost had two: an embassy to the Vatican and a minister plenipotentiary to the Italian state. The minister was Denis Devlin, a distinguished poet who often had literary figures among his guests. One of these when Harry took me there was Alberto Moravia, who looked as if he too might have the evil eye, so I kept my hand out of sight so as to make *le corna*. Another was Archibald Macleish, and a third was an American girl called Peggy, for whom Harry promptly fell. She too was a poet and a protégée of MacLeish's who, together with Devlin, warned Harry, whose reputation was known to both, that she was very special and must be treated accordingly. Or so I heard after Harry and she abruptly disappeared from Rome, took off on a whirlwind courtship in Carthage and Connemara, then got married.

Seán and Silone seemed to enjoy each other's company. I remember several visits by Darina and Ignazio to Knockaderry, and there may well have been others. Seán's bleak memories of the Irish Civil War may have helped him understand – or come as close as anyone could to understanding – the hurts which had soured Silone, and he would, like everyone else, have been charmed by Darina.

I, though, who was soon to start spending less time in Ireland, lost touch with both. Indeed it was only in the late Nineties that I was reminded of them. I was writing a novel about another Italian Communist leader, Palmiro Togliatti, when my husband's friend, the historian and ex-Communist senator, Rosario Villari, asked me if I had heard the recent rumours about Silone who had died in 1978.

I hadn't, so Rosario filled me in. Left-wing Italy, I learned, had been rocked by controversy when letters found in Rome's State Archives revealed that from 1919 to 1930 Ignazio, internationally respected writer and moralist though he was, had been sending reports, first about fellow socialists, and later about Communists, to the Italian secret police.

The most striking of these, written in April 1930, was addressed to the sister of his controller, Guido Bellone, the former Inspector General for Public Security, with whom Silone had apparently had an oddly close relationship. It was signed 'Silvestri', which was his pseudonym with OVRA (the Organisation for Vigilance and Repression of Anti-Fascism) and reads more like a letter to a father confessor than one to a man who, for the previous eleven years, had been paying him to be an informer. The letter says:

I am living through a painful moment. My moral sense, which has always been strong, now dominates me completely; it won't let me eat, sleep or rest. I am in a crisis allowing only one way out: to renounce militant activity. (I'll find some sort of intellectual work.) The only other solution would be death. To go on living in duplicity was impossible . . . I don't think I did any great harm to my friends or my country. In so far as I could, I always made sure to avoid that. I must tell you that you, given your position, always behaved decently. That is why I am writing this last letter, so that you may leave me free to carry out my plan, which has two parts: first to rid my life of all falsehood, double-dealing, shadiness and secrecy; secondly to start a new life, on a new basis, to make up for the harm I did, to redeem myself, to help the workers and peasants (to whom I am bound by every fibre of my heart) and my country . . . I must add that I feel strongly drawn back towards religion (if not to the Church) and that my new way of thinking is facilitated by the cretinous and criminal position being adopted by the Communist Party. My only regret in leaving it is that it is a persecuted party in which, leaving aside the leaders, there are thousands of honest working people.

Silone himself, the letter goes on to say, is waiting for the right moment to break with the Party.

An astonishing document!

It is, says a final flourish, a declaration of esteem for Bellone, whom Silone asks to pray for him if he is a believer. He signs off with his OVRA pseudonym: 'Your Silvestri.'

When evidence of what Silone called his duplicity was made

public, many people tried to deny it. They talked of forgeries, reached for innocent explanations and invented versions of his story in which a hope of saving his youngest brother, who had been jailed in 1928, was the only reason for his connection with the OVRA. But the dates don't support this. Indeed they are as puzzling for those who believe in Silone's innocence as for those who don't. He seems to have begun to sell information to the police even before both the rise of Mussolini and the founding of the PCI (1921). When he first became an informer (1919), he was a socialist. An odd, sad, self-contradicting man! Darina, when asked, before she died in 2003, if she thought he might have really been a spy and a traitor, apparently said that anything was possible, and that the evidence deserved a thorough examination.

She must have sensed many contradictions in his thinking, if he could write a letter like the one quoted without noticing that he was claiming to have done little harm, but needed to make up for the harm he *had* done.

He wrote movingly in *The God That Failed* about the hard choices he and other Communists were obliged to make after the Fascist takeover of Italy:

One had to change one's name, abandon every link with family and friends, and live a false life to remove any suspicion of conspiratorial activity. The Party became family, school, church, barracks . . . Every sacrifice was welcomed as a personal contribution to the 'price of collective redemption'; and it should be emphasised that the links which bound us to the Party grew steadily firmer, not in spite of the dangers and sacrifices . . . but because of them.

Mmm! Noble? Regretful – or a case of split personality?

Yet he published this text thirty years after he first began to bargain with his paymasters for money to betray first the socialists and then the PCI.

On the other hand, how could one presume to judge a man

so patently desperate to help combat the horrors around him? While Silone wrestled with these, the French author, Bernanos, had published his searingly strange novel, *Under the Sun of Satan* (1926). This describes a saint resisting the temptation to let Satan help him save a child from dying of meningitis. It was a time of delusions and coat-turning. Some writers who had flirted with Fascism early on, Bernanos among them, turned their backs on it. Others made the reverse move.

Darina, when asked about Silone's past activities, was reported to have said that she knew nothing about them – which was probably true. They were over when she and he first met in Switzerland. Nonetheless she may have sensed Bluebeard secrets, for the historians who looked into his case in the Nineties discovered that he had, as spies do, given away the addresses, plans, itineraries, photographs, false names and locations of secret printing presses belonging to fellow militants. No wonder that, when he broke with the Party, he felt a need to renew and redeem himself by going into analysis with Carl Jung. Identity, or his sense of it, may have been a problem, for he had had many names: Secondino Tranquilli was his birth name, Ignazio Silone his pen name, Pasquini his name for the Party, Silvestri for the OVRA and, when he worked with Dulles as an agent of the Office of Strategic Services (OSS), he became Len.

Bellone, whom Silone claimed to consider a *galantuomo*, seems to have died in a lunatic asylum in 1948. Well, that was the year when the PCI looked for a while set to win a national election, and the prospect can't have cheered the former Inspector General for Security. Perhaps he would have been comforted had he known that not only was Catholic Europe praying hard against such an outcome, but also, as would later emerge, that the Soviets, from whom the PCI took its orders, didn't want it to take power.

⚭

My time in Rome was more light-hearted than might be suggested by thoughts of poor Silone, and even of Darina, who had gone there before the war, thanks to the same National University of Ireland studentship for which I planned to compete. MacWhite, who had been our ambassador there in her day, was now living in Killiney, and had dropped into Knockaderry several times to warn me not to fall into the clutches of dodgy Italians.

Darina, he told us, had been a thorn in his side in the late Thirties. She wouldn't leave when advised to, did leave for Switzerland at the very last safe moment, and even there took up with the wrong sort of man. His warnings so alarmed my mother that I had trouble calming her. So when one of the surprise-party regulars, an affable man called Beppo Florio, began to court me, I agreed to a low-key relationship which suited us both. I enjoyed whizzing around Rome on the pillion of his Lambretta or Vespa – I forget which he had, but remember with delight the sun-shot lime-leaf-filtered air which began to bathe the city with the coming of spring, and the pleasure of moving from one theatrical setting to another: the Forum, the Colosseum, piazza del Popolo, piazza Navona, via Veneto, the hills . . .

Just as pleasurable was strolling alone along smart streets such as the via Condotti, then up the Spanish steps to the via Sistina which, to my mind, had the best window-shopping in the city. Once a talent scout spotted me and raised my hopes of appearing in a film. Tests were done and I forget how far I got, but the plan foundered.

Garret FitzGerald's brother Fergus, who was with the Food and Agriculture Organization of the United Nations, and his wife sometimes invited me for a meal. Her name was Una which made Italians chortle. 'One what?' they teased. '*Una che?*' The query was as predictable as a bird call.

I was invited, too, by Beppo's mother who, I began to suspect, was sizing me up to see if I would do as a daughter-in-law. His father was or had been a cavalry officer, and may have had access to good seats when the show jumping came to the Borghese Gardens. Either that, or Beppo himself splashed out generously. Those were the years when the d'Inzeo brothers, one in military, the other in police uniform, were winning trophies for Italy, and d'Oriola, a lean, brilliant civilian competitor, was doing so for France. There was also a German called Schockemöhle, but I can't remember any Irish or English names at all, so the winners that year must have all been Continentals.

Everything about the city was thrilling: the shop windows, the shapely women wearing tight emerald green silk when it was warm and – this surprised me – Donegal tweed when cold. Green was fashionable that year, and so was Donegal tweed. This was lucky, for I had had a coat beautifully cut by my father's Dublin tailor in that very fabric. I didn't, however, have the Roman women's swaying walk – their buttocks oscillated like pendulums – and neither, it seems to me now, do today's Italians.

'Whenever we go out together,' Beppo told me, 'I want you to wear that coat.'

I acquiesced. Show mattered. I had learned that on my first trip to Perugia, where the girl with whom I exchanged English conversation for Italian – her name comes back to me, Norma – owned only one dress. It was a nice one, though, and every afternoon at 6 p.m. it would appear freshly washed, ironed and ready for flaunting up and down the *corso*. Maybe going home at nine wasn't only done for propriety? It gave you time to do your laundry as well!

Living in the Prati, I began to see how the less well off lived. I took *mezza pensione*, half-board, which provided fare that was next to inedible. The coffee was made with toasted barley, the bread was grey and the pasta sauce had a definite taste of cleaning fluid. Downstairs from the *pensione*, though, was a small shop which sold tasty take-away dishes which I would later search for in vain when staying in Venice or Florence. Italian recipes are regional, and my favourite Roman specialities, like *supplì* and *carciofi alla romana* rarely turned up in those cities.

On the eve of St Patrick's Day in 1953 an article by Seán appeared in *Life Magazine* and vastly amused the surprise-party regulars. Entitled *Love Among the Irish*, its contention was that puritanism, plus poverty, misogyny and a lack of contraceptives, were on the point of snuffing out Irish sexuality and leading, especially in rural backwaters, to late or no marriage. The article had been written originally for a US anthology called *The Vanishing Irish*, which came out in 1954. The surprise-party guests nodded wisely. Edward, they had noticed, didn't flirt much with girls. A second Irish male student was subjected to close scrutiny, and my standing with Beppo's rather imperious mother may actually have been improved. Undersexed girls, she probably felt, could be easily handled.

Meanwhile, the second Irishman took it upon himself to inform me that Beppo would not be a good bet as a husband, because he had proposed that they share a *garçonnière*. Possibly to protect my good name, Beppo had made it clear that he planned to use the place not with me but with more wanton young women.

'If he's up to that now,' said my compatriot, 'think how it would be later.'

To my surprise, I felt relief on realising, as I hadn't till then, that I had been feeling obligated to Beppo's family because of their invitations to so many Sunday lunches. Now, released from this scruple, I celebrated by spending time with Edward, who, after some months' absence, was back in Rome. He had gone home for Christmas, then, when his mother unexpectedly died, prolonged his stay. Her loss had hit him hard, and his rage with the world was on a hair-trigger. Curiously this, which might have been hard to deal with in Dublin, looked here like an effective way of dealing with the nets and snares of a tightly controlled, Lilliputian world.

Perhaps because he was busy in his bachelor pad, Beppo seemed unfazed by my taking drives with Edward. So we kept going on them, and only gave up when his car fell off the via Appia Antica, leaving us both upside down like capsized beetles inside an equally capsized vehicle. We had been visiting the glass tomb of Santa Maria Goretti, an eleven-year-old who had been canonised two years before for choosing death over the fate worse than death. Edward's irritation at this choice of Catholic role model may have caused the accident.

Back in Dublin, to get in some intensive cramming for the studentship exam, I lay on the flat roof of Seán's new study, wrapped in a rug which could be twitched off if the weak Irish sun came out for even a minute. I was trying for a tan while learning how late Latin developed into Old French. From time to time Eileen, eager to keep my brain fed, passed milk and sandwiches out through an upstairs window.

Getting me to France was as much her project as mine. Indeed her commitment to it was so keen that I wondered how she would cope if I were to succeed and leave her with no fresh challenges.

This guilt was joined by another, when a telegram came from Beppo announcing that he was coming to Dublin to talk to my father about our getting married. With speed and some shame, I sent a reply saying, 'Please don't come.' Marriage, which I couldn't remember either of us mentioning until now, was not on my agenda, and Paris was definitely where I wanted to go next. All six Morandy girls had dreamed of it, and I had appropriated their dream.

'There are', ran a saying which sounds less plausible than it once did, 'more fish in the sea than ever came out of it.' This to my mind applied to men but not to studentships. The one I was angling for only came around every four years, so had to be resolutely landed.

Having got it, though, I found that Paris was furred with grime and as dark as a Gustave Doré engraving. It would be a few years before André Malraux arranged for its house fronts to be cleaned. People were tired, snappish and xenophobic, and aid from the Marshall Plan, which had cheered up Rome, seemed to have made little impact here. There was less elegance in the streets; Sorbonne classes were overcrowded; latecomers were regularly obliged to sit on the floor, and readers to queue for seats in libraries. There were queues for everything, including the one for a student card without which you couldn't queue for anything else, just as you couldn't open a bank account without having an address, nor get an address without a bank account. In the end a letter from the Irish embassy sorted some of that out for me, but I still had to spend hours in the slowest queue of all, which was the nocturnal one outside the Students' Lodging Bureau. Usually you only got one address at a time and, since many landladies stipulated that their tenants must be '*metropolitains*' (code for 'not coloured'), I failed at first to understand this and did not apply.

For a while I stayed in the Foyer International de la Jeune Fille on the boulevard Saint Michel, where my father, true to form, had pulled some American string. But this, like the convent in Rome, shut its doors early. And, as I was planning a thesis on

French theatre and seeing all the plays I could, leaving before the final curtain was not an option. When expelled from the Foyer for trying to bribe its doorkeeper, I took refuge with three Dublin girls who had rented an O'Casey-style slum in an attic on the rue St Louis en Île, a dark and, at that time, unsavoury street which ran down the island's middle like an intestine in a prawn.

Their attic was crammed with bedsteads and dominated by an ancient gas stove which looked, in the smeary gleam from lamps in the street below, like a bull rearing to charge.

Two of the girls, Katherine and Therese, later married the Irish poets Patrick Kavanagh and Tony Cronin. The third, Deirdre, had, like Therese, been an air hostess, and both, as was then expected of air hostesses, were pretty.

Katherine, though not pretty, was passionate and whenever we paused in a local café liked to sing a song about her uncle, who had been hanged by the English thirty-three years before. The waiters, who had no doubt heard generations of immigrants sing about their pride and woes, were tolerant. She sang so often that her song stuck in my memory and here is how it starts:

> In Mountjoy Gaol one Monday morning,
> High upon the gallows tree,
> Kevin Barry gave his young life
> In the cause of liberty.
> Another martyr for old Ireland,
> Another murder for the crown ...

There were several more verses. In the wake of their own poor wartime record, many French people resented the English, and, if they had heard of Ireland at all, liked to think we did too. Katherine was happy to satisfy their expectations.

It was in that same workers' café that Therese, back from a trip to Dublin, told us that she had had offers of marriage from two men we knew slightly and asked which we thought she should accept. I forget whether the others said anything, but I, foolishly, did. If she could really not decide, I suggested she marry the reliable one who might yet become a senator – as in time, one of her suitors actually did. The other, Cronin, was reputed to be a touch too fond of the drink.

'Read his poems but don't marry him,' I no doubt advised, then forgot all about it.

What I failed to predict was that Therese, proud of turning down the high-flyer and revelling in her spotlit moment, would report what I'd said to Cronin.

This had consequences. The first came when I too took a trip to Dublin and went with Seán to a party given by Oonagh, Lady Oranmore and Browne, at her former hunting lodge, Luggala. There, while chatting to an Englishman whom I had just met, I became aware of a gangly figure, loping towards us through contiguous rooms. It was Cronin who, abruptly and without a word, pulled the chair from under me. The Englishman, as taken aback as myself, helped me up. 'Will I fight him?' he asked seriously and, as he looked quite capable of flattening the weedy Tony, I was tempted to accept. But, as I couldn't do that to Therese, I thanked the Englishman for the offer and refused. No doubt he was marvelling at the unremittingly 'brutish behaviour' of the native Irish, which was how the poet Edmund Spenser had described it centuries before.

A more long-term consequence was that Therese, after marrying Tony, took to drink to the detriment of her mental health. 'She's in and out of St Pat's,' old college friends would tell me sadly when I went back to Dublin.

Luggala parties were apt to generate mishaps, so mine at the hands of the brutish Cronin did not rouse much interest. I am unsure whether or not it was that same evening that guests' attention focused on three young people who seemed to be pursuing and eluding each other like figures in a ballet. As they moved through the throng, a ripple of talk revealed that the man was the painter Lucian Freud, the dark woman was his wife, Kitty Epstein, and the red-haired one was our hostess's neice, Lady Caroline Blackwood, with whom he was now in love.

If it was that evening when this encounter happened, Cronin's assault on myself would have roused little attention.

Queuing once again outside the Students' Lodging Bureau in Paris, I was warned by the rest of the queue not to count on having the use of a bathroom. All most landladies offered was access to a lavatory and a basin. For anything else you went with your sponge bag to the *Bains et Douches* which were available all over the city. Rome had had these, too, but struck me as also having better domestic plumbing. This, claimed a Florentine count, whom I knew later, was thanks to the US army having marched up the peninsula in '43 and made itself comfortable as it did. Indeed, he ascribed Italian working-class cleanliness entirely to US tutelage. His own class, he told me, had learned hygiene from generations of English nannies, but, as the new invaders were technologically more advanced, local hangers-on soon were too. Having a fondness for well-scrubbed young workmen, he cared about this. 'It's an ill wind,' as his nanny might have put it, 'that blows nobody good.'

In Paris, meanwhile, reports of the French débâcle at Dien Bien Phu and of troubles rumbling in the Maghreb may have contributed to the prevailing shabbiness, bad temper and poor plumbing. The empire was cracking up. A pair of very young vicomtes, whom I had met some months before, had been laying late claims to its exotic romance, one by enrolling in the École des Langues Orientales, the other by volunteering to fight in Indo-China. Perhaps he died at Dien Bien Phu. Many did, and his good looks were tailor-made for a mourning card. On the day news of that defeat came through, as another young Frenchman drove me up the Champs Elysées, where flags were at half mast, I felt a feather touch of discomfort. Young women, in those pre-feminist times, could be emotionally exploitative, living at second-hand through men. Stendhal's heroine in *Le Rouge et le noir*, who drives off with her guillotined lover's head, is wickedly emblematic. It was the man's head we wanted really: the seat of his mind and soul. Trained to think male minds superior, how could we not be head-hunters?

Eileen's advice had always been to avoid depending on a man. Seán's could be less clear, as when he let me know that he hoped I'd be the sort of woman he liked. Meaning whom? Elizabeth Bowen? Honor Tracy? Or had he someone new? Hurt on Eileen's behalf, my hope was that he no longer saw anyone, and that no one would tell me if he did. But that proved too much to ask.

Shevawn Lynam, an Irishwoman based in Paris, was keen to know the latest Dublin gossip about a falling-out between Seán and Frank O'Connor. Was it true, she asked me, that when Frank and his wife arrived at Dún Laoghaire railway station with his mother's body and found no hearse waiting, they phoned Seán, who selflessly left his desk and came to take charge? And that, later, when Frank's marriage broke down and a woman he had lived with in London arrived to face a hostile Dublin, he asked Seán to look after her?

'Frank himself was in the US just then,' Shevawn recalled. 'Teaching. It seems that when news came that he had met a third young woman over there, and married her without bothering to inform Seán, who was still trying to comfort the English one, the friendship foundered.' She sighed. 'Mind, your Dad's in no position to judge him after his own carry-on with Honor Tracy.'

I pretended not to hear.

'I'm not letting out secrets!' Shevawn grew defensive. 'They were seen together in Venice quite recently. In St Mark's.'

Play acting, I thought with puritan distaste. In a church! 'I don't want to hear.'

'Oh, come on! Anyone would think you were in love with him yourself.'

I hated her.

We stayed on good terms though. Or pretended to. Irish people often do that. Our country is – or was – so small that it was unsafe to fall out with people, since you were bound to run into them again and again.

Before I left home, Eileen had reproached Seán with failing to help keep me from going to the bad in Paris: a fear shared by my French professor, Louis Roche, who had no sooner congratulated me on winning the studentship than he warned me against succumbing to the enticements of Paris and the blandishments of men. The studentship, I should bear in mind, was funded by the state, so I owed it to Irish tax-payers to put it to good use.

Meanwhile Eileen's reproaches had shaken Seán, who drew me into his study and spoke in a way he had not done before.

'Your model,' he told me, without a flicker of irony, 'should be the poor Scottish crofter's son who used to come down from the hills, carrying a sack of oats to keep him in porridge while he was at the university. He'd live on that until he went home again, while spending nothing and devouring his books.'

I was taken aback. 'Do you mean literally?' I asked. 'Like the porridge?'

No smile. Seán was serious. 'It's a metaphor,' he said lumpishly.

I was reminded of the Abruzzesi students and their depressing lives, but this sounded worse. Why, I wondered, did people think me so frivolous? Professor Roche, I remembered, had greeted my arrival for the oral exam with an audible aside to the outside examiner with whom he must have just shared a boozy lunch. *'Voici Célimène!'* was what I heard him say.

Célimène? *Célimène!* The heartless coquette in Molière's *Misanthrope?* Why was I being compared to *her?* There were far more coquettish students than I at UCD. And Roche liked them! Though he could and did play the *misanthrope* with brio, he was notoriously prone to melt when a girl with a tip-tilted nose who played the soubrette in college plays sang songs like *Plaisir d'Amour.* I, however, could neither play the soubrette nor sing anything, least of all *Plaisir d'Amour.* I felt hard-done-by and wondered if someone had been gossiping about me.

Although the studentship had been offered in French and Italian, no warnings, or indeed attention, came from the Italian department, whose few students, apart from Eithne and myself, consisted of some 'blue nuns', who would soon be off to nurse well-born invalids in Italy, plus a handsome member of the Hapsburg family called Claudia and a shy man called Pat who wore a tightly belted mac all year round but loosened up so effectively on stage that he was fast becoming a star of the UCD Dramatic Society.

The professor of Italian, meanwhile, rarely turned up to teach, but could be seen instead sitting for hours in the cafeteria, while we, if lucky, received instruction from some hastily summoned member of his staff, usually a tall, splendid-looking north Italian woman who referred regularly and, we chose to think, wistfully, to 'our patriotic time in Italy'.

('That,' she would reminisce, 'was when we used the *voi* instead of the *lei*, which is a Spanish import, and said *autista*, not *chauffeur*, which is of course French!')

Taking 'patriotic' to mean Fascist, we guessed that UCD had got her cheap and was exploiting her, and that its patience with the absentee professor also had a political source. It was believed – and it may have been true – that in Ireland, as late as the Fifties, sinecures were bestowed in lieu of pensions on people who had been tortured in the Troubles or lost a relative in the nation's service. Maybe our professor's nerves had been so shattered that he couldn't bring himself to confront us more than once a term.

While waiting at our desks to see if he would or wouldn't put in an appearance, we used to elaborate this fable.

'What kind of torture?'

Half credulously someone might then mention the yarn about the man who had been blown up with a bicycle pump in the Civil War.

'Could that happen?'

'People said so.'

'What sort of people?' I asked, and thought of the ones in Gougane who had advised Seán to stick a pitchfork in the hired mare's belly. Perhaps that hadn't been a joke after all but a primitive form of horse-doctoring?

'Country people,' the poet John Montague had told me once, 'are different from Dubliners. For one thing they're sexier.'

But this too could be a joke.

While wondering about this in Paris, a worry struck me. What if Shevawn gossiped about *me*? If anything got back to Professor Roche, might my money be cut off?

This was fanciful, as I was doing nothing gossip-worthy and knew hardly any men apart from three safe solitaries: Stephane,

who was busily preparing to take a double degree in architecture
and urban planning, the poet Richard Murphy, whom I knew
from Dublin, and a Sardinian doctor, whom I sometimes ran into
in one of the subsidised student restaurants and joined afterwards
for coffee. This, if one had a cake as well and sat down rather than
standing at the counter, could cost more than the meal. But then,
students' restaurants were apt to serve horse-meat, and a tea-shop
cake could be delicious. Riccardo Braida was the Sardinian's name
and he was a mature student who claimed to have volunteered for
the Italian Russian campaign as a form of near-suicide after an
unhappy love affair. He was in Paris to take some top-up medical
courses which would, he confided self-mockingly, allow him to
call himself a specialist and charge high fees back in Sassari. Tall.
Melancholy. Very proper. Thin as a pipe-cleaner or a Giacometti
sculpture.

No less thin were the North African Arabs who, now that their
countries were trying to break away from France, were routinely
insulted in the Paris streets. Recognisably the wretched of the
earth, their diffident presence provoked the words '*sales bicots*'
or '*bougnoules*', which I now recalled hearing the Morandys use
of similarly transient figures whom I began to think of as soul-
brothers to my father's generation of rebel Irishmen. Ideologically,
I was on their side, but had been told that friendships with women
wouldn't figure in their mores, and that if I went with them they
would despise me. For a while I risked giving English lessons to
an Egyptian, who confirmed my fears and warned that for my
own sake I should avoid his kind. We worked from an antique
English grammar which he had brought from Egypt, containing
an article about 'new English writers' which mentioned a 'callow,
immature young man called Oscar Wilde'. I coveted it.

On one of our last sessions he brought along a box of lacy
jewellery and begged me to try it on. Was this a test or was I
modelling a gift bought for someone back home? I didn't ask but

did what he wanted, and he apparently derived satisfaction from this for, when he had put it all back in its box, he told me, a little sadly, that I was a *fille bien*. I was getting bored with this. The vicomtes had said it, too.

I started an affair with a man who wouldn't have known a *fille bien* if she had had the words branded on her. His sensuous eyebrows and olive-black eyes gave him a look of Caravaggio's Bacchus. He claimed to be the son of a Spanish Republican mayor who had died a hero's death, and he was in medical school, a Communist activist, who sang, played the guitar and the violin, and spent whole nights in my street checking on my comings and goings. Once he gate-crashed an official reception given for Bertolt Brecht by slipping in through the service entrance to see whether I had come with a man or, as I had said I would, with Sheila Murphy, a diplomat at our embassy. Never one to worry about detail, he joined us just as she and I were being introduced to Brecht. With admirable discretion, Sheila refrained from asking who he was.

Then one night in bed he burst out weeping and confessed that he was not Spanish and that his father had not died a hero's death.

'I'm a Jewish bastard from Algeria,' he sobbed.

He had finally realised that I was, by now, a somewhat tarnished *fille bien* and was overcome. Apparently he had taken me for a call girl. Our two-year affair gave me some insight into the ways of liars. They are, I think, the antithesis of fiction writers in that they neither use their fiction to uncover a devious truth, nor worry greatly about being found out. Jean-Paul – that was my suspicious lover's name – did not, for instance, take the trouble to borrow a dinner jacket when he crashed the reception where he was spying on me. Detail never bothered him, and if one lie failed to convince, he would hopefully try another. Perhaps lies were an attempt to reconcile the men who sheltered in his head? A puritan and a Stalinist ('*J'aime Stalin*,' he was saying ardently just weeks before the old monster died), he would go out on nights when we had no money and try to make some by cheating at poker with lorry drivers in Les Halles – or so he said. I never knew for sure. As a character, he lacked coherence but could have figured with panache in a metafictionist's text. When I wrote a novel about those years in Paris, I didn't use him at all but invented an affair with an Arab. I suppose I was rubbing him out – but then he had often done this to himself.

He interested me, though, and so did the real Arabs who lived in the Maison du Maroc, a men-only rooming house at the Cité Universitaire where he lived and where I sometimes illicitly spent the night. One inmate was suspected of being a spy for the French police. Another had a French girlfriend with whom I exchanged guarded smiles when the men talked politics. Jean-Paul was sure her lover meant to ditch her when he went back to Algeria. He shrugged when I questioned this, saying the break was inevitable – which, though depressing, was no more so than the outlook for the men's own future. Algerians were growing more unpopular and at the Fête de l'Humanité I had witnessed a stand-off between a small group of these and members of the Party's security service who wanted to eject them. Humanity, in the eyes of the Parti Communist Français, seemed not to include working-class Arabs. A year or so later, though, some Algerian Communists, among them a young officer called Maillot, broke ranks and deserted from the French army with a truckful of weapons. Maillot handed these over to the Algerian insurgents, only to be ambushed and murdered some weeks later. He was considered a traitor, just as Erskine Childers must have been back in 1914 when he had used his yacht to smuggle arms to the

Irish Volunteers. There were other parallels between the Algerian *événements* and the Irish 'Troubles', among them the French refusal – it lasted until 1999 – to call what was happening a war.

Once or twice, when feeling out of sympathy with the comrades, I dropped in on a group of American writers who met in the Café Tournon, on the ground floor of what might have been the building where the great Joseph Roth had committed suicide in 1939. They, however, seemed to know no French, and I wasn't in Paris to meet expats. Even the pimp who tried to chat me up in a café on the boulevard St Germain was more interesting, and his offer to fix me up with clients more entertaining.

'The people you're with are no use to you,' he told me.

He was right. The people I was with when he made his suggestion were the Irish rugby team, with whom someone at the embassy had arranged that I should spend the evening. The players knew no French, which left the pimp free to cajole me. Maybe I should have taken his phone number to give to the embassy for future use. He could surely arrange a livelier evening for visiting teams than I had. As it was, the team, tanked up, spilled out on to the pavement, linked arms and bowled down the boulevard singing a song about 'the Muskerry sportsman, the bold Thady Quill'.

Unable to keep up in my high heels, I let them go. If they had duty-free whiskey in their rooms, I imagine they got drunker before falling asleep. Predictably perhaps, their match next day was a débâcle. Meanwhile, feeling less safe without them, I slunk around the block to avoid passing the café where the pimp operated, reflecting, as I did, that having the team to protect me could have been useful after all.

PARIS AND THE COUNCIL OF EUROPE

Seán turned up a few times during my stay in Paris. I now had a room in the rue de Buci, though Jean-Paul kept his belongings elsewhere, and I was able to arrange for the two to meet, as if by chance, in some modest place like the Old Navy. Mindful of Seán's sermon about poor crofters' sons, I avoided better places during his visit. Even so, neither man relished the encounter, and later each marvelled at the other's clothes. Jean-Paul, making an effort, had worn a three-piece suit in a dazzling royal blue, which Seán said afterwards belonged in a musical comedy, while Jean-Paul claimed that Seán's handsome Herbie Johnson hat reminded him of a cowboy's.

Richard Murphy's reaction when Jean-Paul and I ran into him a little later in the Cité Universitaire implied that I had developed a taste for rough trade. He himself had now taken up with Patricia Avis, a pale, nervy, chain-smoking fellow poet who, like himself, was staying at the Maison Franco-Britannique.

'She's too complicated for you to understand,' he told me. 'Brilliant. Neurotic. And very, very complicated.'

On learning that she was half Irish, half South African, I suggested teasingly that as the four of us had Africa and Ireland in common we should all dine together.

Pretending not to hear, Richard quickly started to talk of plans to visit Greece. Perhaps he felt that he, whose father had been the governor of the Bahamas, could not be seen with a man who wore North-African-made royal-blue suits. Or perhaps he already knew that Patricia, though she could be both generous and warm-hearted, was also capable of indulging in Fascist rants.

This sidelight would not emerge until he and she were married and living in Ireland, where her reported outbursts, which I never heard myself, could have been provoked by the priggishness of our more po-faced citizens. In the end allowances were made by and for her, who, due to having belonged when at Oxford to a set which included John Wain and Kingsley Amis, and having only recently wound up an affair with Philip Larkin, had, as Richard acknowledged, acquired a lofty manner and a way of stopping conversations with an impatient 'Yes, yes, we know, we *know*.' This was not calculated to go down well in Ireland, but may have helped dissolve tensions which arose whenever her mega-rich father was gripped by a paternal urge to protect and control. Without stirring from South Africa he contrived to torment her and Richard by dangling offers of financial help tied to unworkable conditions. Dealing with him proved as difficult as dealing with a leprechaun – and he sprang similar surprises. For instance, he bought them a spacious lakeside house in County Wicklow which had belonged to Edna O'Brien and her husband. Then, four years later, when Richard and Patricia had arranged it to their liking, had a daughter and seemed happy, a summons came from South Africa. Patricia flew there – and the marriage collapsed.

Here the old link between money and mating seemed at its most stifling.

Thinking back to how the Morandy girls were kept isolated on their mountain, then forward to Patricia's problems, I wondered why families, though presumably eager to see their bloodlines carried on, were so often hell-bent on stopping daughters taking a hand in the process. Why? Possessiveness? Distrust? Half-conscious incestuous feelings? I suspected that all of these played a role.

In Paris I was sometimes lonely, as I had not been in Rome, where people were gregarious and where, after a very few days in the convent, I had become close friends with my room mate, Romana. She was from Forlì and had come to the capital in pursuit of a *fidanzato* who, on qualifying as a public prosecutor, had been posted there and risked forgetting her. Chasing after him was a bold move for a nice Italian girl so, not long after we exchanged vows of friendship, her mother summoned her home. To my indignation, the gormless *fidanzato* then tried to date me, without even pretending that we would be meeting to discuss Romana's needs. In other words, he neither knew the decent way to steal one's girlfriend's girlfriend, nor had the nous to turn his prosecutor's eye on himself. Maybe, up till then, law exams had taken all his attention. A swot! So – intermittently – was I, but when what you're swotting up is French and Italian literature, you learn a few things along the way about life and love. Not so, it seems, if you plan to be a public prosecutor. By then she and I were fond of each other so, though we exchanged letters for a year, I kept mum about her *fidanzato*'s perfidy.

She adored him. '*Il mio procuratore!*' she used to sigh, and once spent three days queuing to see Padre Capello, a miracle-working priest who, she hoped, could work one for her. The queue outside his confession box was smoothly organised, and numbered tickets were issued to those in need of a sleep or snack or what sports commentators call a comfort break.

After Seán's plea, 'Leave your Frenchman, or your mother will leave us both,' I flew home so often to argue my case that even long afterwards the view from a plane circling Dublin Bay could trigger stomach cramps probably as sharp as those which the sight of Martello towers scattered along its coast had been designed to provoke in Napoleonic invaders. Back then, though, many Irishmen hoped the Frenchies *would* invade and trounce the Brits. Madame de la Tour du Pin's great grandfather, General Arthur O'Connor, had been all set to help.

There are said to be about fifty of these towers along our coast, each built in sight of the next. From a plane they look like squat wine corks, or the chess-pieces known as rooks. Most are in disrepair, as I and Grace found when in our student days we threw a party in the one on Dalkey Island. We hired boats, prepared a picnic, got men friends to drive my father's old wind-up gramophone to the harbour, lug it into a boat, row to the island, then carry it up into and through the high, narrow opening in the tower. With hindsight this was a ridiculous enterprise, as we had no lights apart from the smoky flicker obtained by lighting a fire.

In those days, however, we would do anything for a party, no doubt because ours was a tame generation for whom parties became vital escape valves. Even in our twenties most of us still lived with our parents. Few had money and none had a job. The Irish state had given too much power to the Church, which used it to bully its flock, with the result that the flock, lured by emigration, failed to stay home and develop a robust secular state.

I and my friends were lucky. We got through college. Yet I can name ten of us – maybe more – who emigrated as soon as they graduated. Not all went back either. I read recently that 'Over 500,000 people left independent Ireland' – meaning what is now the Republic – 'between 1945 and 1960.' We didn't just leave to find jobs. We needed to be with a peer group and decide who we were. So parents who tried to postpone the break were infantilising us as, in another way, was the father of another friend, a circuit judge who went away regularly leaving his house available for three-day parties: a dangerous move, since crashers could arrive and squat. Crashers were gangs of young people who, on learning from some loose-lipped barman that a party was planned, would turn up at the planners' house with crates of drink and hope not to be turned away. Often they were hard to get rid of, though we never thought they'd crash our picnic. But our plan leaked out and a group from Trinity College managed to hire a rowing boat and join us. Well, the tower was not our property, and our male contingent, being Dramatic Society aesthetes, were no good as bouncers. So the invaders climbed in unopposed and, as we had by then occupied the best stretch of floor, had to make do with one where sections were starting to give way. We learned this too late. At the time it was too dark to see the danger, and the first we knew was that several crashers had crashed, i.e. fallen down four or more feet onto jagged rubble.

If this happened today, several people would have mobile phones with lights. We were lucky to have matches. A pretty Trinity girl was found to be injured. Medical students to the fore, some of the more muscular men hauled her from the hole, then gave her whiskey for the pain while others rowed to the mainland for help.

It was dawn before an ambulance-boat was sighted being rowed towards us by men in dark uniforms. The white-swaddled stretcher looked like an image from a film, and before the hurt girl, by now knocked out by pain or whiskey, could be laid on it she had to be lifted down through the steep slit of the tower's entrance. She didn't respond when we tried to commiserate.

Grace reminded me in a whisper that she and I had given our addresses to the boat-owners so, if any laws had been broken, it was for us the police would look.

'Will we take a boat and make a dash for it?'

'There's no point if they know our addresses. Anyway,' I reminded her, 'I can't leave my father's gramophone. He doesn't know I took it.'

Just then a group which had managed to get that gramophone down from the tower put on a Neapolitan record. One of Seán's, it reminded me that he would soon be up and that, when he was, it would be hard to get the cumbersome thing into his study without his knowing.

Out over a pink, satiny sea floated the syrupy music, afflicting me with that yearning which tells you that this would be a perfect setting for amorous adventures. But, although people in our group knew, liked and trusted each other, there were few couples among us.

Oddly, the song we were hearing on one of Seán's 78s was about a girl whose parents didn't want her to make love.

> *Mamma non vuole, Babbo nemmeno.*
> *Come faremo a fare l'amor?*

I doubt if there had been much chance of *amor* at that picnic.

In the end returning the gramophone discreetly proved impossible. Coming face to face with two of my men friends crunching down our gravel path with it, Seán got them to say where we had been.

I expected an explosion, but instead he was eager to share the experience. How was the injured girl, he worried. Did we know her name? 'I', he mused, 'feel responsible. Maybe I should phone to find out how she is?' Clearly our company made him feel young.

'Ah no!' As they edged past him, the gramophone-bearers' arms strained under its weight. 'Best not encourage crashers, Mr O'Faolain,' they warned. 'They'd be knocking at your door with a "God save all here" next time you had friends in.'

Seán laughed and invited them to join us for breakfast. What may have pleased him about our mishap was that it could have featured in an old-time *Boys' Own Annual*, innocent of sex and impropriety.

Remembering this later, when hostilities in our house were at their worst, I concluded that he hadn't wanted me to grow up.

It was then that both Eileen and I got stomach cramps and were diagnosed by our GP as having ulcers. I disputed this. Dr S, a small-town misogynist, had, I knew, always thought Eileen's illnesses imaginary and in an attempt to forge a male alliance with Seán he advised him not to worry his head about her. I suspected him of giving her placebos, guessed that 'ulcer' was code for 'women's notions', and greatly offended him when I asked for a copy of the X-ray showing *my* alleged ulcer.

'I want to show it to a French doctor,' I told him.

He refused angrily.

I explained that the food in the students' restaurants in Paris would aggravate whatever was wrong with me unless I could prove my need to eat at one reserved for people with a delicate digestion.

When he offered to write a letter about this to the French authorities, I pointed out that it would have to be in French. That foxed him and he surrendered the X-ray.

Back in Paris I took it to the doctor who could get me a card for the special restaurant. There were technicians with him who asked to see what sort of work the Irish did. Holding up the X-ray to scrutiny, they opined that what our Irish GP had taken for an ulcer was a photographic blip.

I felt some shame for, though S might be a poor doctor, *I* had committed the capital sin of letting the country down in front of foreigners.

Meanwhile Jean-Paul and I were having rows. Although these had been set off by Seán's asking us to keep away from each other for a year, even when that year's start had been postponed to let me produce sample chapters to show my thesis director, we met rarely. This was due both to Jean-Paul being unable to join me for meals in the invalids' restaurant and to my having furtively begun to date the doctor. This, I knew, would enrage Jean-Paul if he found out, since he was only a medical student, whereas Dr P was a hospital consultant and, being neither North African nor a Communist, might appeal to my parents. I despised myself for harbouring such thoughts and was in a fix since, having insisted that I was in love and knew my own mind, how could I now unsay this?

Did I want to? Yes and no. No because I mustn't let them think I had been mesmerised – as their letters implied – by sex which, according to them, confuses the mind. Had I ever, they asked, seen the old woodcut of a naked whore riding astride an equally naked Aristotle who, down on all fours, was letting her flout his sense of decorum? They had a reproduction of it somewhere. Here it was. Take a good look. Did I suppose my defences were better than his?

With hindsight I see that my relations with Seán and Eileen were more important to me, both in good and bad ways, than anything I felt for either Jean-Paul or Dr P, with whom, because I disapproved, priggishly, of two-timing, I had gone out only four times, one of which, having started as a medical visit, didn't quite count. But I was attracted, I found him pleasingly adult and had let him kiss me while strolling along the *quais* where anyone could have seen. It would have been *un*-adult, after all, to have dragged him behind a tree or a *vespasienne*. Worse, we hadn't been all that far from the École de Médecine, so I must be more careful next time if there *was* a next time, which I guiltily wanted there to be. Like it or not, deciding which man I preferred was going to require *some* two-timing.

∞

Meanwhile, Professor Moreau, my thesis director, put my typescript into his briefcase and proceeded to give a class to the half-dozen of us who were taking his course in *Méthodologie*. How discussion of a literary figure whom he described that day as 'a sincere hypocrite' fitted that heading, I forget, but I remember fearing that the definition fitted myself and that, when he produced examples from novels by Bernanos and Mauriac, my stomach pains grew worse, either from guilt at having gone out with Dr P, or from eagerness to do so again.

A 'sincere' hypocrite? Was I? Remembering my prim disapproval of Romana's *fidanzato*, I felt ashamed. After the class I went into Gibert's bookshop and bought a novel by Bernanos which had featured in Moreau's discussion, and, on reading it, was shaken by the fanatical and possibly heretical Catholicism by whose standards the writer judged his protagonist, Monsieur Ouine – whose name suggests weasels, *fouines* – and the village where he lived. This was said in the novel to be in the grip of evil and described by its new priest as 'a dead parish' which, when the book first came out in 1943, may have been taken to stand for France itself. For all their talk of Cartesianism, the French, I was starting to think, could be more excitable, not to say deranged, than the earthy Irish ever could be. Intrigued by this, now that I could see my way to finishing my main thesis, I had asked Professor Moreau whether he thought I could write the obligatory subsidiary one about some aspect of the poet, playwright and actor, Antonin Artaud, a mad but seminal figure whose work I had been reading with fascination in the Bibliothèque Nationale. Moreau sent me to talk with Artaud's sister, who was understandably reluctant to speak about her brother's drug addiction, eccentricities, spells in mental homes, possible schizophrenia and general oddity. Why, I asked myself, should she let someone as unenlightened and self-deceiving as myself discuss him? He intrigued me, though, and so did his manifesto, *The Theatre of Cruelty*, in which he explained that by cruelty he meant no more than a resolve to force audiences to know what they didn't want to know and rid them of 'the false reality which lies like a shroud over our perceptions'. No wonder Ireland had appealed to him.

My worst fight with Jean-Paul happened on a bus where, when a priest took the seat opposite us, Jean-Paul put a possessive hand on my thigh then, when I removed it, retaliated by making anti-clerical comments. I stood up and told the priest that I hoped he would forgive my companion's ignorance of big city ways.

'He's from the colonies,' I told him, then pulled the overhead wire and, before Jean-Paul knew what I was doing, had stepped from the bus as it moved off.

Soon my cramp was worse. Self-punishment? Or – oh dear! – an ulcer? I was tempted to go to confession for what would be the first time in years: a notion which must have come from reading Bernanos, whose novel was clogged with words which coalesced in a vision of a cold, temporal hell. Recurring ones were 'glacial', 'nothingness', 'indifferent', 'hollow', 'malign', 'empty', 'muddy', 'inactive'. I wondered why Moreau had headed me towards this bitter writer, then remembered that it was my Dublin professor who had sent me to Moreau. Perhaps dealing with Irish Catholics was a speciality of his, and the French Right a terrain where he felt we would be at home. Today, when I think of the relatively recent German film, *The White Ribbon*, which portrays a sick pre-Nazi society, it is hard not to compare it with Bernanos's *Monsieur Ouine* which describes an even sicker pre-war French one, remnants of which still lingered in the Fifties and which lay fermenting in the old magazines, obituaries and reviews of pre-war plays that I combed through in the Bibliothèque de l'Arsenal, a library specialising in drama. Hindsight could sharpen their thrust, as happened for me in the case of Robert Brasillach, a brilliant theatre critic whose work had been delighting me for months before it occurred to me to find out about his life. When I did, he turned out to have been the only man executed after the war for 'intellectual crimes', i.e. editing a newspaper called *Je suis partout*, which favoured collaboration with Germany and gave away the whereabouts of hidden Jews. De Gaulle, ignoring an appeal signed by, among others, Valéry, Mauriac, Cocteau, Camus, Colette and Claudel, had refused to commute the sentence. And a current newspaper supplement which I happened to buy showed a murky photograph of Louis-Fernand Céline lurking behind a barred gate clearly intended to suggest a prison. Some people must have wanted *him* executed too. Having grown up on Irish Civil War stories about fratricidal murder, this should not have upset me, but did because I admired Céline's novels and suspected that extremists on both sides had had more in common with each other – passion, activity, eagerness for change – than with people who condemned them, but themselves did nothing at all. This, I had to admit, was a notion I'd inherited from Eileen.

The topic of my main thesis, suggested by Moreau, was Gaston Baty, a Catholic theatre director who had roused hostility by keeping his theatre open during the occupation and welcoming the German ambassador to the best seats. He died in 1952, thus entering the pool of artists on whom university theses might be written. As an *animateur*, his chief characteristic was the primacy he claimed for directors over playwrights and his belief that actors should be as pliant as puppets. Clearly a martinet, his stage productions were as hard to assess in retrospect as a vanished sunset.

Rows were eroding my feeling for Jean-Paul and no doubt his for me. But, being in no mood to placate him, I rang Dr P to ask if he had something for stomach cramps, saying that if he phoned a prescription to a chemist, I'd pick it up.

Instead, he took me to dinner and insisted that a glass or so of wine could hardly hurt me.

'You haven't got an ulcer,' he reminded me. 'It's just stress. Why are you stressed?'

I hadn't the nerve to say. And when he offered to walk me back to the rue de Buci, which was a worrying move, since we risked running into a visiting Jean-Paul, I found myself crying, which must have persuaded Dr P that I was a bit unbalanced. Stress?

'Sorry,' I said. 'Sorry.'

'What's the matter?' he asked gently. 'Can't you tell me?'

I should have said, 'It's because I find you attractive.' It was on the tip of my tongue and would probably have gone down well. Most people, after all, like to be liked.

What stopped me was seeing Jean-Paul over his shoulder. Real? Imaginary? Was guilt making me hallucinate? Fearful of finding out, I thanked Dr P for dinner, rammed my key into the lock in the door of my *porte cochère* and went in, closing the door behind me.

I left for Dublin that week and did not meet Jean-Paul again until some decades later when he saw me on French television promoting the translation of my novel, *No Country for Young Men*, got in touch and invited Lauro and me to dinner. We accepted and spent a pleasantly sedate evening with him and his pretty wife in their house in Bourg-la-Reine, outside Paris. Jean-Paul, who didn't in the least resemble his old self, was now a psychiatrist and clearly living comfortably. The occasion was, however, a trifle odd. The word Communist was not mentioned, and he seemed to have forgotten that he had ever loved Stalin. In his eyes the unique purpose of our meeting must have been to show me that Seán had been wrong to think him a poor match. The four of us agreed, while saying good night, that his wife and he would come and dine with us in London, but they later called off the visit.

In Dublin in 1956 I decided to burn my thesis, which Moreau had more or less approved, though I did not. Gaston Baty as a topic didn't really appeal to me, but I had discovered this too late. My plans for a subsidiary thesis had collapsed, too, for I had given up on Artaud as being thrilling but daunting – as any assessment of an artist subject to spasms of frenzy must, I imagine, risk being. So before leaving Paris I asked Samuel Beckett if I might write instead about him. He discouraged me, as he did everyone until fifteen years later, when Deirdre Bair, who was obviously more persuasive than I, made the same request and this time he agreed.

I was disappointed, because I had been enjoying his work since 1953 when a mutual friend gave tickets to the poet David Gascoyne and myself for the first production of *En Attendant Godot*, then lent me Beckett's novels. It was a time of experiment in the Paris theatre, where Beckett was bracketed in people's minds with Adamov, Ionesco and Genet, whose opacity was equally intriguing. I loved both opaque and open-ended narratives. They left you wondering. I didn't necessarily think of Godot, for instance, as God. The Italian verb, *godo*, fitted just as well, and when the play was in English gave it the title 'While waiting I come', which was pleasingly paradoxical and connected with the play-acting with shoes (*godasses* in French) by the two tramps.

Play melts barriers, as our family had learned on wet days in West Cork when, rather than chat, we played cards so as to let monolingual Gaelic- and English-speakers join in.

Back in Ireland, having freed myself from Baty, I emptied my mind by hiring a horse and learning to jump double fences from an ex-jockey. Unfortunately he taught me to ride with my bottom in the air and the shortest of stirrup-leathers. When I said I wanted to do a sitting gallop instead, he pooh-poohed the idea with a leer.

'Listen to me, ma'am,' he argued, 'the ones that sit back are in the military and, sit back so as to be able to draw their sabres. Now you don't have a sabre, am I right?'

At Christmas it snowed, and Patricia and Richard, who were now living by a lake in a close-by bog, invited Seán, Eileen and me to dinner and, as there were said to be deep snow-drifts into which Seán's small Wolsely could slip and disappear, Patricia's brother, Keesje, who was staying with them, fetched us in a jeep. He and his two small sons were in Ireland to try to calm the despair which had gripped the three of them when the boys' mother unexpectedly died in South Africa from a freak malady. Patricia had conceived a mad hope that I might help console Keesje, but Eileen, who had sat next to him on the drive through the snowy, starlit bog, confided later that his clenched profile had made her fear that, at any moment, he might swerve off the road and kill us all. She had, she said, sensed a doom hovering over him, for she claimed to have a feel for such things and often slept with a scarf over her forehead to prevent her third eye from detecting forces which it was as well to leave undisturbed. She had learned about the third eye from an Indian who lived in Howth.

Men were trouble. She didn't want me taking up with another one. What she *would* like, she told me wistfully, was for me to take a crash course in Gaelic and become proficient enough to get a job in my own country – ideally in the diplomatic corps, which would allow me to travel but always bring me home.

'Like a dog on a long leash!' I teased, and, though we laughed, I knew she meant it. My failure to learn Gaelic, which other people's daughters did with ease, struck her as perverse.

'A crash course,' she wheedled. 'The Sacred Heart schools are no good at Gaelic. We should never have sent you to them. There must be lots of good teachers around, so why not give it a try?'

Instead, like generations of emigrants before me, I went to London.

It seemed to be full of people obsessed with what they wore. A school where I taught for a term made the girls change several times daily, and the taste for uniforms persisted into adulthood. Men wore defining ties, and boys couldn't wait to get into the rig of pinstripe and bowler to strut down the King's Road. A man who was then a radical, but later became a Thatcherite peer, came with me to Trafalgar Square to hear Nye Bevan denounce British action in Suez, then took me to tea in the Ritz. He had been to a wedding earlier and wore a morning suit, which struck me as a sign of readiness to turn one's coat. The suit bore the message 'Don't count on me; I'll revert to type'.

Patricia, over on a visit, warned, 'Don't talk politics. People here don't like it.' I found this baffling. How, if not in such talk, did you test your views? Jean-Paul's head had been brimming with emphatic ones, and, like Stendhal's heroine, I had borne off what was in it. Much of this was compatible with my own heritage: radical sympathies spliced with disillusion, which was rampant that year. The discrediting of Stalin, the invasion of Budapest and the divisiveness of the Algerian War kept it on the bubble. Nobody, however, cared to discuss this, so I began numbing myself with work and took two jobs, a daytime one as a supply teacher working for the London County Council, and a late-night one as a short-order cook in a place called the Moo Cow Milk Bar opposite Victoria Station. One of the waitresses there claimed to be a refugee from the troubles in Kenya and talked darkly of native savagery. Taking an Irish view of this, I wondered if the truth might be more tangled, and, sure enough, learned long afterwards that, when opinion in the Moo Cow Milk bar and the British press was ascribing atrocities to the Kikuyu, that tribe was being tortured and massacred by Brits at twice the rate at which the French were killing native Algerians. The difference was that French atrocities were known about, thanks both to the outraged French Left and to General Massu who claimed the right to torture anyone who had information which could save his men's lives. English misdeeds, by contrast, were kept lengthily under wraps. No wonder people here didn't like to talk about politics.

Edward McGuire had asked me to look up a girl in London with whom he was in love, but whom his father had forbidden him to see. Rita was the most beautiful woman I ever met, but had no instinct for self-preservation. She was said to have been chosen by the film director Michael Cacoyannis for a major part in a film, but to have missed her chance by failing to turn up to an appointment. There was a series of such stories, including one about a youth who had so adored her that he built a shrine in her honour.

'Yes, but she's been around too long,' shrugged a cynical friend. 'Nobody will marry her now.'

Rita kept begging me to assure her that Edward *would* marry her, but I thought it wise not to raise her hopes, if only because of the emphasis with which he cursed his father for being 'a bloody businessman!' '*I'm* a painter,' he often complained with pride. 'But to paint I need money.' And it was clear that he wanted the best of both worlds and that his father wouldn't let him have it, possibly because he himself, from what people told me, was a good amateur painter who may once have faced the same choice as Edward and chosen business over art.

Rita, meanwhile, lived from hand to mouth, doing odd jobs in boutiques and restaurants up and down the King's Road.

On one of my evenings off from the Moo Cow Milk Bar, I filled in for her by waitressing in a place run, or perhaps owned, by a sprig of the Anglo-Irish gentry. It was Friday, and some Irish construction workers, who had clearly strayed from their familiar beat, came in for dinner asking for fish. The sprig thought at first that he had none, then located some ancient prawns.

'Have they a pong?' he asked me sotto voce.

'Yes.'

'Are you sure? They seem all right to me.' He was as feckless as the squireens whom Maria Edgeworth so brilliantly described in *Castle Rackrent*. 'I'll slosh brandy over them,' he decided. 'That'll hide it.'

Meanwhile, five or six Irish heads, all as pink as peony buds, were converging in consultation – possibly about walking out.

'Quick,' said the sprig, 'pour them some Guinness. Tell them it's on the house and that the prawns will be ready in no time.'

'They're really off, you know,' I warned and mouthed the words 'fish poisoning'.

But he had the bit between his teeth. 'Nonsense,' he said, 'that's just how prawns smell.'

Since Rita could have lost her job if I warned the Irishmen, I kept mum, though I was tempted not to. The restaurant, I consoled myself with thinking, was unlikely to survive long if its owner sloshed brandy and Guinness around so readily. It would have been cheaper to make his customers an omelette.

Patricia had given me an introduction to a man called Poldy von Loewenstein-Wertheim, who said he had a claim to the English throne through the Stuarts and the House of Bavaria. He mocked himself amusingly, translated tales from the German and paid me to check his English. As he and his wife, formerly Diana Gollancz, gave me lunch whenever I did this, it made me feel a touch guilty, since Poldy and she were clearly short of cash. Later I heard that his son by a previous wife had become a financial adviser to the Rolling Stones and, thanks to his financial savvy, prosperous. Clearly the source of the savvy wasn't genetic, but I hoped some prosperity would go Poldy's way. Patricia, however, who came from a rich family, had a pitiless little smile when I mentioned my scruples. 'Diana', she told me, 'spent her youth darning her dressing gown and being bullied by her father. Anything is better than that, so don't worry about either of them.'

About this time I got work as a translator at the Council of Europe in Strasbourg. I went out there whenever the European Parliament was in session, and in between came back to work for the LCC, filling in for absent teachers all over London. I stayed for what felt like a long time in a Dickensian school in the East End, where they couldn't get teachers at all, and only left when one of the mums, a large, muscular woman, barged into my class and threatened to beat me up. Upsettingly, her son, though disruptive, was also one of the brightest children in my class and, when I put him out of the classroom for using four-letter words to a little girl, he had been found and caned by the headmaster. It was a violent place, jammy with soot, and had been scheduled for dismantling years before.

In soothing contrast, friends of Seán's took me to clubs in the West End and, in Rita's company, I idled in its pubs. That I had lost my protective colouring as a *fille bien* became clear on an afternoon when I paused in Paris on my way through from Strasbourg. Patricia Murphy, the poet, happened to be there, too, and so did the literary editor of the *New Statesman*, John Raymond, who was over to interview some woman writer, I think Marguerite Yourcenar. The three of us had a drink at the Deux Magots and, when I went down to the lavatory, a man was waiting for me. It was Lucian Freud, who some weeks before had tried to detach me from my escort at the Gargoyle Club in London. He looked a bit like a gargoyle himself, and in the Magots lavatory the flush of plumbing reinforced an impression of spitting rage.

'You should know,' he said, 'that since you polluted yourself with that disgusting creature, John Raymond, I no longer desire to sleep with you.' With that, he turned and sped up the stairs.

An odd encounter, given that neither man meant a thing to me. I had thought neither of sleeping with Raymond – who was unlikely to have thought of it either, since he was a Catholic convert – nor about Freud, except to remember that he had been a mentor to Swift and McGuire. My mind was on my own past; so learning that I might figure in, and even 'pollute', other people's fantasies, gave me the mildest of jolts. The self-absorbed are hard to ruffle. Slowly, though, irritation surfaced. After all, had I not spent my childhood trying to cope with the coercive fantasies of my Gaelicising parents and their dreaming generation? Being reproached for failing to play a role for which I had not volunteered was a replay, and, as replays do, it helped get the past in focus.

In the Magots' lavatory, however, my first reaction was annoyance at the male habit of defining women in terms of the men with whom they're seen.

But I wished that Dr P had been half as enterprising as Freud.

❖

Seán's letters kept urging me to give up the Moo Cow Milk Bar and try writing. So I did both, to the indignation of the Moo Cow manager, who claimed that I was wasting my training, since I could have had a future in the business and that, after the way I had let him down, he would never hire another graduate. Unworried by this – the pay had been risible – I began to write a radio play about a private boarding school for girls where I had taught for a term. It was located in St Albans and staffed by geriatric lesbians.

'*They're* all varsity women!' the headmistress had boasted, while glancing with disdain at my Irish-Roman-Parisian CV. She claimed she couldn't afford to pay me the Burnham scale, a rate of pay on which her staff were all too old and tottery to insist. We haggled, and my determination stiffened when I learned that I was to replace a French teacher who had unexpectedly dropped dead. In the end I enjoyed a small triumph at being the only one in this Do-the-Girls Hall to be paid the legal salary. Nicole, the resident mademoiselle, was young, freshly arrived in England and disgracefully exploited. Half stupefied with boredom, she told me, she had volunteered to wash and lay out my dead predecessor, and had no doubt been underpaid for that, too, if she was paid at all, since it was not the sort of job whose rate of pay one tends to know.

'It interested me to do it,' she admitted. 'It was a challenge.'

Staying in that school was itself a challenge. The food was appalling: far worse than anything I had tasted in Ireland, let alone in London state schools where lunches were good, and pupils unlikely to accept anything as foul as the bread and dripping served here as elevenses to both staff and pupils. Yet several of those girls' brothers were at Eton, and the sisters revelled in reporting their doings. Nicole and I amused ourselves by imagining other economies which their families might impose on their daughters so as to help stump up Eton fees for their male offspring.

I can't recall whether I used any of this in my radio play, which was broadcast while I was in Strasbourg, and for which I eventually received a cheque from the BBC. Next I wrote a story about meeting Romana in the Roman convent, and the *New Yorker* took that. Both pieces were crude caricature and had no doubt been accepted only because they were taken to be reports from the youth front. I also sold something to American *Vogue*. Later I grew ambitious, tried to write better, and sold nothing for years. I had made a false start as a writer, and the real one would not come into being for nearly another decade. Meanwhile I worked as a translator, taught languages and considered trying to get work as an interpreter at the UN. This would have required me to add a third 'official language' to my French and English, since you needed three to apply, and Italian did not count. Hesitating between Spanish and Russian, I made a stab at both. Meanwhile I also fiddled at writing. Why, I sometimes wonder, was I so slow to take off? Perhaps because, in an attempt to train myself in simultaneous interpreting, I developed a habit of turning news items read or heard on the radio from or into French and Italian. My mind at times was a clutter of cliché in three languages.

Stints in Strasbourg combined work and conviviality. Money flowed, and even translators were booked on 'champagne flights' – you could drink all you liked! – and put up in comfortable hotels. Pay was lavish, or seemed so to me. One sensed a barrier, though, between the grand, who were MPs or ministers, and the less than grand who were sometimes typists – though a few of these, thanks to family connections, were grander than anyone. Translators came in between and, despite their linguistic skills, tended to cluster in Anglophone groups. Perhaps living in Strasbourg had made full-time ones homesick. One old stager who cast an occasional eye on my work found French manners an affront. When I translated an account of a ceremony in the European parliament in which two male politicians embraced, he argued that this could not have happened.

'But,' I told him, 'I saw it from the public gallery.'

'*L'accolade?*'

'Yes.'

'And they *embraced?*'

'They kissed.'

'My God!' He shook his head. 'The French!'

As similar thoughts sometimes struck me about the Irish, I knew how he felt.

David Kelly, who was in Strasbourg to learn about journalism, could touch these off. He had attended the Benedictine boarding school from which my brother Stevie had had to be rescued, and I wondered, with some embarrassment, if he knew more than I did about why. To my relief, though, David never brought the thing up. He and I sometimes took walks, during which he warned that, if he were to unexpectedly climb a lamp post, I should know that this was one of his Benedictine mentors' cures for the troubles of the flesh. At first I took this for a joke, then saw that it wasn't. Recalling how, when our family was worrying about Stevie's mishap, there had been hints that 'sex came into it', I wondered if he too should have learned to shin up lamp posts.

In May 1957 I finished my work in Strasbourg, so my parents suggested we meet in Florence, hire a car and explore the countryside. They loved wandering around rural monasteries and rousing sextons from their siestas. Tuscany, at that time, was a sleepy place.

On their last day we drove to San Gimignano, a hilltop town

spiked with tall, slim, mediaeval towers. Smaller and surely cheaper than Florence, it would be a good place to settle in for a while, and try to write. Why didn't I do that? Eileen coaxed hopefully. So while Seán lay drowsing on a bench with his hat over his face, she and I agreed that, if I stayed in Italy, they would come back in the autumn.

Then I drove them to the station where no sooner had their train pulled out than I began to miss them. Now that we had no reason to quarrel, we enjoyed each other's company, though I was already having doubts about staying in San Gimignano. How could I forget the woman in Forster's *Where Angels Fear to Tread* who is so charmed by a small Italian town that, unable to imagine its winter dullness, loneliness and underlying misogyny, she marries a local dentist? As one enticement quickens another, she walks straight into the trap laid by the narrative. Best, mindful of that warning, to stay somewhere at least as big as Florence.

What I needed, if I was to do that for any length of time, was to find someone who could point me in the direction of cheap *pensioni*, *tavole calde* and the like. So I headed for the National Library where I asked an American girl for advice. With some pique, she asked how I had known she was an American and, when told she looked like one, pointed out that everything she was wearing had been bought here. I tried to soothe her, learned some useful addresses and left to follow them up.

Clearly we were not going to be friends.

Americans in those years did stand out, but it is hard to say how. The words 'open-faced' and 'bland' come to mind. Globalisation was unheard of and national characteristics pronounced. French faces were often intensely focused, and American mens' shorts gaudy, while English ones tended to be army surplus and bell out like lamp shades; Italian men wore tight suits . . . I regretted annoying the American girl.

Next day was my twenty-fifth birthday when, according to

an old French saying, girls *coiffent Sainte Catherine*, i.e. become spinsters. Thinking about this, I realised that, though I no longer missed Jean-Paul, I did miss Paris and Rome. Both are enlivening and protean, and my learning their languages was no accident. France in the old songs was Ireland's friend, and I had been ready to love it. I think, too, that I am drawn to cities which developed a complexity which our bit of the Roman Catholic empire failed signally to achieve. It is satisfying, when you have only known fragments, to encounter the realised model, though liking a Catholic metropolis can have less to do with belief than with codes and jokes which belong to an *anti*-Catholic backlash. When I visited Latin America in 1980, it was the satirical talk which made me feel at home.

Yet the man whom I was now about to meet would take me to a place with which I feel little affinity. Notoriously the US West Coast has its own beauty, but for my taste it is too spread out, lacks shadow, and is insufficiently urban; its oral skills are poor and I would never have gone there but for Lauro.

So back to my birthday.

Having dined alone, I walked out into the summery, noisy June evening and there he was, a lean, dark-eyed young man, wearing a seersucker jacket which marked him out as an American, sitting in an outside café in a group which included Anna Maria, the girl I had annoyed the day before and was now – though I didn't realise this – annoying even more. She and I greeted each other, which enabled the men to invite me to join them and within minutes, when the other man said he was the librarian at the Villa I Tatti, which Bernard Berenson had bequeathed to Harvard, one or other of us mentioned Ford Madox Ford's *The Good Soldier*, and soon we were all bickering about books – as

Lauro and I still do. He is a historian and was then writing his doctoral thesis for Harvard, but he had also been to the Kenyon School of English, where he had worked under Kenneth Burke and William Empson, and had an approach to reading a text which impressed me. I had not majored in English, and at home there had been an anti-academic bias, a romantic approval of the writer as 'inspired idiot', even a notion that the brain hobbles the imagination. Some of this may be traced to the cult of 'the people' and some to my father's reaction against the dry discipline of his own time at Harvard. There is truth in it, too – at least there is for me, but it is a small, limited one. I enjoy research but find that it can shrivel my ability to invent. This belongs to a part of the mind that takes over when the critical part closes down. Then, in a sort of dream, it gets to work on the raw material – facts – that have been left for it like offerings to a capricious daemon. Later, the dreamer's work is checked by the monitor. You need both, and it was Lauro who taught me to use the second.

We met for lunch the next day, shared more meals and some days later – Lauro did not go in for climbing lamp posts – went to the station and tried to buy tickets for the next train.

'To where?' asked the ticket-seller.

'Anywhere. We want to leave on the next train.'

This turned out to be bound for Arezzo, so that was where we went. In those years Piero della Francesca's *Pregnant Madonna* was housed in a small free-standing chapel in the open countryside, so we visited and became particularly fond of this painting which, like all this painter's work, has a thrillingly luminous tranquillity. We were to revisit it often.

Back in Florence, we moved into a flat on the Lungarno Vespucci and five months later were married in the local parish church. I was no longer a Catholic, and Lauro had never been one, though, by luck, he had been baptised in a Catholic church. I say 'luck' because now, in one of those appeals which blend cynicism with piety, Seán begged me to get married in the Catholic church.

'What difference can it make to you?' he pleaded. 'It will mean a lot to your mother and me.' I knew the argument. Ireland was run on its dodgy track. It reconciled the irreconcilable, shirked change and must have darkened many minds, but in the land of 'great hatred, little room' was a necessary tribute to tribalism. I tried it on Lauro. 'What', I challenged, 'can it matter to you?'

He conceded the point but, with American candour, warned, 'I won't lie to that priest. I'll let him know that I don't believe in God.' This baffled Monsignor Marani. Why, he plainly wondered, would an unbeliever *want* to marry in his church? Might I, he worried, be an heiress and Lauro a fortune-hunter? While he dragged out the paperwork, our landlady told us that his wariness was due to his having been duped in the past by a couple who, since the Italian state did not yet allow divorce, had chosen to marry in the Catholic church as it has always been prepared to annul a marriage if either spouse can prove to have contracted it with 'a mental reservation'. Proof that, in this case, the bride had done this was established when she was found to have written in shorthand next to her signature, 'This is all balls.'

'*Palle!* Excuse the expression!' Our landlady's lips twitched in amusement. 'It's what she wrote.'

'In shorthand?'

She quenched a smile. 'The monsignor couldn't read it.'

His worries about us may have festered when no relatives attended our wedding. Lauro's were in the US, and I had fallen out with mine. This happened when enquiries about Lauro, which Seán had made through Harvard friends, stirred up gossip and revived a small scandal.

A year earlier Lauro had had a fling with an undergraduate

called Nina who, when checking out of her Radcliffe dormitory to spend two nights with him, mistakenly specified that she would be away for one. When she overran her exeat, the authorities fussed, made indiscreet phone calls and then expelled her, as they had the power to do. They had none over him, who was a PhD student living off-campus. However, the difference in the way the two were treated looked unfair, and the Dean of Students, McGeorge Bundy (later US National Security Adviser to Presidents Kennedy and Johnson), had Lauro on the carpet, and told him that, if it had been up to him, he would have clawed back the Sheldon Travelling Fellowship which Lauro had won and which was to take him to Florence.

What may have given this tittle-tattle legs was the fact that Nina's father was Leo Castelli, a New York art dealer who would be described in a subsequent biography as having 'revolutionized the status of the artist in America and changed the rules of the art market'. He and her mother, who would later become a still more successful gallerist, pleaded with the Radcliffe authorities, reminding them that, though Nina was a prize-winning student, being kicked out of Radcliffe could prevent her from getting into another élite college. And indeed, this happened, and she had to settle in the end for New York University. New England Puritanism was making a late, last stand.

All this, condensed in the misleading phrase 'he got a girl into trouble', was hyped by Harvard professors with a verve which village gossips could not have bettered.

Seán, who even before meeting Lauro had been seeking grounds to discourage our marriage, now had them. Why, he challenged me, were we rushing it? The answer was that I was doing so because of him, who, I suspected (rightly as it would later turn out), had asked his Harvard contact to find an obstacle that would justify his and Eileen's opposing it.

A maxim she liked to air gives a key to this. It runs, 'Your son is your son till he marries, but your daughter is your daughter for life.' I have since heard Englishwomen complain of the burden put on them by such expectations, but in Ireland, from which daughters had been emigrating since the Famine, these were often foiled. I once visited an Irish retirement home where a tearful widow beckoned me over and told me that I reminded her of her daughter in Australia. Other residents took up the lament. Their daughters, too, were far away, and one of Seán's letters, written that year to a Harvard friend, comically cursing 'the entire American nation for stealing my daughter', echoed an ancient dirge. He could, he added, make his peace with the marriage if Lauro found work in New England, but feared we would both go mad if we ended up in the Middle West.

His concern, this implied, was not only for me but also for Lauro, with whom he now began to exchange letters.

'I find', he wrote in his second one (the first had been tougher), 'that despite my concern for Julie which remains well based considering the harsh sort of impressions (just or unjust) that you can evoke in and about Harvard, I can also find room for much sympathy for you.'

This letter, which I still have, is typed, but the word 'much' has been inserted by hand. A puzzled afterthought? Did he mean it? If so, he may have been wondering on which side of the fence he now stood. With defiant youth as he had in the past? Or not? The excerpt quoted concedes that he may have been casting too cold an eye.

AN AMERICAN IN FLORENCE

Lauro and I, meanwhile, were heading for Edward Albee territory, just four years before *Who's Afraid of Virginia Woolf* was first put on.

Like that play's setting, Reed College in Oregon was animated by brainy drunks, some of them as articulate as his leading characters. It was a pastoral playground for the clever young, staffed for the most part by ageing intellectuals who had somehow got stuck in a place which, though stimulating for students, was less so for them. Consequently they drank. And when accepting their hospitality, so did we. Dinner was often served a good hour or two after the one for which guests had been invited so as to allow time to have several stiff Martinis. Reed was reputed to be Red at a time – we reached it in 1958 – when a hangover from McCarthyism still poisoned the air, and the local town, Portland, ostracised Reed people. It was said that the children of successive central committees of the USCP had been educated there, but I can't vouch for this, for when I, riding Lauro's coat-tails, got a job there teaching French, the students struck me as unlikely to be politically active. They were polite, self-absorbed pre-hippies from places like Boston and New York, devoted to free love, bare feet and a tolerance which could have put Radcliffe to shame. Reed's one drawback was that, as Seán and Eileen must have seen with dismay on the map, it was a long way from Europe. We stayed for four years – just as the students did.

I guessed from their style and ease that most of them were more emancipated than I had been at their age. But then, at that age I had just emerged from a convent school, where we had

had to wear grim, grey gymslips with matching stockings and bloomers, whereas Reed girls didn't even have to wear shoes. This distinguished them – perhaps deliberately? – from the local teenagers who flaunted lipstick and large plastic hair curlers at Portland bus stops. Perhaps Anna Maria, the girl I had annoyed in Florence, had feared I might think she looked like these girls. US snobbery, I learned, was, if anything, touchier than ours.

Thinking of Florence reminded me that of the five guests at our modest wedding reception there, three had been damaged by their elders. Of these, the one least likely to recover fast was probably Yvonne. A Cambridge (UK) graduate now working as a governess in a Florentine marchese's family, she had been seduced by the marchese. Convinced at first that the sheer banality of her plight would protect her, she had found that even a playful replay of *Jane Eyre* could generate hurt. When we met the marchese, we saw she was right, for his talk of seeking a Mexican divorce from his wife was clearly an outing from reality. He enjoyed raising Yvonne's hopes and liked showing off his English, but would not, we guessed, rock his domestic boat for her sake. Though a lot older than she, his sexual antics must have been vigorous, for once, leaping over her in bed, he almost broke her neck.

Both of our male guests were called Roberto and the one we called Roberto V was at odds with himself. He is the man I mentioned earlier who at the end of the war was beaten up by Reds because his father had died fighting in Mussolini's army. Oddly, this led to his becoming an ardent Red himself, who sang lefty songs and strummed his guitar with what struck people who knew his story as displaced rage.

The other Roberto too had troubles stemming from the past. He was a general's son which, he assured us, was a hard thing for an Italian to be. He claimed to have been repeatedly tormented by envious bullies, but never told us why. Had the now-dead general been a Fascist or a post-war democrat? We didn't ask and Roberto didn't say.

His sisters came to tea with us once, but refused to drink any. He explained later that they never used a lavatory outside their own home, so were fearful of ingesting liquids. I began to see why the bullies had felt irked.

Another man we met in Florence was a Harvard friend of Lauro's who would later become a psychoanalyst and may already have been practising. He told me that what I should know about Lauro was that, though prone to losing his temper, he was always sorry at once.

I remembered this when we began having culture clashes over beggars. These started when we were still in the flat on Lungarno Vespucci, near the Grand Hotel, a smart area where beggars would count on getting generous alms. This meant that I, who had promised to help stretch our funds to keep us in Florence for another year, felt two-way guilt when giving stingily to the needy who knocked on our door. Lauro, who spent his days doing research in the State Archives, at first knew nothing about them.

Back in Ireland beggars had had an acknowledged foothold in society. They brought entertainment to bored households and for years Eileen had regulars to whom she would sometimes give a meal, some cast-off clothes and a few coins. I particularly remember a man from Ballinasloe, where she had taught school for a while, who used to amuse her with tales of figures from its past. The glitziest of these was Belle Bilton, who was remembered in that bleak, boggy region long after her death. A popular English music-hall singer, she had so bewitched aristocratic young bloods that members of a group of these were said to have tossed a coin for her.

'What I heard,' Eileen liked to recall, 'was that the Earl of Clancarty won her at cards, then took her to Galway.'

'No, ma'am!'The man from Ballinasloe sometimes corrected. 'It was on the toss of a coin. He was Viscount Dunlo then and only became earl when his da died.'

'They say the da opposed the marriage?'

'He did indeed, which is why it took place in secret and why he tried to get it declared void due to the boy being a minor. When this failed he stopped his allowance and sent him to Australia. That left Bilton without a penny and obliged to take up with an old admirer.'

'Falling into the wicked earl's trap?' Eileen could be all for young love.

'True for you, ma'am!' The beggar tended at this point to pause and chew a mouthful of Irish stew then, sustained by this, take up his story. 'When news of the admirer reached Australia, Dunlo started proceedings against her for adultery and set off for London, but no sooner did he get there than the pair were reconciled. She could twist him round her finger.'

'The old earl must have been beside himself!'

Thoughtfully, the beggar would now wipe bread around his plate. 'The queer thing was that he dropped dead the next year. That roused talk. But once Bilton was Countess of Clancarty it died down.'

'Was it true she had no talent?'

'Divil a bit!' Cheered by the thought, the Ballinasloe man laughed. His name – it comes back to me – was Fleming. He must have been descended from a soldier brought to Ireland by the Williamite wars.

✄

Bilton's story used to thrill me but, knowing I couldn't pass the thrill on to Lauro, I didn't try.

Then one day he came home early with a headache. I was out, so he fell asleep, but was woken by someone ringing our door bell so persistently that, on seeing that the man outside was a beggar, he flew into a rage which was still on the boil when I got back. The beggar, according to him, had said, 'I won't deal with you. I want to talk to the signora.' Lauro asked how much I used to give, and, when I wouldn't say, we had our first major row, which was followed, over the years, by others.

I don't remember any at Reed, but later in Los Angeles, when I found what seemed to be a dying man on our lawn, the only thing that stopped me hauling him up our steps and into the house was his weight. Hoping for help, I rang Lauro in his UCLA office, only to be told that sane people did not bring strangers into the house. Next I appealed to our neighbours who agreed with him. Then I rang a helpline, only to learn that the only help on offer was from the police who would lock the man up. I was protesting at this heartlessness, when a glance out at the lawn revealed that the dying man was gone. No doubt seeing me telephone had led his thoughts to the police, too.

My credibility shrank on the spot and vanished for good when we moved to London, where a man who claimed to be collecting for cancer research proved to be a fraud. I had reached the front door ahead of Lauro and by the time he joined me had handed over two twenty-pound notes in memory of a friend who had died of cancer. The self-styled charity worker had a collecting box and badge showing his ID, but Lauro rang the research charity anyway, which confirmed his doubts. The man, it turned out, *had* worked for them – hence the ID – then been fired for larceny and now, with the ease of the Artful Dodger, had slipped from sight.

I saw no logic to this. Lauro *should* have been wrong, so I refused to believe that his rightness proved anything other than the world's meanness. He couldn't explain how he had come to distrust the man – or rather he could, but only by saying that I attracted con men and imposters who could *smell* my gullibility. This, need I say, prolonged our row when I observed that I had, not so long ago, attracted *him*.

In other ways, Lauro was more prone to melt than I. Not only did he weep in cinemas, but the very touch of 500-year-old documents in the Florentine State Archives set him agog with pleasure. Learning to decipher their Latin and Italian abbreviations did, too, and this was partly why his thesis was taking so much time, despite his often working on it until 3 a.m. His Harvard professor – the man whose reported gossip had upset my parents – had been little help, having known nothing about the archives until Lauro himself, who learned of them from a student of Theodor Mommsen's at Princeton, submitted his project. There was, though, a stimulating peer group of young researchers who revelled in their work and, when in Florence, often got together for after-dinner drinks to share their excitement. A favoured venue for these sessions was the flat of an English scholar who had married the daughter of a *fattore* employed by one of the great Tuscan estates. Sometimes she took us down to her father's wine cellar, whose rows of shelved bottles were like another archive. Some of these were venerable, in wine terms, so could turn out to be either delicious or disappointingly past their prime. For the researchers the city, too, was like an archive, since what most of its street names commemorated was itself: a proud, tight, in-turned, provincial world, which in spite of its architecture and past eminence reminded me of Dublin. Both places were self-absorbed, obsessed by memory, treasured small scandals, retold puns and gave the impression, when I first knew them, of disproving the dictum that one cannot step into the same river twice.

Yet changes did take place. On our first return visit to Florence we spent a week in Elba where, lying in a vineyard on a warm evening, we saw Sputnik orbit high above us, winking its prophetic way, like the star of Bethlehem, across a cloudless lapis-blue sky.

Not only was it exciting to watch and wonder at, it would, at surprising speed, affect our lives when US authorities, shaken by the Soviet success, started to realise that academics, hitherto regarded as near-useless citizens, not to say arty-farty frills on the body of a serious, commercial society, could on the contrary affect the space race and the Cold War. Scientists' salaries were promptly raised, and some trickle-down reached the humanities too. As a result we, who had two salaries during our Reed years, were able to pay off debts contracted during our year together in Florence and even to save. Things became easier still when in our second year at Reed we moved to a house on campus. It was airy and roomy, surrounded by trees and, once I had painted its inside walls and hung home-made, pin-striped roller blinds on its windows, struck me as charming. Others were less impressed. Kick Erlanger, a rich New York friend of Seán's and Eileen's, flew out to see us and, judging by a subsequent letter from Seán praising our 'fortitude', was taken aback by what she saw. But then Kick's standards were high, as she owned two mansions, one in East 64th Street, New York, and the other in New Jersey.

Months later, when our son, who had been born prematurely weighing less than three pounds, was big enough to come out of his incubator, Eileen also visited. By then the place must have looked better, for she showed no signs of shock. But then in the Twenties she and Seán had probably been no better off in Cambridge, Massachusetts. And meanwhile, gifts had come from Kick: electric cooking appliances, a Balenciaga coat for me, a nappy-laundry service for three months, a baby-carrier and several dresses from Bergdorf Goodman.

This mix of grandeur and thrift seemed amusingly bohemian. Geoffrey Taylor, when poetry editor of *The Bell*, had, I now remembered, lived in a house full of furniture made from tea chests and butter boxes. I, who must have been about nine when I was first taken to visit it, had been thrilled to see adults playing house and now had my chance to follow their example. Furniture from charity shops was easier to recycle than butter boxes and when re-upholstered looked, I considered, rather well. We had brought a dozen antique champagne glasses and two baroque porcelain candelabra from Florence, and Eileen arrived with a gift of Staffordshire pottery from her friend Norah McGuinness, which both soothed our nostalgia for Europe and added style.

Meanwhile letters brought news of friends. Among them came a copy of the first number of a magazine called *Nonplus* from Patricia Murphy, who had founded and funded it and enclosed a covering note reporting – tartly – that Patrick Kavanagh had taken up with Katherine Moloney 'because he wanted a nurse'. What Patricia herself had wanted was a poet. Accordingly, when she came to the end of her affair with Philip Larkin, she had married Richard Murphy, with whom she had been living when I last visited them in a revamped Lake Park which he had turned into a setting fit for poets by adding such features as a Yeatsian flight of seven granite steps.

The lake itself, though, struck me as gloomy. Wicklow water is often filtered through turf, and though bright as honey on your skin when you are swimming in it, can look, from afar, as dark and restive as a flock of starlings. Perhaps because of this, the two had now divorced and Patricia was living in Dublin near the Grand Canal.

The copy of *Nonplus* contained three prose essays by Patrick Kavanagh and seven poems – a contribution seen by his biographer as 'extraordinarily generous'. My own sense was that the generosity was Patricia's, who clearly felt an urge to protect Kavanagh. Many Dubliners had succumbed to that impulse, including my father, John Betjeman when he lived in Dublin, and, more surprisingly, the tyrannical Archbishop McQuaid.

His soft spot for Kavanagh was the first benign thing I ever heard about him, and the explanation which springs to mind is a second. For Kavanagh was unworldly, though perhaps less from choice than because the world was too much for him. His view of it could be caustic. Take the lines:

> To be a poet and not know the trade,
> To be a lover and repel all women,
> Twin ironies by which great saints are made,
> The agonizing pincer-jaws of heaven.

He did not himself repel women. On the contrary, verse like that is guaranteed to attract them, and there were reports of women who circled around him. But the hyperbole has a drum-beat which echoes the Metaphysical poets and some vernacular hymns – and may well have appealed to John Charles McQuaid. I suspect it might have pleased Seán, too, for he sometimes quoted early Gaelic poetry whose monosyllabic metre thumped out an even more insistently spasmodic rhythm.

The unlikely connection between poet and bishop was watched with interest by neighbours who exchanged stories about 'the Arch' arriving in his chauffeur-driven car to call on Kavanagh who, not wanting his patron to see the squalor in which he lived, allegedly piling up empty sardine-tins and used tea leaves in his bath tub, once sent down word that he couldn't receive him because he had a woman in his flat. The Arch, to his credit, is said to have smiled and remarked that the woman, if there was one, was no doubt a saintly do-gooder. And indeed Katherine Moloney, the same one who used to sing about her martyred uncle in cafés on the Île Saint Louis, seems to have done Kavanagh good, for in 1966 the two married. Before that, though, Patricia too extended largesse when he arrived in the small hours at her door in Wilton Terrace, drenched and shivering after either falling into the canal or – his version – being pushed. Patricia, a qualified doctor, knew how to help and did. She bought him a tweed outfit the next day, too, and now that she was his near neighbour often had him in for a drink. Judging by what we know of her relations with Larkin, she relished challenge when dealing with poets, whether lovers or protégés. And indeed, Desmond Williams, her last companion, was both brilliant and badly disabled. I saw her once feed him his dinner with a spoon, as you might feed a child.

Maybe Kavanagh also welcomed disability. Here is a scrap of his verse which I learned in my pious childhood when he used to visit Knockaderry on Sunday afternoons. While my mother made tea, he and I would show each other our poems:

> We have tested and tasted too much, lover.
> Through a chink too wide there comes in no wonder.
> But here in the Advent-darkened room
> Where the dry black bread and the sugarless tea
> Of penance will charm back the luxury
> Of a child's soul, we'll return to Doom
> The knowledge we stole but could not use.
>
> We have thrown into the dust-bin the clay-minted wages
> Of pleasure, knowledge and the conscious hour –

I don't remember having learned or even read the last two lines. Perhaps, when I was a child, they meant nothing to me. But 'clay-minted' has the ur-Kavanagh ring. In his verse, earth and 'the stony grey soil of Monaghan' are out to destroy him. His hell substitutes fire with clay.

I have a notion that he may have courted my mother, not only because of those afternoons when he walked the ten or twelve miles from the city to Killiney just for a cup of tea, but because of five neatly handwritten poems which I turned up when going through the papers left in Rosmeen Park, the cul-de-sac where Seán and she lived at the end. One is dedicated 'To Eileen O'Faolain'. Here are a few lines:

> There was no miracle of sky or earth
> The dream-witch high astraddle on her broom
> Vanished – and we had only slave mirth
> To cheat the Master of the Hags of Doom.
> Without the gate were we, talking of all
> The love green meadows lying somewhere south
> Where the black-faced Frustrator cannot thrall
> Pure souls. Or break the word in Passion's mouth.
>
> Two children in a desert place were we
> Remembering there was once a fruited tree.

Neat and copperplate though the writing is, I may have misread some of it. 'Hags' for instance could be 'Hogs'. But the motifs are familiar. Is the broom phallic though? If so, Eileen might have failed to guess this.

The two events which marked our time at Reed were the birth of our son, Lucien, and the publication of Lauro's first book, *The Social World of the Florentine Humanists*, which, thanks to his archival work, was able to relate the thinking of fifteenth-century Florentine intellectuals to their economic and political circumstances. The book went to press in 1962 and thanks to it – and perhaps to Sputnik – he got a grant to go back to Florence, and later more grants, so we were able to stay there for four supremely happy years while he worked on a second book and I did some translating from Italian, taught in the Scuola Interpreti and began to write short stories. As I write this, it is 2011 and *The Social World* is about to be reissued by the University of Toronto Press. Seán, Lauro reminds me, was both reassured and surprised when, on a trip to the US, he ran into a historian who told him what a good book it was. He had nourished divided feelings about Lauro and reproached himself for this.

The Florence we now came to know was livelier than the one we had known before. For one thing, thanks to the Italian 'economic miracle' of those years, people had more money and, for another, Lauro was now a fellow at I Tatti, so at its lunches and other junketings we met Florentine figures such as Berenson's old friend and lover, Nicky Mariano, and her sister 'the baronessa', who invited us several times to her house in Vallombrosa. From time to time Harold Acton invited us, too, and so did Count Neri Capponi, who was an advocate at the Sacra Rota and a professor of Canon Law. He and his wife, Flavia, had links with Ireland, she because she had spent time there when her father was ambassador and had, to judge by Edward McGuire, left teasing memories of her young self with a generation of wistful young men. Neri's connection was earthier, in being through his nanny who, he told us, had taught him how to say *póg mo thón* which is Gaelic for 'kiss my ass'. Like the Capponi, other old Florentine names – Ricasoli, Corsini, Strozzi, Ruccellai, Gondi, Guicciardini, Antinori and the like – still belonged to the owners of the matching palazzi. We didn't meet them all, but those we did were friendly and so were the owners of villas in the hills.

To make a small, token return for their hospitality, we decided to give a drinks party. The flat we were renting on the via San

Niccolò didn't lend itself to dinner parties. It had a spacious reception room, a large, airy bedroom, and a large terrace canopied in wisteria season with mauve blossoms; but its kitchen was one floor up, at the top of a steep and narrow stairway down which anyone carrying trays of food could slither and fall. Cautiously, therefore, we stuck to drinks and invited everyone we knew. This proved to be a major gaffe, since it was now the Sixties. Academic friends tended to be left-wingers and the aristocrats wouldn't talk to them. When, ignoring my invitations to mingle, the party split into two hostile phalanxes, a guest took me aside to explain why. He was Count Giovanni Buoninsegni Tadini who had driven up from his villa near Lucca.

'Julia,' he scolded, 'you have invited us with Communists and people who plan to destroy us. You can't expect us to socialise with them. It's different for you. You're foreign. But they want our property.'

Viewed from the British Isles, such Cold War terrors had rarely seemed real, so Tadini was almost the first person I met who took them seriously. Besides this, Communists in France and Italy had been arguing for so long that they must 'wait for the right moment' before trying to get into government that few now thought this would ever happen.

Next time we met, Tadini spoke more freely about his dislike of the Left. It was not entirely based on fear. There was also distaste. Florentines, he told us, fell into five groups, only some of which could be mixed. There were aristocrats like himself. Then there were the rich foreigners who lived in villas like Acton's La Pietra, Violet Trefusis's Villa dell'Ombrellino, and I Tatti in Berenson's day. Both groups were his friends. Even foreign academics like Lauro were acceptable, because, unlike Italian ones, they knew how to handle a knife and fork. But Italian professors – 'mostly Reds anyway' – were out, and so were prefects, mayors and so forth, who weren't too good with knives and forks either. The fifth category were the demonic Communists, a few of whom, like the aristocratic, but also Communist, film director Visconti, were class-traitors to boot.

Tadini was the man I mentioned earlier, who liked to contend that the US army had taught Italian workers to wash more hygienically than people like himself, whose now outdated sanitary know-how came from English nannies. He was self-mocking, entertaining and could have written a lively guide to his own world. Mindful, however, of Poldy Loewenstein's father's riposte when the young Poldy wanted to become a doctor – 'we do not become, we *are*!' – I did not encourage Tadini to take up the pen.

He was right about cutlery, though. As another Italian friend remarked when rummaging in a London street market for long narrow spoons with which to serve osso buco, a supremely Italian dish, England was the place to find them, because it was deeply middle-class, and that class had invented table manners. Sure enough, the osso buco spoons turned up in London. Meanwhile Tadini's view of Florentine manners was bolstered by a scene I glimpsed in a trattoria where a man whom the waiter had addressed as *professore* was instructing his children about that topic. Manners, he told them, were essential, and, to endorse the point, waved his knife in the air.

Left-wingers had their own snobberies. The Communists who ate regularly in a trattoria on a corner of the piazza della Signoria – a party-member owned it – were neater and cleaner than many aristocrats. Indeed, in their white shirts and perfectly ironed summer suits, they had an evangelical look, were exceedingly proper and called each others' wives *signora*. They were easily shocked. Once Lauro and I went out to dinner with a couple of them and had a marital squabble in which I used a four-letter word. The wife didn't know English, and the husband was so fascinated by my impropriety that he couldn't wait to tell her about it. Here was scandal. Here was bourgeois decadence. 'What the Signora just said,' he told her excitedly, 'is VERY strong! *Molto, MOLTO forte!*' His mouth trembled as though the wicked word were threatening to jump from it. Perhaps he wanted to use an Italian equivalent, but shrank from letting us know that she, too, knew it. I imagined him saying it when they were alone. Perhaps he would use several words to vent his pique at having had to wait. Which? *Fottere? Fica? Chiavare? Inculare?* Which did he pick? I didn't like to ask.

Sometimes I was shocked as well. One evening Lauro and I went to hear the thrilling film director, Francesco Rosi, give a talk at the Circolo di Cultura, where he complained that the Neapolitan crowd, which he had recently used in his movie *Hands Over the City*, had been filmed so often that its members had lost all authenticity and now cartooned themselves. Self-cartooning was understandable, but his next comment surprised us. 'That lot,' he sneered, 'are the lumpen!' This contempt for what I had been brought up to think of as 'the people' confirmed rumours of left-wing big shots privately despising the masses. I had not expected this from Rosi. So when he went on to make some of the most darkly prophetic political films of the Sixties and Seventies, my memory of his dismissing fellow-Neapolitans as social scum – 'lumpen' – would add to the films' unsettling impact. What was striking about them was that, though they often took the form of investigations, they refrained from answering the queries raised. Their narratives, several based on novels by the scintillating Leonardo Sciascia, mirrored an Italian reality which had begun to throb with indignation at the deceits which many people sensed, but for which fiction could only with difficulty provide coherent solutions. Anarchy was soon to usher in what would come to be called 'the years of lead'.

Those would be seriously frightening, for the word 'lead' stood for bullets and random killings, as impatience with the PCI's reluctance to take power led to its being outflanked by smaller, more trigger-happy groups.

Back in the mid-Sixties, though, at Harold Acton's table, for instance, polemics were still as light-hearted as ping-pong games. Harold enjoyed teasing people whom he suspected of disagreeing with him, and didn't mind saying why. The dimming of his popularity as a writer rankled. Criteria had shifted while he was absent from England and he seemed puzzled by this. Fine writing, he complained, was now despised. The definition had become a reproach. Why? Political correctness puzzled him, too. Blacks, he stated once, had only just come down from the trees. Or did he call them 'niggers'? Quite possibly. He lived in a congealed expat world which was more courteous, but could also be rougher, than the one which had replaced it. He was a generous host, but Florence – in this, again, like Dublin – was a prickly place.

His guests could be prickly too. At one of his lunches John Sparrow, then Warden of All Souls, took a shine to Lauro and, on hearing that he had been taught by and admired William Empson, began running the man down. He and Empson had attended the same school, Winchester, where, Sparrow sneered, Empson had been a scholarship boy with ringworm in his head. Turning next on me (I may have been looking chilly), he guessed that I admired Roger Casement, which I did. I may even have annoyed him by quoting Yeats's poem about 'that most gallant gentleman who is in quicklime laid'. The English had hanged Casement after he was caught trying to run guns from Germany in 1916. Well, said Sparrow, Casement's *Black Diaries*, which the Irish had claimed were British forgeries, were proving to be genuine and so exposed him as a homosexual. Since both Harold and Sparrow were also homosexual, it was hard to know how to respond. Maybe, with luck, the pudding arrived to distract us. If it was riz á l'impératrice, which was often served at Harold's, it would have appeared in what looked like a caramel-coloured glass bowl which, to the shock of first-time guests, a footman would shatter with a smart blow from his spoon. This was a trick, for the bowl was not glass at all but made of caramel, slivers of which would now be served with the rice to sweeten our tempers.

Just below Fiesole, on the brow of its hill, was another elegant villa. The Albergo Villa San Michele was an ex-monastery which its French owner, Lucien Teissier, had furnished with fifteenth-century antiques and turned into the smartest hotel in Florence. His wife, Maura, was an old UCD mate of mine, so Lauro and I enjoyed the privilege of joining their lively group of polyglot friends. Maura, who had modelled for Balmain, was, and is, a tall, rangy beauty, and so were some of her fellow mannequins whom she sometimes invited to stay. Lucien, who adored the Tuscan countryside, often organised drives through it to places like Pienza (named after its founder, Pope Pius II) and Montepulciano, two elegant hilltop towns whose architecture we would admire before enjoying a lunch enlivened by generous amounts of the excellent local *vino nobile di Montepulciano*.

On another Florentine hill, in the Villa dell'Ombrellino, lived Violet Trefusis, daughter of Edward VII's mistress, Mrs Keppel, who was herself to achieve notoriety when Vita Sackville West's son, Nigel Nicolson, published his account of her ardent lesbian affair with his mother. From delicacy he waited to do this until Violet had died, so what we knew of her at first came mostly from herself. She was an entertaining narcissist. Once, on arriving for dinner, we were led by her friend John Phillips to a viewing spot at one end of an enfilade of rooms at the other end of which stood Violet, whose copious grey curls had been arranged to resemble an early Hanoverian monarch's wig. When we reached her, she instructed John to take Lauro aside 'to tell him who I am'. The two duly left the room and returned minutes later to let her know that Lauro had been enlightened as to her royal blood. This, of course, had long since been checked out by those Florentines who took an interest in such matters, and declared non-existent. The dates didn't fit, so she was not the king's daughter. But play-acting amused her, perhaps more than a serious claim might have done. It kept people talking.

One New Year's Eve she threw a black-tie dinner party whose guests, when one of them fell ill, threatened to number thirteen. She asked Maura to lend her one of her own house guests to deflect bad luck, which Maura kindly did. But throughout the day, as Violet's guests kept phoning to report mishaps of one sort or another, number thirteen continued to loom, so the borrowed guest – an amiable Irishman called Billy – had to be put off, then re-invited, then disinvited again. At the very last minute, Lauro and I were asked to drop round to Villa San Michele to collect and drive him to Violet's, whose fear of what the penny catechism used to call 'charms, omens and dreams' must have been acute. This fear, as fear can, may have magnetised trouble, for early in the meal, she collapsed and, in my – unreliable? – memory, fell face first into her hors d'oeuvre. Her guests had to leave, and we were lucky to find a trattoria where we and Billy could see the old year out.

Violet, though, continued to entertain. Company revived her who, at times, could be conviviality itself, as she recycled anecdotes which didn't spare the dead. A favourite one recorded a triumph over Berenson, whom she suspected of having tried to poach her titled guests.

'I let him know,' she told us, 'that if he wanted to invite them, there was no need to send his butler to meet their train to try to lure them away. *I* could give him their names. Then *he* could invite them – and it would be "tit for I Tatti".'

Even at the end there were triumphs. On a happier New Year's Eve she had a house party whose guests' names rang like those of characters in Proust. Among those I remember were the Duc and Duchesse d'Harcourt, the Comte de Ségur, a couple called Sheremetyevo who explained that they had not been called after Moscow Airport. No. On the contrary, *it* had been called after land which the husband's family had owned. These guests impressed, not just by their pedigrees, but by their dramatic haute couture clothes. Being in a room with them felt like being a sparrow among humming birds. The Duchesse d'Harcourt, who was young, Spanish and a beauty, was particularly glamorous. So Violet was in her glory. She might be in her seventies and wobbly, but she could still give house parties which dazzled Florence.

Parties at the Teissiers were livelier and more French, with guests like the novelist Roger Peyrefitte, the banker Michel François Poncet, assorted girlfriends and other clever Parisians. The villa owners invited each other's house guests, so now, remembering, I am unsure in which we were when I sat next to Philippe Jullian or James or John Pope-Hennessy or Emilio Pucci. Probably at Violet's. I Tatti guests were more apt to be academics, or else to have been invited with an eye to fund-raising. The villa needed endowments, and its successive Harvard directors had the US talent for attracting them. Harold Acton, who complained about the failure of English institutions to compete, may not have grasped the difficulties. He had wanted to leave La Pietra to Oxford, but, on learning that Oxford feared that it would not be able to find the money needed to keep it up, left it instead to New York University. Fund-raising in England is hampered both by a tax system which gives insufficient tax breaks to donors, and a habit of giving titles to the rich, which curbs any need they might otherwise feel to embellish their names by endowing art collections. When I was one of the directors of the Susan Blackburn Memorial Prize for women dramatists, which is offered both in the US and UK, our US colleagues found it far easier to raise money than we did in England.

In the palazzo where Lauro and I rented a flat for four years in the Sixties, everyone's business was known to everyone else. The owner, Marchese Stiozzi-Ridolfi, was said to be an unlucky gambler, which may have been why he needed to take in so many tenants. Besides ourselves, there was the porter's lodge, the Stiozzi-Ridolfi's own area, a family upstairs called Cini, and, at the very top, three generations of a working-class one consisting of a matriarch called Nonna Rosina ('Granny Rose'), her daughter, and several men whose relation to each other I never sorted out. Janet and Roger Rearick, the I Tatti fellows who had had our flat before us, warned us against having anything to do with Nonna Rosina's daughter, who was a thief. She had been their laundress until Roger saw her son in the street wearing one of his best shirts. She claimed she hadn't known, protested her innocence, swore that she'd kill the boy, and put on a dithyrambic scene which it amused Roger to mimic.

Meanwhile *our* son, Lucien, needed a babysitter, and Nonna Rosina set out to win his heart. She did this in the mornings while he waited for the car which would take him to kindergarten, and the *portiera* kept an eye on him while getting on with her chores. One of these consisted in killing chickens by catching their heads in a drawer, then slamming it shut.

Lucien might conceivably have taken the chicken-killing in his stride, if Nonna Rosina hadn't seized the chance to cuddle and coddle him while scolding the *portiera* for doing such a thing in front of a sensitive child. Her concern flattered him. So before we knew it, a bond had been forged and she was his babysitter. Then two weeks later something of ours went missing, which left us feeling so unpleasantly vulnerable that we severed relations with the manipulative Nonna Rosina, who pleaded with us to reconsider. Lucien, now called Luciano, did, too, but we held firm. The *portiera*, perhaps in revenge for the scolding, told us about a respectable widow who lived close by and would love to look after a pretty child like him. Nonna Rosina raged at her, bad-mouthed the widow, and took to ambushing us in *cortile* and street to confront us again and again and argue her case. Neighbours laughed at this story, improved it in the retelling and teased Lucien whom they called *il dottorino* because he looked so comically like Lauro, who was known as *il dottore*.

The widow told us to call her Tata Rita, and the first correct – and passionate – Italian sentence I remember Lucien using was '*Non voglio andar da Tata Rita,*' meaning, 'I don't want to go to Tata Rita.' He repeated it for weeks. Then she too won him over – and he changed her way of life. She had been one of those black-clad widows who used to be seen all over Italy, whose mourning was so prolonged and deep that it isolated them from ordinary living. She hadn't been to a cinema since her husband died several years before, fearing lest people disapprove. Now, though, she had an excuse: Lucien. She could go into cafés with him, too, and for walks in the park, where strangers complimented her on her attractive charge. Unfortunately he was so frightened by the wicked queen in *Snow White* that he had to be carried out wailing. This dashed Tata Rita's hope of seeing how the film ended. Lucien also wanted to see this and begged for another chance, so we provided a second set of tickets, then a third, when the same thing happened again. But,as far as I can remember, neither he nor Tata Rita ever saw the end of the film. Instead she started taking him on a long – remorseful? – bus ride to the cemetery to put flowers on her husband's grave, and to Mass and various other church ceremonies. He loved these and to this day is drawn to the religion which both Seán and I had managed to escape.

I wondered if he had inherited my childhood addiction to terror.

1966, the year we left Florence, was the Year of the Flood. It came just months after our departure, and when we returned the next summer, mud marks on the walls showed how dangerously high the Arno, often a mere muddy trickle, had risen. Artisans, whose workshops were usually on street level, had suffered most, and museum artefacts were still being restored with the help of experts from a number of countries.

We, meanwhile, had spent the winter in Los Angeles, where Lauro was now a professor at the University of California (UCLA), and where Piero Bargellini, the mayor of Florence, came by to thank US donors whose money had helped repair flood damage. Remembering that his daughter-in-law and I had been colleagues at the Scuola Interpreti, he asked me to interpret his speech which, as he must have given it many times on his way to the West Coast, was by now highly polished. I still remember a wry Florentine joke which he told with panache. It described two artisans meeting in the street. One was holding a picture frame around his head, and the other asked why. 'Oh,' said the one with the frame, 'I'm pretending to be a ruined work of art. All the money goes to those. Live people, like you and me, don't get any.' This went down well with the LA audience, who, with any luck, coughed up some funds specifically for the artisans. Documents in Florence's State Archives had also suffered badly, due to having been stored underground and to the building's being just beside the river. But, as the archivists pointed out, the last time trouble threatened had been during the war, when it had been expected to come from aeroplanes.

Surprisingly the flood, despite all the damage caused, did a few good turns and one person who benefited was Tata Rita.

She, whose flat was above flood-level, had come into her own during the catastrophe. She had taken in needy neighbours and lodged and fed them and rejoiced in her own usefulness. Now, she told us, she had friends whom she might otherwise never have got to know. We hoped she had found some with whom to go to the pictures.

Ordinary Florentines were often more quick-witted and friendly than any of Tadini's five categories of citizens. The greengrocer near our palazzo was a jolly, gossipy woman who added free, well chosen herbs – *odori* – to season whatever you bought. Tata Rita and even Nonna Rosina were warm-hearted, and the most flattering tribute I ever received came from Ida, the maid we shared with the Stiozzi-Ridolfi, who gave a farewell dinner for us in her garden before we left. It was actually a banquet, for she joined several tables together, invited a throng of neighbours and cooked enough food for a village fête – good food, too, as Florentine food almost always is. I was delighted, for I had always enjoyed chatting to Ida, who had the same playful feel for Florentine turns of phrase that Eileen did for Hiberno-English.

Catherine and Marie de Medici, two Florentines who married into the royal house of France, are credited with having brought teams of cooks with them to Paris who taught the culinary arts to the French. This is sometimes disputed, but I find it persuasive for two reasons. One is that, to this day, regional and home cooking often seems better in Italy than in France. The other is the delight which Florentine housewives take in passing on their knowhow. In my first year in Florence my cooking standards, being still those of the Moo Cow Milk Bar, were so shamingly inadequate that I nerved myself to ask a fishmonger what to do with a slim, silvery fish on his counter which he told me was a *palombo*. Within seconds several of his customers had surrounded me and were asking practical questions – did I have an oven for instance? No? A hob then? Good. I could do a pot-roast. In no time, thanks to the clarity of their advice, I was able to go home and follow it with such ease that pot-roasted *palombo* with appropriate *odori* became my favourite stand-by. Only dictionaries let me down when I left Florence and learned that the English names were dogfish, mudfish or shark, all of which sound a lot less palatable than *palombo*.

Towards the end of our four years in Florence, Seán, Eileen and I took Lucien to be baptised in the city's ancient and lovely baptistery. Lauro, though not opposed to the ceremony, was, as usual, busy in the archives and did not attend. Lucien, who was now seven, showed himself, according to the officiating priest, to be *un bambino pieno di giudizio*, meaning, I suppose, a wise child, and, perhaps because of this, his affection for Catholicism still survives.

I forget whether it was J. B. Priestley or V. S. Pritchett who wrote that, to children, their parents' friends can look like comic monsters. The dispiriting thing is that it is when the adults' brains start to fail and they struggle to hide this that the comedy can turn monstrous – or, at best, depressing. Seán, in his last years, hoping to keep Lauro and me from being upset by his slip-ups, turned these into anecdotes. He had, one letter confessed, poured boiling water into a freshly filled tea-caddy instead of the teapot, and another admitted having astounded his barber by offering him sixpence for a haircut, which had not been the going rate for years. Then, when I was visiting him in a hospital not far from Dún Laoghaire, where he was having tests, he asked whether we should let Eileen know that he was in Ennis.

I marvelled. Ennis was the small, western town where he had got his first teaching job back in the Twenties, when the IRA Civil War fizzled out and he, like the rest of the defeated side, was scrabbling for any work he could get.

When I got back to Eileen that day, I reported thoughtlessly, 'He thinks he's in Ennis.'

She was horribly upset. Being used to taking her worries with a pinch of salt, I had failed to notice that she was now hiding them – especially Seán's gaffes, for which she provided cover when she could.

'Dan Binchy', she told me, 'wants you to phone him. Seán is too ashamed of his deafness to go to the phone when Dan rings. My excuses are sounding thin, and Dan is hurt.'

I had by then given up taking Seán to see ear specialists, who insisted that they could do nothing for him.

But when I phoned Binchy to say Seán was in hospital, I could tell he took this for a fib. 'He dodges me,' Binchy accused. 'If he does that with everyone, his mind will close down.'

The truth, Eileen guessed, was that Seán couldn't bear to be pitied by a clever old friend like Binchy, whereas people who meant less to him were welcome to drop in and chatter.

Both Seán and she were now showing their age. His chief symptom was an incipient mental decline, and hers was rheumatoid arthritis. When this became unbearable, she needed two wheelchairs, one upstairs and one below, and, to enable her to move between them, a lift shaped like a vertical coffin which had the look of a theatrical prop. This was not in Knockaderry, which they had reluctantly sold in the early Seventies after it had been burgled several times. They would, they had promised, stay on if there was any chance of my coming back to live there. But I said there was none, and persuaded them that they would be better off in a smaller, more manageable house close to doctors and shops. So they bought one, near both the sea and the centre of Dún Laoghaire, and put down a green carpet in their living room which, in certain lights, so exactly mimicked the grass outside, that the garden seemed to have crept indoors.

The first time I looked up to see Eileen descend, feet first, in her lift, I was shaken. Knowing that those feet were deformed by arthritis sharpened my distress, when I thought of the medals she had won for Irish dancing as a girl or remembered that I had not always been patient when she grew difficult, as invalids do. On our last trip to Italy, for instance, when we were booking into a hotel on a hot evening in Taranto, she had urged me to ensure that there would be no air-conditioning, as she couldn't stand draughts.

Missing the point, the receptionist replied with a smile that *of course* the hotel had excellent air-conditioning.

'Can it be turned off?'

'No, no,' the girl assured happily. 'It's centrally controlled.'

'Not even in my mother's room?' I pleaded. 'She has bad arthritis.'

But plainly the process functioned like the bag of winds in the *Odyssey* and could not be modified.

In the end Seán and I had to leave Eileen alone in the hotel lobby, cocooned in a shiver of shawls, while we trudged from one hotel to the next, proffering our troublesome request. As the hours passed, I wondered what people thought a couple like ours was doing looking for a room after midnight.

'Have you really got *no* room without air-conditioning?' I kept pleading, only to be told snootily that if there *had* been one, it would be no cheaper. That wasn't the point, I argued – then, on realising that to hotel employees it was the only point, I asked to be directed to somewhere sufficiently unimproved to use ceiling fans equipped with a switch or plug. This, when found, solved our problem.

The next year we went to Mouriès in Provence, a pretty village in the hills, and took rooms in a hotel there which suited us perfectly, being within driving distance of Aphonse Daudet's windmill, and Avignon and Arles, in whose Roman amphitheatre we guiltily watched a riveting bull fight. I don't remember the air-conditioning trouble recurring, but was mindful of it when, a year or so later, Kick Erlanger's daughter, Sally, generously offered us the loan of a villa she owned in Portugal.

Kick had died in 1969 and Seán, who clearly needed to talk about this, told me that for years he had secretly been her lover. I suppose I could have guessed, but hadn't let myself do so – as was perhaps the case, too, for Eileen. Indeed given that she favoured accepting the loan of the villa, maybe she never guessed at all. I, however, refused to join them on this jaunt – which, as they had come to rely on me to be their guide, translator and driver, scuppered it. I was sorry to disappoint them, but, remembering Taranto could all too easily imagine myself failing to cope in Portuguese with whatever hitches might arise. To my ears, Portuguese sounded intractable.

I fear that Eileen may have died holding this refusal against me. Seán, though, thought this unlikely.

She was, he reminded me, a lot tougher than she seemed. After all, her childhood, in her own accounts of it, sounded like Huckleberry Finn's. In one memory of when she must have been about seven, her brothers, who had stolen a pile of apples but had no way to carry them, had taken off her dress to use as a bag and made her walk home in her underwear. In another, they killed wood pigeons, covered them with clay, then baked and knocked this off so that the feathers came with it. Fictions? Perhaps. Eileen liked to enhance things. Her maiden name, Gould, for instance – in Irish *gall* rhyming with 'owl' – meant, she chose to think, 'Norse' or, better still, 'Viking'. Wild ways appealed to her, though it is fair to add that Seán, whose own childhood had been dull, agreed that hers had been eccentric. Her mother had died when she was three, leaving her to the care of her father, an ex-seaman who, in his youth, had gone round the world picking up foreign tastes. One of these was for snails which he fed on lettuce leaves, then purged and cooked himself.

Eileen, who adored him, may or may not have shared his culinary tastes, but sadly she did inherit his susceptibility to bad flares of arthritis, which led to them both being bedridden for long periods during their final years.

PORTLAND, OREGON

Watching friends wonder at my concern about Eileen, I suspected them of thinking me retarded. No doubt they themselves had snapped the umbilical chord faster than people did in my generation. Rather than react against our parents, we admired them for having fought both the English and the compromisers in the Civil War, whereas we, who had fought nobody, felt untested.

Memories of Oregon had led me to think the US dull, but Los Angeles in the Sixties proved different. Having rented a house in Venice, LA's equivalent of Haight-Ashbury, Lauro and I were soon living in a carnival where identities were shifty and the most ragged people you saw on the boardwalk were often the very rich, while the poor lived unimaginable lives.

My Mexican cleaner, Señora G, was one of these, and, to me, her view of Catholicism was astounding. Mention of priests made her titter. *Los curitos!* Who could take *them* seriously, she marvelled, but wouldn't say what they had done to amuse her. Grabbed her? Teased her? Made her, who was as fat as a corn dolly, feel desirable? Ah dear! *Diosito!* What a laugh!

She may have been an illegal immigrant or even a small-time smuggler of illegals. When not working for me, she was employed for less than the minimum legal wage, ironing trousers in a sweatshop where she had to stand with her weight on her varicosed legs for up to ten hours at a stretch.

Her laugh could also be set off too by mention of her husband.

Señor G, the villain of an ongoing saga, pursued a resilient taste for under-age girls up and down the US–Mexico border. He had been jailed on both sides of it, beaten up by outraged fathers, and almost forced into bigamy on several occasions.

'But', said the Señora, 'none of the marriages could come off because he's married to me!'

The humour of this broke her up. *Machismo* and concern for the honour of daughters were trumped. Exploited she might be, but she foiled these fine principles by simply existing. Titters swelled. I saw tears. Was this sorrow? Glee? She must have been the fattest skeleton any Don Juan kept in his conjugal cupboard. I laughed, too, sharing her ambiguous outlet, and drank thin beer with her at the end of her charring afternoons. We were both homesick.

'*Mi tierra*...' she sometimes sighed. She made frequent trips to its border, driving there in a nephew's truck to pick up coloured cakes, ceramic pots and other oddments. Sometimes there would be new nephews when she came back: alert young men whom I might glimpse once or twice, and then no more. Illegal immigrants? If so, she wasn't making much from them. Her small house was built, like those of the less provident of the three pigs, from unreliable materials. It was cheek by jowl to the one we were renting, for Venice, which had not yet become fashionable, mixed up social classes, just as the Stiozzi-Ridolfi palazzo had done.

Once she invited Lucien and me to her daughter's birthday party and fed us excellent home-made enchiladas, tortillas, re-fried pinto beans and bright green guacamole, and there, while playing some game, I looked through a crack in a shed and saw two bewildered eyes blink out at me. Another nephew? The party rioted on and, presumably, whoever the eyes belonged to went back to sleep.

'Learn English so as to live better,' nagged an ad on a Spanish-language radio station: Radio Amor. Señora G hadn't time to learn English, but her daughter spoke like a little Californian.

Conchita, who got straight As in school, looked like a mini model of her mother and was the focus of her hopes. She hoped to become a doctor so that the two could return in pride to Mexico: a long haul. She was twelve the year we attended her birthday party, and didn't laugh the way her mother did. She was grave, half a *gringa* already, responsibly grappling with life and, unlike her mother, in need neither of irony nor alienation.

When the sweatshop was raided, Señora G and other *indocumentadas* were rushed out the back. Later, to make up for time lost, they were obliged to take stimulants and work through the night.

When I was leaving for Europe, she gave me a delicately hand-painted water pot which I still have, and a glass necklace which might have suited a child of six. Then she brought a nephew with a truck to collect whatever household gear I wouldn't be taking. Her last bit of advice, given over our goodbye drink, was that I should one day visit Mexico.

'You'll like it,' she said.

I knew that. Long before I went there, it figured in my geography of romance, just as Spain, Scotland and Italy did for eighteenth-century travellers. Prejudice is potent, and the appeal of my chosen heartlands is rooted in an education whose message was that victims may be godlike. Our first role models – Celts and Christ – had been losers, so in pious moments we saw loss as noble. In practical ones we were, need I say, as competitive as anyone.

Countries known for their ruined grandeur offer a paradoxical thrill. Featuring among them for me were Egypt, Mexico, Peru and, in its small way, Ireland, where picnics often climaxed, once we had tidied away our rugs and thermos flask, in a search for some half-overgrown *fothrach*.

This Gaelic word is best said fortissimo, lest breath whistle through without registering any consonants. It means 'ruin'.

Seán didn't frequent what has sometimes been called 'Dublin's literary underworld', meaning, I suppose, McDaid's, a grubby near-Hogarthian den. He did, though, like meeting old friends in restaurants quiet enough for him to hear them and would bring home reports about the activities in which they were still engaging. Sometimes, when Eileen's poor health kept her from such outings, he took me instead, with the result that the Dublin I first knew belonged to his generation rather than mine. This started when I was a schoolgirl and lasted into the Seventies when I flew from LA to join him at a festival in the Playboy Club in Chicago, where V. S. Pritchett, Alex Haley, Alberto Moravia, Dacia Maraini, James Dicky, Kenneth Galbraith and Seán himself read from their work. I forget who else was there, but remember the event as manic, and only mildly marred by VSP's and Seán's chagrin when told not to talk to the bunnies whose chaperons – 'bunny mothers' – took their role seriously.

Another slightly odd gathering to which I was bidden, this time in Minnesota, featured the brilliant *New Yorker* humorist, J. F. Powers, whom I had seen once or twice in Knockaderry and whose short stories anatomise the predicaments confronting RC priests in the land of Mammon. Rereading them now leaves me wondering whether the carnal innocence of the clerics depicted represents what Jim Powers actually saw around him. Pride and covetousness were the sins he flagellated. But, as we would all learn later, worse was going on.

On the evening in Minnesota he, Seán, and several well-heeled clerics, flashing cufflinks the size of quarters, dined with a gusto that, if Powers had himself been chronicling the occasion, might have augured a sobering outcome. I wondered if he was harvesting copy by stealth and, if so, who – hunter or prey – was footing the bill?

I was reminded of an earlier occasion in Dublin, when Peadar O'Donnell invited Seán and me, again as Eileen's proxy, to dine in what was then the city's best restaurant, Jammets, to meet a man whom Peadar took to be a US Communist. A chill descended when it emerged that the guest, Max Eastman, was on the contrary a Trotskyist. In the Spanish Civil War, where Trots and Commies had bloodily confronted each other, Peadar had been responsible for raising a small anti-Franco contingent from Ireland, so squandering pieces of silver to feed a Judas must have rankled.

Once when I missed an interesting lunch, Seán later described it so fully that even now I can summon up the scene.

'That's what he says,' I heard him tell Eileen, that evening, as we came down to supper.

'Who?' I asked, taking my place at the table.

'The actor, Michael Mac Liammóir', Seán told us cheerfully – not to say gaily! – 'wants me to write what he calls "an Irish *Corydon*". I'll be counting on you for tips if I agree. I hope you've read the original? By André Gide? No? So why did we waste our spondulicks sending you to Savoy?'

I reminded him that my hosts there, the Morandys, would have refused house-room to books by Mauriac, let alone Gide.

Next, mimicking the actor's diction, Seán reported that Mac Liammóir, whose birth name was Alfie Willmore, had come to lunch wearing greasepaint. 'I'll supply the background,' he had apparently promised. 'We could start our dialogue with you and me sitting here whispering. What's wrong with us? I'll tell you what. The confessional has the country ruined – though there are rum stories about what can go on there. Wishful thinking I'd say. Mostly we lack nerve.'

'So why', Seán claimed to have challenged, 'ask me to write what you could do better yourself?'

His flattery was sincere. Mac Liammóir was multitalented and in the Sixties was to devise, deliver and tour around the US a one-man show about Wilde entitled *The Importance of Being Oscar*. This was both a pleasing reminder of Charles Dickens's successful readings of his own works, and a discreet defence and illustration of a way of life which would stop short – wisely in those years – of revealing that it was Michael's as well as Oscar's.

'Why do you need me at all?' Seán said he had asked.

'To help us *find* our nerve,' he was told. 'To challenge people to defend a way of life that is losing its best camouflage which in the old days was people's ignorance. I had a landlady one time in Cork City who told me that, though she wouldn't let a fine-looking man like myself share a room with a girl, boys were OK. Now, aul ones like her are getting so savvy that we need to defend our right to be as God made us.'

'God?'

'He's the homophobes' big asset.'

'But I'm not . . .'

Eileen had gone out to the kitchen.

' . . . one of us.' Seán lowered his voice to let me know that he was now speaking as Mac Lammóir. 'Of course you're not, which is why, for you, defending those who *are* is no risk. Being a known ladies' man, you can afford to show that your choice is more risqué than ours.'

In a fusion of fancy and memory, I see the two revel in their topic. Light gleams on Seán's specs, and the actor's greasepaint is as bright as a blush. Notoriously, he wears it off-stage as well as on. 'I was twelve,' he confides sadly, 'when I made my first conquests. I was a beautiful youth.' He wears a wig. Indeed, Dublin gossip claims that he wears several, one when he wants to look as though he has recently had a haircut, others when the hair must seem to have grown.

'Tell me', Seán teases, 'how *you* know what goes on in confession boxes.'

Michael mentions a fling he had with a young policeman. 'Tell me, Donal,' he says he asked once when they were in bed together, 'when next you go to confession, will you confess what we just did?'

'Oi,' replied the cop in an indignant, singsong Cork accent, 'wouldn't tell a priesht a dirrty ting like dat.'

Eileen, back from the kitchen with a bowl of fruit – arthritis, in this memory, has not crippled her yet – sends me for water to wash it. By the time I bring it, Seán has finished quoting Michael-quoting-the-cop, and is telling about a journalist who reportedly went into a confession box in Rome, with a hidden tape recorder, then later published a provocative exchange with the priest.

'Italians', Seán reflects in his own voice, 'lived with popes for so long that they learned to defend themselves against them. *They* developed nerve.'

Watching Eileen, I remind myself that if something off-colour strikes her as earthy, she will accept and enjoy it. Admiring earthiness is part of the cult of the people. We are a contradictory lot: gossipy though shy, indiscreet though prudish and, as I reflect on that now, it strikes me that it would not be until the late Sixties that reading gay literature led me to understand enough to even wonder what Michael and his policeman lover could have been doing in that bed.

Earlier, saving face had been de rigueur and drove a tenacious English lover of Michael O'Donovan's – alias Frank O'Connor – to change *her* name to O'Donovan by deed poll, before daring to join him in Dublin along with their infant son. Frank, though, possibly alarmed by her nerve, took off shortly afterwards for the US, where he met and married someone else. Both Mac Liammóir and Myles na gCopaleen had other names – as indeed did I who, when teaching in London, called myself 'Miss Whelan'. So who or what did we all think we were? Chameleons?

A deeper dilemma was mocked by Myles – alias Flann O'Brien alias Brian O'Nolan – in his savagely funny novel, *The Poor Mouth*, in which Gaelic-speaking natives of his imaginary Corcha Dorcha grow so bewildered by the misery of their lives that they wonder if they are human at all.

When Lauro and I reached LA in 1966, we discovered that we, who, when last in the US, had had to show ID before buying alcohol, now belonged to a reviled older generation. 'Never', ran a slogan, 'trust anyone over thirty.' The US had changed. Hippies, Black Panthers and anti-war movements, Pacifica Radio, *Ramparts* magazine and Angela Davis were part of a new scene where it seemed hard to know whom to support. Black people, clearly, had legitimate complaints, and so did young men who risked being more or less press-ganged into fighting in an unpopular war. But what about the druggy, flower-toting hangers on? They struck me as narcissistic. Maybe I was square? Maybe one should be? None of the street demos I had attended in Paris and London had doubled as picnics, and participants represented a cross-section of society. Here many seemed to be spoilt, frivolous and middle class.

Disciplined young policemen, sent to keep order at UCLA anti-war gatherings. were regularly insulted by students, who needed no provocation to barrack and jeer 'Up against the wall, mother-fucker' at the under-privileged boys of their own age who stood to attention and stared stoically ahead. My grandfather, I remembered, had been a cop. I hadn't known him, but did know that in the Ireland of his day, joining the army, the police or the church was a classic step up the social ladder. Nobody, I was sure, had called recruits 'mother-fuckers'.

A hippie we knew asked us to adopt his under-age girl friend so that he could get the detention centre in which her biological parents had put her to release her to us, so that he and she could continue their love affair. We refused. What did he expect? We – and he – were over thirty – and *she* looked thirteen .

We stayed some years in the house in Venice where groups of hungry hippies occasionally dropped in for whom I might make pasta or omelettes. Drugs, someone explained, sharpened the appetite. So who did I think I was? Cook? Protester? Possibly a decorator, for I painted the walls, made bookshelves from planks and tables from doors and, in free moments, joined the anti-war rallies surging and merging up and down the boardwalk. Meanwhile some furniture which we had bought in Florence had arrived and raised the tone. A dealer we knew there used to drive around Tuscany looking for solid walnut cupboards and chests which country priests had in their sacristies and were often eager to sell or even trade for a TV set. The designs were timeless, since provincial cabinet-makers hadn't changed their prototypes in five hundred years. Cheap Mexican pieces, available in LA, though far more crudely knocked together, used some of the same patterns.

All week Lucien and the children of our French and Italian friends attended the French Lycée, wearing the claim *cogito ergo sum* picked out in gold thread on their blazer pockets, and learning to use the subjunctive so that, like good Europeans, they could feel and voice doubt. At weekends they sometimes dressed as hippies.

When we first reached LA, friends from Reed College who had preceded us there sat me down and filled me in on the history of SNNC (Students' Non Violent Co-ordinating committee, pronounced 'snik'), CORE (the Congress of Racial Equality) and the Civil Rights Movement generally. These friends were Bahais whom we had seduced into drinking alcohol at Reed parties, only to find them, two hours later, making for their car on all fours having turned out to have no resistance to the stuff at all. Now they had reverted to being teetotallers and wouldn't have drink in their house. Pomegranate juice was supplied instead, but the friendship languished.

The query 'Who do you think you are?' could be as hard to answer in California as in Corcha Dorcha. And *cogito ergo sum* didn't help, since neither thought nor identity was stable. Luciano Z, a professor of medicine, was the first of our friends to illustrate this, when he fell for a hippie called Pauline, changed her name to Paola, divorced his Italian wife, implored her not to tell his mother what he had done and proceeded to remake the Californian Paola in her predecessor's image. LA at that time was full of adults who, bemused by the youth cult, tried to relive their own first, fine careless raptures and start afresh. Wives, children and dogs fell victims to the impulse and, in our case, the scapegoat was our pet.

Lorenzaccio, a young Labrador whom I had rescued from the pound when I first came, had nowhere to go when it was time for us to give up our Venice bivouac and head for London where we planned henceforth to spend six months of each year. Some of

Lauro's colleagues joked that he was now a jet-setter, then began spending half of every year in Europe themselves.

This was before the English anti-rabies regulations were relaxed to allow dogs to travel. So feeling that Lorenzaccio needed a steady home, we began looking for a responsible, dog-loving family who would take him over.

As his great joy was bounding through ocean surf, barking at seabirds, and our friends the Wohls lived by the beach, we entrusted him to them. Unhappily no sooner had we left the US than Bob Wohl quite unforeseeably divorced his wife and, in the ensuing reshuffle of property, Lorenzaccio was given to a passing Japanese. By the time I learned this, we were in London, and all trace of him had been lost. I tried not to wonder whether it was the Japanese – surely not? – who ate dogs. Koreans perhaps? But could the Wohls, who were Swedish, distinguish between them? Anyway, what right had we to blame anyone for anything after letting down our trusting dog? Lucien, too, I'm afraid, found moving to an English boarding school a bit of a jolt.

Shuttling between London and LA and renting houses through the UC housing bureau led to our spending time in every part of that city. Looking back over twenty or so years, I remember staying in Westwood, Santa Monica, Bel Air, Beverly Hills, The Hollywood Hills, Laurel Canyon, Beverly Glen, Pacific Palisades and even Malibu where the Irish novelist, Brian Moore, had a seaside house which he and his wife Jean sometimes lent us. Our social profile changed with the luck of the draw, and we could feel delighted or horrified on first pushing open the front door of a new house. The smartest one we rented belonged to a scientist and was so high up in Bel Air that the hawks which hovered on the lookout for prey were sometimes below us. Wildlife in some of the ravines was almost tame. Deer, racoons, coyotes and possums were common and so were hummingbirds. The climate changed too as we drove up from sea level to the cool hills.

Friendships matter when you are living far from home and in a country you don't much like. In LA, though, they could be hard to maintain.

Its residents were prone to move on, and when our close friends Josie and Franco Fido left, we felt bereft. In their case, the momentum propelling them to the East Coast was powered by a rumpus which hardly involved them, yet led to their leaving as neatly as two balls side-swiped by another one can be shot across a snooker table. What happened was that ageing Fascists who had been cocks of the walk in the LA Italian community in the days of Mussolini, and resented being replaced by young, lefty Italians, got wind of a row in the UCLA Italian Department, where teaching assistants were said to be swopping As for sexual favours. Eager to make trouble, the old Fascists described the department to the local media as a *covo di comunisti* – a communist lair. Franco was the department chairman just then, so his relations with UC fund-raisers may have grown strained. All I know for sure, though, is that not long after being fingered on TV as the head of a communist lair, he left and that, cheeringly, his career may well have benefited, for exile took him to pleasant places such as Brown in Providence, Rhode Island, where we spent a delightful Christmas with him and Josie in their elegant Greek Revival house, then to Stanford and Harvard. But until Lauro and he retired from teaching and we all moved back to Europe, we saw far too little of them.

Meanwhile in 1980 another friend, this time an entertaining and erudite Parisian called Pierre Pathé, fell badly foul of the law, and a letter from Maura Teissier reached me in LA, reporting that he had been arrested and charged with being a Soviet spy. Though this sounded like a joke, it was backed up by newspaper clippings in which 'Freelancing for the KGB' was a recurrent headline. Later another friend sent a set of notes taken at Pierre's trial which I still have and which make clear that he was actually charged with being a 'disinformer', a word so new at the time that the press thought it might have been invented – or translated from Russian – to fit his case.

Article 80 of the French penal code, however, provided for people like him. You could, it specified, be jailed for up to twenty years 'for having had secret dealings with agents of a foreign power intent on harming the military or diplomatic status of France or its economic interests'. Public indignation was sharper than might otherwise have been expected because of Pierre's background. His father, Charles Pathé, is credited with having 'industrialised' the film business, and one of Pierre's brothers-in-law at the time of the trial was the head of Renault and would be appointed French ambassador to Washington the following year.

Pierre Pathé, noted *Le Figaro*, 'knew a lot of people. He moved in the highest circles, among the most prestigious political and scientific personalities of France, who sought him out because of his brilliant conversation and his superior intelligence. He was the perfect carrier of disinformation.'

So his connections did him more harm than good. They roused the wrath of the state prosecutor who, after harping on Pierre's privileged origins, asked, 'How does a man like you come to betray?' then added oddly, 'I use the word in a literary, not a legal sense.' There are gaps in the notes I was given, some explained by the word 'inaudible'. And some comments seem oddly self-referential: 'You', reproached the same prosecutor, 'were my age when you chose Soviet Russia,' then referred to his own 'modest career in the law . . . I didn't read your book about the Soviet phenomenon,' he noted, 'lest it poison my mind.'

Listeners might have wondered if he was echoing the harangues of the ferocious old Paris witch-finder, Jean Bodin, and poisoning his own mind. 'Taking legal proceedings against someone because of their possible influence,' the prosecutor went on, 'is unknown in the West. This is the first time a court has sentenced anyone for such a crime. So we are creating jurisprudence.'

Did he hope this would look good on his CV? Perhaps it did.

By the time I got to France, Pierre had spent months in Fresnes jail, a short train ride from Paris, facing a five-year sentence – though the prosecution had asked for ten. The supposedly influential intellectuals who had spoken in his defence may not have helped him much, for France – as ever – was fiercely divided and, as even the prosecution acknowledged, the case was odd.

What had started the trouble was that the Direction de la Surveillance du Territoire, France's MI5, had been keeping an eye on a soviet diplomat attached to UNESCO. They knew him to be a member of the KGB, and, on seeing him with Pierre, began watching Pierre too. While doing this, they saw him in a café in a working-class part of Paris handing documents to the Russian and accepting an envelope in exchange. They then arrested both men. The Russian was promptly deported and Pierre, who admitted having received modest sums of money from Soviet contacts to help finance *Synthesis*, one of the magazines he ran, was accused of complicity with an agent of a foreign power. He explained that the cash was payment for articles he had written for the Soviet press – and indeed what he had just handed to the

Russian proved to be a fresh selection of these. The prosecution's admission that they did not regard him as a spy, but were setting a precedent by pursuing him as an *agent d'influence*, might seem to have weakened their case. Yet there he was in Fresnes. 'Serving as a scapegoat?' queried left-wing newspapers. Several editors and heads of academic institutes spoke up on his behalf, but this backfired when opponents said he was dangerous precisely because he was friendly with – and in some cases related to – people of influence on whom *his* influence could have a bad effect. *Synthesis*, they claimed, had a dual purpose: it was both cover and a way of passing on information. 'Very clever!' sneered the counsel for the prosecution.

People at Amnesty International, whom I phoned to ask for help when I got back to the UK, were pessimistic. Pierre had no constituency, explained the man who came to the phone, and when I asked if this didn't prove that he was unlikely to be either dangerous or engaged in a conspiracy, the answer was that it made it hard to rally support.

When I visited Pierre in jail, neither of us alluded to the fact that a jail was where we were. Instead. we chatted about friends and Ireland and my novel, *No Country for Young Men*, which had recently appeared and he had read. Ironically, he complained that my depiction of my compatriots was 'harsh', which made me wonder whether he felt that I too had betrayed my country. Poor Pierre! He looked ghostly. The prison walls were painted a pale grey and he, who was wearing a sharply tailored, grey summer suit – clearly not prison issue – seemed to merge into them. He was sixty-nine.

It was painful at the end of my visit to leave him in that bleak place, where we both assumed that he had almost five years still to serve. Luckily, as it would turn out, Mitterrand and his Socialists took power the following May and had him released.

Pierre's sentence had been tougher than his friends expected, for not only had he proven to be older than we had supposed, but his motivation for acting as he had seemed to be a romantic Russophilia, which was noted even during his trial, when he spoke throughout of 'Russia' rather than of the Soviet Union. To the customary query as to whether he had anything to say, he had replied, 'I would like to tell counsel for the prosecution that I never thought ... that the Soviet model of socialism would suit France.'

That, Maura Teissier and I agreed, was bewildering.

'Just as well', she told me, 'that you didn't take him too seriously.'

'Nor you.'

'Nor Berenice nor Rosemarie, wouldn't you say?'

'And certainly not Chantal.'

Over a number of years, Pierre had fallen serially in love with five of us, four of whom were Irish, and seemed to have romanticised Ireland in much the way he had Russia. We, he assured us, were more idealistic than Parisian women.

'Did you notice', Maura wondered, 'what the minutes of the trial say about his ex-wife, "Miss Russia of Paris"?' She seems to have attended it – or tried to. Apparently she sat with the press on the first day, but on the second was asked to leave by one of the defence lawyers.

According to the news clippings, even the psychiatric expert who had been brought to assess Pierre agreed that he had an unusually brilliant mind. But clearly – and this reminded me of the flower-children of a dozen years earlier – he had not, as my mother would have put it, 'a pick of common sense'. This was obvious in small ways. Once, when I was staying with the Teissiers and Lauro was elsewhere, Pierre had flown to Florence to urge me to get divorced and marry him. 'You', he told me, 'are the woman I should have married.' And he refused to believe me when I protested that, in fact, Lauro and I were well suited. This may have been due to Maura's telling him that, like swans, Irish women mated for life.

He was, said the expert, emotionally cold and secretive by nature. This could be in reaction to his father's notoriety, but he had no psychiatric troubles. Then she talked of Lacan's theories about the importance of fathers, but the notes left these out.

Before he left Florence Pierre had told me, as though I had not discouraged him at all, that when married we would not have much money because he meant to go on publishing *Synthesis*.

'But,' noted Maura when I told her this, 'he'll have no money now for that either.'

Another paradox:

Shortly after this I took part in a literary festival in Japan, where the liveliest person I met was an Irish Sacred Heart nun who told me that when first taking vows she had asked her superiors to send her to work with the poor, but instead, – perhaps to test her will? – was sent to teach in the order's school for aristocratic girls in Tokyo, which she now ran. She invited me to dine with some of her former pupils who had become elegant adults, whereas she – whose will seemed startlingly intact – chose to appear in a cardigan which might have come from a car-boot sale. If her mentors ever let her switch back to her first vocation, she already had the kit.

Since Eileen had resented both my not going to Portugal and my taking off for other places, I suspected her of testing me when, in 1988, she rang me in London to say she was going to hospital and needed me to come straight to Dublin to be with Seán. She had made such requests before, and I had always come. This time, I had a house guest and didn't. Misinterpreting the situation, I took it that her anxiety really *was* about Seán. But as their housekeeper had offered to move in and look after him, I couldn't see why he needed me to be there as well. He and Eileen, having good health insurance, made so many trips to hospital that I thought of these as routine, and, oddly, she didn't disabuse me. With hindsight, I now guess that she feared to worry him, as he could have been listening on the telephone extension. Sometimes, moreover, she could be fiercely demanding – less for herself than, as I assumed to be the case on this occasion, for him. They propped each other up, as ageing couples must.

At this time, Lauro and I were juggling a tricky life style. Our house – a Victorian wreck when bought the previous year – was only now ready to be redecorated so that I could let it before the spring term started in LA so as to bring in enough income to cover whatever rent we would have to pay there. With this in mind, I had stayed in it while Lauro was in the US, and struggled to keep the builders from taking on other jobs before finishing ours, as builders like to do. Even now they were behind schedule, so I was reluctant to leave London, though I would have if I had known how ill Eileen actually was. Perhaps she had been too ill to argue when asked whether their housekeeper, who had had training as a nurse, wouldn't be more help to Seán than I could be.

'Well, wouldn't she?' I pestered.

Eileen sighed and put down the phone.

She died in the small hours the next morning. Seán's mind gave way under the shock and never quite recovered. This, however, was not clear at first, for though he was nearing ninety, he could still be funny, as though mimicking a younger self. Indeed, when I flew to Dublin to help with her funeral and memorial service, he seemed to be on the mend.

Lauro, Lucien and I spent Christmas and New Year with him, and watched anxiously when he grew paranoid or mistook me for Eileen. His personality was now as volatile as a kite, and he grew angry when discouraged from wandering into the streets late at night, as he liked to do when he couldn't sleep. He tended to have stuffed hundreds of pounds in loose bundles into his coat pockets and flew into a rage when told that this was dangerous. Dún Laoghaire, local people kept warning, was not the sedate place I had known years ago. It was now full of druggies. Even churches had to be locked because of people shooting up in their gardens.

When we finally left, first for London and then LA, where Lauro was still teaching, letters from Seán's neighbours caught up with us to report that a woman had been visiting him, and had persuaded various literary hosts that he was eager to attend their functions and needed her as an escort. This, warned the neighbours, was destabilising him. What was more, she was arousing him sexually. They had seen her do so through his and their front windows. And when the housekeeper remonstrated with him and he chased her into the street, attacked a neighbour, then had to be confined in St John of God's mental hospital, fresh letters accused the temptress of having, literally, driven him mad. The doctors, however, put his troubles down to a series of small strokes and a lack of folic acid. They said it might not be safe for him to be let out of hospital for months.

Meanwhile, his house was burgled by well-briefed thieves, who reached it through another empty one whose back garden adjoined his. They must have had a van nearby, for they moved a hunt table and a two-tiered glass-fronted book case through both gardens without being detected. After that, with or without the housekeeper, there could be no question of his moving back there to live.

Helen Fahy, our generous neighbour and friend, was immensely supportive when I flew back to visit Seán in St John of God's and to vet the secure nursing homes to which its doctors were prepared to release him. Aclare House, the one he chose, was close to the Fahys, so Helen became a target for frequent, unannounced visits. Yet even when he forgot having already dropped in on her twice on any given day, then did so a third time, she welcomed him warmly and once the Aclare House staff decided it was safe for him to come out she drove him and me all over Wicklow to see the familiar scenery, after which the three of us had numerous lunches and teas in his favourite hotels. Over one such meal he told us what he thought had been happening while he was in St John of God's. He had, he gravely stated, been confined in 'a colony of blacks run by priests'. He proffered this as an accurate account of his experience, but seemed relieved when we managed to convince him that it amounted to a dream.

Interestingly, he had allegorised his confusion by turning the doctors who had locked him up into priests, and fellow inmates into blacks. The old Republican distrust of the clergy, plus an Irish sense of ourselves as perennial victims, help explain these notions, though Helen and I wondered whether the bit about blacks could be a theft from Roddy Doyle. Either way, the past was dominant, and we noticed that what gripped Seán's attention, and burrowed through it like a thorn through wool, was an increasingly early past. Early and angry. The schoolyard jeer, 'Cowardy, cowardy custard/ Stick your head in the mustard', which he disconcertingly took to chanting, seemed to be aimed at himself.

For how long, I wondered, had he been angry? And afraid?

He had, I remembered, been subject to nightmares as long as I had known him and might in his youth have suffered from what is now called post-traumatic stress. In the late Seventies, when I visited him and Eileen in their last house, in its small, cruelly metaphoric cul-de-sac, she used often to be upstairs in bed, knocked out by the painkillers which would eventually kill her, while he, below in their living room, cheered himself with gin. I would go up and down, chat with each, try to comfort each and exchange the small doses of gossip which are often what the housebound crave.

During these visits his mind tended to take plunges into memory, and in the course of one he shyly revealed that in May 1968, when the French anarchic maelstrom had briefly made travel impossible, he and Kick found themselves stranded somewhere near Paris. Kick by then had terminal cancer, so they were enjoying a last fling – or perhaps no more than a memory of one – when private sorrow was overtaken by the *événements*, which prevented their getting back to their homes as planned. Unknown both to them and me, we could easily have run into each other, for I may not have been far from their hide-out. Lucien and I were spending the summer with Chantal, a French friend who has a son his age. The boys were boarding at a local riding school, while she and I stayed close by in a house which she had rented near the Forest of Fontainebleau. The idea had been for the four of us to lunch together at the weekends, then ride in the forest, or else visit nearby châteaux like the exquisite Vaux le Vicomte, which had been the model for Versailles. And this is what we did until the fine May morning when Chantal, who worked for Radio Free Europe, turned on the radio at breakfast time and, hearing the news, took a piece of bread in one hand and her car keys in the other and drove hell for leather to her office in Paris to cope with it.

Some months later she would have to leave still more urgently when the Soviets invaded Czechoslovakia.

Eileen liked to dissect her past and, when Seán grew deaf, she enjoyed chatting with people who dropped by and were prepared to join her in doing so. After the move to Dún Laoghaire the droppers-in were different from those I had known in Killiney, though some old friends, like David and Ita Marcus, came by, and so did American visitors, the writer, James Plunkett, and neighbours like Helen Fahy who rarely arrived 'with one arm as long as the other'. This Irishism refers to the practice of bending one's arm to accommodate a gift. Helen's was usually a home-made cake.

Talk, though, was what interested Eileen. 'Can you tell me', I remember her asking a historian who sometimes came, 'how my Gaelic-speaking grandmother came to lose her property?'

'How do you know she had any?' I asked, for I thought of rural Gaelic speakers as likely to be penniless.

'She used to ride to hounds,' Eileen told us proudly. 'And she had a bit of land. But somehow she lost everything quite suddenly. She was so terrified of Protestant clergymen that if she saw one approaching, she would cross the road. Why do you suppose that was?'

'Tithes,' said the historian who, it strikes me now, may have had this conversation with Eileen before. 'She must have failed to pay them.'

'Tithes?' marvelled Eileen, playing her part.

'Yes,' he reminded her. 'Until the 1870s everyone had to contribute to the upkeep of the Protestant Church – the Church of Ireland, as they still call themselves. But back then it was still the established church and everyone had to cough up money to keep it going.'

'Even Catholics?'

'Catholics, Dissenters, Jews, everyone. If they didn't, they could be fined.'

'So you think that's how she lost her bit of land.'

'I do.'

'God help us, weren't they savage when they had power.'

⚭

In 1990 Lauro and I spent six weeks at the Villa Serbelloni, the Rockefeller Foundation on Lake Como, where we were each granted a residency to get on with our writing. Meals were designed to enable us to 'interact' and, while my neighbour and I at one of these were trying to do so, he brought up the topic of paedophilia, which he said was rampant among RC priests. I was incredulous.

'That surely can't be true?'

'I'm afraid it can,' he insisted. 'From what I hear, they're all at it!'

Perhaps I looked peeved, for his query as to whether I planned 'to return to the fold' was acerbic.

Hoping to avoid a religious wrangle, I remarked that, whether or not one believed the Christian story, belief seemed to do wonders for those who did. Then I quoted what a Catholic journalist had told me, about how a priest from Cork had described his experience under torture in Buenos Aires. 'My Christian faith became very real to me,' he had told her. 'In such suffering Christ is almost physically present . . .'

To change the subject, I turned to the man on my other side. He, however, had been listening and wanted to talk about the Pope's charisma which was also being described as 'physical'. Well, I told him, I had gone on the journalists' train to Knock in County Mayo which was said to have been one of the more magnetic of John Paul II's appearances.

'And felt the magnetism?'

'No. Just the crowd's excitement.'

'So how explain that?'

I said I thought crowds generated it themselves, as sports fans did.

'Going back to what you say about paedophilia,' I said to the first man, 'if it's true . . .'

'It is.'

' . . . the Vatican will lose support.'

A shrug.

We left it there, for I wasn't sure I wanted that to happen, since the Church *had* comforted some people, viz., the priest from Cork.

It didn't comfort Seán though. He, who had struggled against it when it was at its domineering worst, died in 1991, yearning for belief in an afterlife which evaded him, and feeling the ire of a man who has paid dues to a club which welshes on commitments.

I was upset when Mrs Jones, who ran the home where he died, told the press that he had gone back to the Church. I didn't believe her, for he and I had discussed his disbelief – and the distress it was causing him – quite close to the end.

A more down-to-earth truce, however, worked out better.

In 1978 the Lord Mayer of Cork, Gerald Goldberg, invited him to accept the Freedom of the City: a move designed to patch up quarrels with long-dead Corkonians. At first Seán refused the offer but, when it was repeated ten years later, accepted it. Sadly, when the day came, he was not well enough to travel, so I went to Cork to represent him. Meanwhile in 1986 he was elected *Saoi*, a newish honour then (I think Sam Beckett was the only one to have it before him) and still defined today as the highest one which Irish artists can confer on one of their number. Patrick Hillery, then president of the country, came to the house to present him with a torc – a Celtic ornament – which symbolised it. Garret FitzGerald visited too.

For as long as Seán could be taken for drives, visits to Killough remained a ritual. I don't know whether anyone still lived there, but he took a wry pleasure in pausing at its gate to stare, probably not at what was before him, but at a remembered self aged thirty-three, which was the age he was when he and Eileen moved there. A few years later, it was the house he came home to when he had been betraying her with Elizabeth Bowen.

This reminded me of one of his own short stories.

'An Inside Outside Complex' is about a man who, having fallen out with his wife, brings her a peace-offering. It is a mirror which proves too big to bring through her door, so is left leaning against the hedge outside her window. As the two look out of this and see themselves looking in, their conflicted need to be together and apart is briefly resolved. It is a perfect metaphor both for the way Seán's yens did and did not work, and on how the mirror of narrative changes what it reflects.

Sometimes, standing with him at that gate, I too slipped back to a time when he used to exorcise the thrills and terrors which Eileen's stories conjured up. These, being gleaned from the Gaelic, had come either directly from native speakers in West Cork or from tales collected by the Irish Folklore Commission, which she translated, retold in English, and sold to the Oxford University Press in the Fifties.

Once, she told me, she asked a woman from whom she had got some fairy tales whether she herself believed in fairies, but the woman was too proud to admit this.

'Yerra no!' she denied. '*I* don't. But mind, they're there all the same.' This answer enchanted Eileen – and showed that belief in Ireland had often been dodgy.

Whenever I was back in LA, Helen Fahy sent me reports on Seán's health, along with warnings that Maurice Harmon, a

UCD professor, who was writing his biography, would read any letter I sent.

'So write nothing private,' she warned.

This recalls another short story, one by Robbie McCauley, and is about a man writing about a writer he has not met – which makes him an unconvincing Boswell. When the story opens, though, the writer is to visit him and will, with luck, reveal something of himself.

Setbacks accumulate when the academic learns that he has been mispronouncing his guest's name – which, when colleagues find out, will turn him into a laughing stock. Next, the guest has a stroke and dies.

Setback or bonus?

Bonus, of course. Now nobody need know about the mispronounced name, and the biographer can write what he likes and footnote it with the claim, 'learned in a private interview'.

'So,' Helen repeated, 'write nothing private.'

But nothing *was* private now for Seán, whose ability to read or think flickered unreliably. Worse: old letters to friends, most of these now dead, would be quoted in the biography. He had sold them to the Bancroft Library in Berkeley, where biographers could consult them whenever they chose. Gossip, in a town like Dublin, would lose nothing in the telling.

Recalling the reticence of Antonin Artaud's sister when I, as a brash doctoral student, wanted access to facts about her brother's life, I felt retrospective shame. And, on reading about the venom which James Joyce's grandson displayed when scholars wanted to make use of Joyce's family papers, I realised that relations between relatives and biographers are bound to be fraught, with self-interest on both sides masquerading as *pietas*.

Maybe it's as well, I tell myself, that fewer people now write letters at all. Think of what happened to Joyce's 'dirty' ones to his wife when they were left with Brandeis University on the understanding that nobody was to copy them. People did. They memorised, took furtive notes, and wrote down their unreliable recollections. So in the end it was thought safer for Dick Ellmann to publish the letters openly and officially, since this, at least, deprived poachers of the glee of the chase.

So now the 'dirty letters' display their ancient, salivating excitement on the Internet.

With considerable rue, then, I made my letters to Seán impersonal, knowing that the experience of slitting open the envelopes would probably bring him as much – or little – pleasure as an exchange of views about anything at all. Even before his breakdown, I had seen him puzzle for up to half an hour over a single page.

Eileen, who unlike him had stayed mentally sharp until she died, had concealed his mental deterioration from me, which was what made it impossible for him to join Lauro and me while we were still commuting between London and LA

However, once settled in Gloucester Crescent, I suggested that he pay us a visit, and offered to give a party for him and invite anyone still alive whom he would like to see. His old friends, V. S. Pritchett and his wife, Dorothy, were living just around the corner from us in Regent's Park Terrace, so would surely come. I was hoping to replicate a dinner party we had given for him in the Seventies, which had been attended by Elizabeth Bowen, John Betjeman and some friends of my own. Cecil Day-Lewis and

Jill Balcon were to have come, too, but Day-Lewis died just days before that first party.

The second one never happened – or rather did not include Seán, although he had claimed to be looking forward to it. At first this was due to his doctors' warning that he might have a fit when the plane took off and create a disturbance, which could oblige the pilot to return to the airport. They then got the idea that if a strong young man were to travel with him, to handle any trouble which might arise, he *could* come. Mrs Jones volunteered her son for the duty, but, for reasons which I was never told, Seán now backed out. VSP and Dorothy came to dinner anyway and we had a good, if slightly subdued, evening.

Seán had meanwhile developed a crush on Mrs Jones and sighed at his failure to make any impression on her. Why, he asked me, when confessing this, were some women standoffish? Was it to do with power? I mentioned age, which set him brooding.

'How old *am* I?' he asked after a while. 'Am I a hundred?'

'No, no,' I reassured. 'Only ninety-one.' I was glad he had a woman to dream about. After he died, I gave Mrs Jones a watercolour by Norah McGuinness to thank her for the kindness, which must, I guessed, have won his heart. McGuinesses, I saw, some time later, were selling well, so with luck Mrs Jones got a good price for hers.

Seán died two and a half years after Eileen.

They had made their wills at a time when the Church was forbidding Catholics to leave their bodies – 'temples of the Holy Ghost' – for research, which meant that Irish medical schools were in urgent need of such legacies, but in defiance of 'Holy Mum', as some fitful convert – possibly Graham Greene? – used to call the institution we knew as 'Mother Church', both had done so. This meant that once the research was done, the memorial services were over and I had scattered their ashes on similar grey days in Lake Gougane Barra, there was no place dedicated to their memory, so less reason for me to visit Ireland. I did so a few times, nonetheless, to judge literary prizes or see friends, although lively members of our diaspora were often easier to see elsewhere: Maura Teissier in Paris and Positano, Brian Moore in LA, and many more in London.

Then our LA connection ended too.

This happened during an economic dip, when UCLA invited senior professors to take early retirement in exchange for better pensions, since its pension fund was more solvent than the one for salaries.

Lauro accepted the offer, retired to London, and started to write livelier narratives, one of which was actually a novel and won a prize. Even when writing history, he now felt more free to vary his interests and topics. He also gave seminars at the École des Hautes Études, which meant that we needed to find somewhere to stay when in Paris. We did this by swapping a sojourn in Gloucester Crescent for one in the rue Saint Martin, where the American writer Edmund White then lived. We did this exchange several times and, in between house-swaps, did the same thing with the Italian theatre critic, Rita Cirio. She took our house for less time than we wanted to spend in her Paris flat, so, to make things fairer, she brought parties of friends with her. Her flat had a pleasant roof terrace, overlooking the Senate building, and both arrangements worked so well, that even when the connection with the Hautes Études ended, we went on spending time in Paris. The Eurostar has now brought it so close that we have almost as many friends there as in London.

∞

April Blood, Lauro's book about the 1478 conspiracy to murder the Medici brothers Lorenzo il Magnifico and Giuliano in Florence cathedral did well both with his academic peers and with a popular readership. He followed it with *Scourge and Fire*, an account of the struggle between Florentine Republicans, animated by Savonarola, and Medici partisans, who, though banished from Florence during the years covered by the book, were doggedly plotting to get back. Reviewers were surprised by Lauro's view of the Dominican friar, who is often presented as an unlikable puritan but emerges here as an idealist. His end – he was hanged and burned at the stake – darkens his story. Yet it strikes me that to see him as a forerunner of today's Liberation theologians brightens it with the reminder that the Church has, repeatedly, found the ingenuity needed to sidestep its own dogmatism. I saw this in action when the canon lawyer Neri Capponi advised Maura Teissier that if she had any Irish friends who needed their marriages annulled, they should apply not to the bigoted Irish hierarchy, but directly to Rome. This advice was on a par with his way of dealing with Italian tax collectors who, assuming that everyone lied, allowed for this when calculating what people were likely to actually owe the state. This, Neri noted, obliged *all* citizens to lie, since those who did not risked being excessively penalised to the detriment of their families.

'So,' we asked him, 'one reaches for truth through falsehood?'

'Why not?'

Well, since religion is the realm of paradox, indeed why not? '*O felix culpa!*' goes the hymn celebrating the redemption necessitated by the Fall. The liking for happy endings may originate right there.

Scourge and Fire was Lauro's tenth book and, as I write, he is finishing his eleventh.

Once freed from our annual commuting to and from LA, we were able to visit, among other places, Egypt, Syria, Cambodia, Turkey, Russia, Sicily and different parts of Spain. This was more fun than toing and froing between the UK and US. Also, from time to time, we separately enjoyed 'freebies', such as my visits to Japan, to the Adelaide Festival, and an earlier one to the lavish Harbourfront festival in Toronto, where the Faber publisher Charles Monteith turned up with his star writer, William Golding, and his wife, and encouraged me to join their group.

This was generous of Charles, since I had by then left Faber and gone to Allen Lane with my novel *No Country for Young Men*, which was shortlisted for the Booker Prize in 1980, when the prize itself was deservedly won by Golding's *Rites of Passage*.

Charles was not only generous in this. He had been stoical ten years earlier when my first novel, *Godded and Codded*, had to be withdrawn because of a libel threat. That taught me the cost of words – mine and the lawyer's. His were so expensive that I hardly dared speak to him.

'*Did* you commit libel?' he asked.

I wasn't sure. True, I had taken something from life: a bed so infested with termites that the bed had become termites and termites the bed, and this, claimed the woman who was suing Faber, tied her to the novel, which presented her, she said, as 'a ludicrous and lecherous female'.

'The story's fictional,' I told the lawyer hopefully. 'And the characters are composite. The bed's a metaphor really.'

'That's *worse*!' he told me. 'If you'd stuck to truth we could have pleaded "fair comment".'

It was too expensive to argue. Besides that, the litigant was a woman who had once, at a party, loudly described Honor's and Seán's affair in terms quite close to 'ludicrous and lecherous'. Had I, consciously, been taking revenge? Guilt hovered. I had, undeniably, turned one of her own comic turns against her, whose lovers, she often joked, perhaps to forestall other people's jokes, tended to be damaged. 'My lot', she liked to say, 'are the halt and the blind. I seem to attract them.' The words were hers! Could I claim that she had libelled herself? Better not try.

The question arises, why use reality at all? I can only say that, for me, it provides a ballast which allows the imagination to levitate. When grounded in everyday life, I feel able to write without too much planning, which is how I prefer to write. There *is* a fear of drying up, but there is also the hope of something unexpected happening on the page. I got the idea for *No Country for Young Men* from hearing of an old Dublin lady from a nationalist family who had gone astray in her mind and fancied the year to be permanently 1922. This scrap of gossip was a talisman. Explosive with parable to anyone who knew Ireland, it was also blessedly commonplace, as avatars ought to be.

The gossip used in *Godded and Codded*, in contrast, led to that novel's being scuttled. Shaken by this, I eagerly agreed when Lauro suggested that we collaborate on a documentary history of women. Its title, *Not in God's Image*, echoed St Augustine's notion that 'separately ... woman alone is not the image of God; whereas man alone is ...' We spent a year and a half doing research in the British Museum, using law codes, court cases, wage scales, diaries and the like as criteria for judging ordinary women's status. Our subtitle was *Women in History from the Greeks to the Victorians*. As I educated myself in the history of domestic mores, the pleasure of seeing how societies work became a fillip to fantasy. I was learning a new trade, and the tricks of all trades are useful to novelists. I was interested too in the workings of the Church which has so often controlled society and more especially women.

Feminism was in the air, and animated my novel *Women in the*

Wall, which came out in 1975. Set in sixth-century Gaul, it focused on the role of convents in misogynist warrior-societies where they could sometimes provide women with a refuge from violence as well as scope for ambition, self-realisation, self-mortification and an aspiration to become deaconesses. Clearly my mind was partly on the quarrels of the Seventies. What drove the narrative, though, was a suspicion that violence like that described in the sixth-century chronicles was likely to be internalised by the women too. And, indeed, the particular story which I chose – that of Queen, later Saint, Radegunda – shows the nuns in her convent inviting in the very ferocity which their convent had been founded to repel.

Among new strings to the RC bow was left-wing Catholicism which grew increasingly courageous in the Sixties and Seventies. As priests became less diffident about criticising Rome and it began to be said that the Church was now frankly divided, I used my own perceptions about this in a long historical novel. *The Judas Cloth* is set in the last years of papal Rome before the Italians took it over in 1870. I got the idea from a pun made by the vicar general of a mountainous diocese in Ecuador, when his Indian flock teasingly called him '*el Cardenal*'. Not only did he deny having that title, he also reminded them that the princes of the Church who did have it had often afflicted the poor as cruelly as the weals (also called *cardenales*) left on peasants' bodies when landowners beat them in the bad old days. As Pope John Paul II was then discouraging left-wing priests from engaging in politics, I felt that it was the Roman *cardenales* who had often supported right-wing causes who were most likely to provide good material for fiction.

'But why', people who despise that sometimes ask, 'write or indeed read it at all?'

Well, we all have our habits. The English invade other people's countries; Italians design elegant things; the French dream of revolutions, and we Irish tell stories to amuse and console ourselves.

∽

And Again? was Seán's last novel: published when he was eighty, it consoled him for his loss of hope in a Christian heaven by imagining an offer made by the gods of Mount Olympus to a man not unlike himself. The offer is to let him grow younger instead of older, forget his past, enjoy successive erotic adventures with his daughter, his grand- then great-granddaughter, and so on. The gods' interest is in discovering whether humans learn from their mistakes and, as the younging protagonist – whose name is Robert Younger – makes the same ones again and again, the message can only be that they don't.

Reviewers were surprised. It was unlike anything Seán had written before. 'This rueful hymn to life', *Publishers Weekly* concluded amiably, 'is funny and sad and true.'

Eileen hated it. Her own writings had always aimed to hold on to her happiest and most intense experience when, in her teens, she discovered what seemed to be a still vital, Gaelic culture, surviving in the hills and islands of the west. Seán had shared the discovery, so turning his protagonist, Younger, into an Englishman possibly seemed like a double betrayal.

'I don't like it,' she murmured to me behind the kitchen door. 'His book! I just – don't *like* it.'

What could I say to comfort her? I couldn't think of anything. I may have agreed that the novel was – *did* I say this? – a mite self-indulgent. But I suspect I didn't, since admitting his need to indulge himself could have made her feel worse. People were reading the book as we had by then, so we couldn't put his impudent genie back in its bottle. I wasn't keen either on admitting that the notion of serial incest came uncomfortably close to revealing wanton impulses which, though fictional, were recognisably his.

'I don't like it either,' I said to show that I was, for once, completely on her side – and that ours was in no way a literary discussion.

'No?'

'No.'

She haunts me now: warily, sometimes leaving behind a tenuous shadow of herself. When I awake from wool-gathering or sleep, she – or the shadow – slyly conveys an awareness that she has been in and on my mind. Like the trespasser she used to be, she is elusive. And by the time I begin to focus, both she – and the certainty that it *was* she – have dissolved.

Seán's last invention, then, was a Faustian fiction in which his alter ego could enjoy a new and scruple-free youth. 'Daydreaming' had, after all, been the favourite hobby he chose to name in his entry in *Who's Who*.

Eileen, instead, enjoyed evoking the myths of the country's youth. Looking through her papers, I found after her death that, despite her arthritic fingers, she had been working on a new collection of these.

As for my own love of fiction, I contend that trying to slip inside and understand an alien reality keeps the imagination supple. Perhaps, too, impelled by memories of childhood fears that I might not exist, I write to exist *more*, to extend my scope and get a better look at life than you do while living it. Like one of those high-speed trains that don't stop at your station, it streaks by too fast. One has to piece together the broken images and try for new patterns – that's fiction writing. In my case I suppose, too, that I write because Seán and Eileen did. *Je suis un enfant de la balle* – I ply my parents' trade.